IN THE PRESENCE OF MINE
ENEMIES

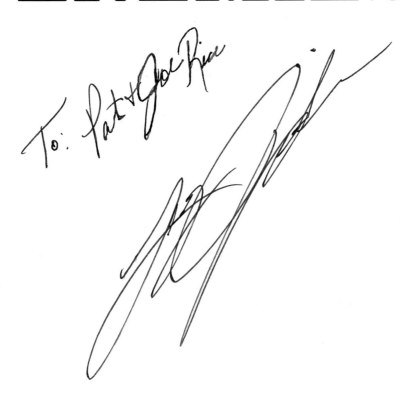

To: Pat & Joe Rice

IN THE PRESENCE OF MINE ENEMIES

*The Story of Evangelist Leroy Jenkins' Betrayal and
Ultimate Redemption in a SMALL SOUTHERN TOWN*

LEROY JENKINS

Co Author June Buckingham

WINTERS
PUBLISHING GROUP

Published by Winters Publishing, LLC
2448 E. 81st St. Suite #4802 | Tulsa, Oklahoma 74137 USA

Book design copyright © 2013 by Winters Publishing, LLC. All rights reserved.
Cover design by Jan Sunday Quilaquil
Cover photos by Michele L. Allen
Interior design by Jomel Pepito

Published in the United States of America

ISBN: 978-1-62902-136-2
1. RELIGION / Christian Theology / Eschatology
2. RELIGION / Christian Theology / General
13.09.24

DEDICATION

For my pastor, friend, and employer of nearly
forty years, the Rev. Leroy Jenkins

CONTENTS

PREFACE

I first saw the Rev. Leroy Jenkins when he brought his revival meeting to the Civic Auditorium in Dayton, Ohio, in 1971. I had never seen anyone like this spell-binding evangelist, preaching and parading across the stage in what I later learned was the time-honored style of many a Southern man of the cloth. Dressed in a tuxedo that matched his coal-black hair, his diamond-studded fingers grasping the microphone, he crooned gospel tunes with a voice that bore a remarkable resemblance to Elvis Presley's. *This is show business*, I thought, *not church*.

But I found myself relaxing as the waves of the deeply spiritual music washed over me. I became renewed and refreshed by the Bible verses I heard. The people in the seats all around me were *excited* about knowing a man named Jesus. And they danced and sang and raised their hands in joy.

On that day, I saw my first healings. I can't say I accepted the healings without reservation. After all, those things didn't happen in my church. Yet it was biblical, as much as salvation or the infilling of the Holy Spirit. I went home that day exhausted, elated, and energized by what I had seen and heard. And I had a feeling that somehow my life would become intertwined with the lives of those people and that evangelist.

That was more than forty years ago, and since that day, I have served the Leroy Jenkins Evangelistic Association in the business of the ministry, along with many other dedicated employees and volunteers, seeing to it that the tents are raised, the television programs paid for, the mail answered, and the prayer requests prayed over daily.

It has not always been easy. There have been trials and tribulations as in any ministry built around a strong, charismatic personality. But the rewards are impossible to convey in words. When you see thousands upon thousands of desperate people receive healing and salvation according to Scripture, it is a feeling with no equal.

That is what makes writing this book both so painful and so poignant. None of us who love our pastor and have worked hard for the ministry could ever dream that he would one day be sent to prison after having been entrapped and framed by federal agents on a flimsy conspiracy charge and convicted of a crime he did not commit.

As the widow of a respected Dayton, Ohio, attorney, I saw a side of the justice system that almost crushed my faith in humanity. It is only through God's grace, the prayer of thousands, and one man's faith in his Lord that this story has a happy ending.

I have faithfully tried to recreate conversations as I remember them and as related by others. Naturally, there will be variations in syntax and grammar. Some offensive words have been left out. Some conversations may have been shortened or edited for clarity although they are faithful, in spirit, to the original. For the sake of clarity and consistency, I refer to myself in the third person as June Buckingham or Mrs. Buckingham (see photo on page 266) throughout the book.

Newspaper articles have been reprinted with permission of the publishers. I have tried to omit no item of criticism, innuendo, or charge aimed at the Rev. Leroy Jenkins, even if it has been proven false by an independent source or deemed to be false by me but have endeavored to shine the light of day on all aspects of this remarkable story.

While attempting to present a fair and honest account of the events surrounding the imprisonment of the Rev. Leroy Jenkins, I make no claims to impartiality, nor do I apologize for the injection of my personal observations into the retelling of a story I consider to be a tragic miscarriage of justice.

J.B.

PART 1:
THE HOMECOMING

The LORD is my shepherd; I shall not want.
He maketh me to lie down in green pastures:
he leadeth me beside the still waters.
He restoreth my soul:
he leadeth me in the paths of righteousness for his name's sake.
Yea, though I walk through the valley of the shadow of death,
I will fear no evil: for thou art with me;
thy rod and thy staff they comfort me.
Thou preparest a table before me in the presence of mine enemies:
thou anointest my head with oil;
my cup runneth over.
Surely goodness and mercy shall follow me all the days of my life:
and I will dwell in the house of the LORD forever.
— Psalm 23:1–6 (KJV)

Note: On September 28, 1993, the South Carolina Board of Probation, Parole and Pardon Services absolved the Rev. Leroy Jenkins of all legal consequences for which he was convicted and restored his civil rights. This is the story of everything that happened before.

STOCKMAN STREET

Greenwood, South Carolina, is an alluring and picturesque community just a step from the foothills of the Blue Ridge Mountains. A stranger can't help but be seduced by the area, especially in the springtime when the fragrance of honeysuckle and jasmine clings to the warm air and when the splashes of pink azaleas are nearly blinding.

The Rev. Leroy Jenkins was no stranger to Greenwood. It was his home. Granted, he had not lived here for decades. But now, in the middle of his years, he felt a strong pull from the place of his birth. He was still a Southerner, after all. He savored the politeness of the people, he enjoyed food flavored with salt pork, and he eagerly wrapped himself in the subtropical climate after many winters in the icy Midwest.

The reverend had spent his youth on Stockman Street, a short, unimposing residential lane tucked just behind the downtown business district. Only blocks from the banks, retail establishments, and professional offices that line the parallel main streets of routes 25 and 34, it was a convenient address. (see photo on page 258)

But the neighborhood had always been dreary; the ten little, wood-frame homes were unpainted and in disrepair even back in the late 1930s when Willie Mae Jenkins, the reverend's mother, settled her young brood there. She had been grateful to find a place for herself and her five children. The Stockman Street address was one of the few rental homes she could afford on her modest salary from her job in the sewing shop at the cotton mill.

When the Rev. Jenkins—referred to as Rev by most of his friends and employees—returned in the summer of 1977, the homes looked as if they might topple over from neglect. Some of them had no plumbing or sewer connections, so the waste ran out onto the ground beneath the houses. According to the only people still living on the street, the landlord did little more than collect the rent.

Surveying the shabby street, the Rev. Jenkins was reminded of a vow he had made years before. As a child, he had felt the scorn of some of Greenwood's "good" citizens who looked down their noses at the "lint heads"—people who worked in the cotton mills. He resolved to make something of himself so he could one day return to his hometown a man of means. When that day arrived, he would buy every house on Stockman Street and fill them with his friends and family. For himself, he would buy a mansion. And no one would ever look down on him again. It was a natural-enough childhood wish. (see photo on page 278)

The Rev. Jenkins made good on that vow. His *Revival of America*—a half-hour show of healing, singing, and preaching—aired on eighty-seven stations nationwide. His following rivaled that of Billy Graham. The ministry was bringing in about $6 million a year. He was at the top of his game.

This day, as he stood on Stockman Street in his tailored silk shirt, the long fingers of his finely manicured hands pointing out landmarks to friends, he made a decision that would change his life forever. He decided to fulfill his childhood vow and resurrect the neighborhood of his youth from its crumbling decay.

It was an audacious thing to do, of course. But it wouldn't be the first time the Rev. Jenkins would do the unexpected.

A LUKEWARM RECEPTION

Leroy Jenkins was thirteen years old when he abandoned his boiled-peanut-selling business and left home to seek his fortune. When he returned, it was as a well-known evangelist who counted among his friends such icons as Mahalia Jackson and Mae West. Politicians, including Clare Boothe Luce, sought him out. Liberace turned over the keys to his home when the Rev. Jenkins visited California. Dale Evans sang for a crusade at Madison Square Garden. Jerry Lee Lewis performed his trademark rockabilly hits on the reverend's grand piano. Rev seemed to enjoy spending time with other celebrities because they understood the trials and also the blessings of living in the public eye. (see photos on pages 268-272, 277)

Many of Greenwood's residents welcomed the prodigal son, enveloping him in their charm and Southern hospitality. Others, however, were not so hospitable. For one thing, people don't just come into Greenwood and start changing things. Next to God, Southerners worship tradition more than anything else. In Greenwood and its surrounding communities, textile workers had traditionally lived in "mill villages" built by the mill owners. They had their babies in the mill-owners' hospital and worshiped in the Baptist church named after the mill-owner's mother (which came complete with the mill owner's handpicked preacher to guide people down the path to virtues such as obedience and "umbleness" and knowing one's place.)

Even now, textile manufacturing employs thousands more workers than any other industry. And people here, like anywhere else, remember on which side their corn bread is buttered.

Greenwood residents are proud. A newcomer is quick to learn that more revolutionary war battles were fought in South Carolina than any other state, although these days most of the fighting is done on the college football fields. And there is still a stubborn and pervasive undercurrent of resentment over losing the War Between the States.

Folks don't take kindly to interlopers telling them what to do. So when the little boy from the wrong side of the tracks returned with his new clothes and his new, audacious way of doing things, some people were not pleased. And the people who were the least pleased were the town leaders. The reverend had a way of shaking things up, Greenwood officials knew. He didn't mind challenging the "powers-that-be" when he felt they were wrong. He had created a stir in Atlanta years before when he brought blacks and whites together under the same roof to worship. And despite threats to his life, he continued this practice.

Greenwood officials knew he wasn't just a lot of hot air. They knew about the packed auditoriums in places like Detroit and Chicago. This man had influence. When he announced his intent to run for governor of Ohio in 1977, there was sufficient interest in his candidacy that the statewide political parties were eyeing him with the possibility of nabbing him as their candidate. The Rev. Jenkins soon found politics not to his liking, but that didn't stop his occasional tirades against anyone from the local dog catcher to the president if he thought they were doing something wrong.

He seemed to delight in poking the underbelly of entrenched local governments whom he viewed as standing in the way of his ministry.

The Greenwood establishment knew this. It wasn't long after his return home that a diabolical conspiracy seemed to form with the intent of ruining a well-meaning, if outspoken, man. Endangered also was a ministry that had helped thousands receive God's healing and salvation.

When its facade of manners falls away, an outsider sees Greenwood in a different light. Then, the fragrant creeping vines begin to cloy, the humidity saps all vigor, and even the mocking birds that dwell in the cedar trees become a maddening annoyance.

THE MIRACLE ARM

Leroy Jenkins first left home for Texas, then Georgia, where he met and married young Ruby Garrett. They settled in Atlanta, where Mr. Jenkins bought a home and established a business selling pianos.

Though outwardly successful, he was not happy. His heart hungered for meaning in life. Like Saul on the road to Damascus, he found it in an unexpected way. As he was replacing a plate glass window in his home, it fell on him and splintered, nearly severing his arm at the elbow.

In the emergency room, doctors wanted to amputate the arm to save his life. Mr. Jenkins refused and went home fully expecting to die from the gangrene that would almost certainly set in. An article about the incident ran in the Atlanta newspaper with the headline "Young Atlanta Businessman Refuses Amputation, Faces Death."

When a friend told Mr. Jenkins about the Rev. A. A. Allen, a well-known evangelist who was holding a crusade in town, his sister, Polly, drove him to the tent meeting. His arm was held together by a cast and was, by then, reeking with infection. His swollen fingers were useless; his tendons, mangled.

That night, A. A. Allen singled him out, called him up on stage, and the twenty-year-old Leroy Jenkins received the blessing of the Holy Spirit in full measure. He was healed by his faith in the power of God. All at once, he was saved, healed, and granted a vision of his own ministry. As a result of this remarkable event, many thousands of people would receive the gift of salvation and healing in tent meetings, auditoriums, and churches across the nation and throughout the world.

HOME SWEET HOME

After years of traveling the country, holding tent meetings, the reverend settled in Ohio where he bought a beautiful mansion and remodeled it into a church. People came from all around to attend meetings at the Holy Hill Cathedral. But the pressures of running such a large operation became overbearing. Eighteen years after his healing, the Rev. Jenkins returned to Greenwood where he longed to find respite from the heavy demands of his Ohio ministry and where he fully expected to be welcomed as the accomplished man he now was.

As if in an attempt to rewrite history, he tore down half of the Stockman Street houses and salvaged the remaining five, remodeling them into charming brick cottages.

His dream was to transform his childhood home into a museum, which would house the hundreds of braces, crutches, and canes that had been left behind at the crusades by those who had been healed. He would furnish the museum with furniture and collectibles from the 1920s and '30s, as well as lovely Victorian pieces.

The other homes along the street were sold or rented to employees of the Leroy Jenkins Evangelistic Association. The Association also purchased a duplex on Magnolia Street, just around the corner from Stockman Street, and remodeled it into its Greenwood headquarters.

Under the Rev's direction, workers tore out the tangled underbrush that had grown up around the houses and replaced it with flowering trees and bushes, including hundreds of azaleas. Roses now climbed the new fences; and cherry, apple, and dogwood trees shaded each lawn.

Fifty towering flagpoles lined the street, flying alternate American and Christian flags. With his passion for green space, the Rev. Jenkins created two parks. In one, he built a small white chapel, with a copper steeple, where he occasionally conducted marriages and other services.

By Christmas 1977, the Stockman Street neighborhood came alive for the first time in years. Loudspeakers chimed hymns to every home, while church members decorated an imposing tree in the park. The reverend himself handed out toys to neighborhood children who had been invited to the festivities.

News of these improvements spread, and cars carrying folks who had never set foot on Stockman Street began to cruise up and down the road to see what the reverend had made of his boyhood home. The Rev. Jenkins was so elated with these events he decided to move his entire operation to Greenwood.

JENKINS MOVING MORE OF OPERATIONS SOUTH

Delaware Gazette, July, 1978

Personnel at the Rev. Leroy Jenkins' offices are packing up the computers and business operations as the controversial evangelist prepares to move his operating base to Greenwood, S.C.

Linda Myers, Jenkins' business manager, told the Gazette this morning that she expects the computers to be on their way to Greenwood by Tuesday, arriving in the South Carolina city by Friday.

Jenkins' prayer line has also been moved to Greenwood, Ms. Myers said. She did not know whether Jenkins' health food store would remain in Delaware after the evangelist completes his move.

Moving the computers to Greenwood, Jenkins' boyhood home town, will complete the shift of the evangelists' mailing operations from Delaware.

Ms. Myers said Jenkins advised the 270,000 people on his mailing list to send mail for the evangelist to Greenwood several months ago. The Delaware post office reports that Jenkins has been sending mail to his followers through the local facility. However, those mailings may change with the moving of the computer mailing list to Greenwood.

The Columbus Dispatch reported Jenkins' impending departure from his Holy Hill Cathedral Thursday and quoted the evangelist as saying Delaware "is the most unapprecia-tive little city I've ever seen in my life. "Of Delaware, Jenkins said, "I despise it."

Ms. Myers said this morning that Jenkins will be in Delaware Sunday for an 11 a.m. worship service at Holy Hill Cathedral.

She said that Jenkins will visit Delaware for Sunday services "as often as his busy schedule permits. "She said the evangelist has a series of crusades in the Midwest scheduled for this fall.

The Holy Hill Cathedral has been open for services since July 2 after Jenkins complied with the state and corrected a series of building violations for which the structure had been closed.

Copyright © The Delaware Gazette

A BABY GIRL IS HEALED

It was so hot the blacktop bubbled, as car after car filed into the Greenwood Civic Center parking lot. Cadillac cars parked next to rusty old pickup trucks as their occupants spilled out and joined in a diverse pilgrimage, making its way to the auditorium where the Leroy Jenkins Crusade would soon begin. There were laughing women of color, their faces shaded by broad-brimmed pastel hats, followed by old men pushing walkers. There were little old ladies dusted in lavender talc and working men, their rough hands clasping a treasured family Bible. Catholics, Pentecostals, and AME—pious, sinner, and skeptic—all marched in agreement with at least one thing: they all believed, or dared to hope, that God was still in the miracle-working business.

Among the first to arrive for the crusade that August Sunday in 1978 were a man and a woman who had driven all the way from Alabama. They had seen the Rev. Jenkins on television and had heard him say many times, "Prayer works, and Jesus never fails." On faith, they struck out for Greenwood, searching for a miracle of their own.

In her arms, the woman held a baby girl gaily dressed in ruffles, tiny white booties, and a pink bonnet. The only blemish on this tender family portrait was a narrow plastic tube running into the baby's nostrils.

The reverend's employees were anticipating the family's arrival. Someone had mailed the office a copy of an article from a Florida newspaper describing the parents' plans to bring their baby to the Greenwood crusade. Without a miracle, the article said, she would die.

An employee spotted the family waiting at the entrance and led them into the auditorium to the front-row seats that had been reserved for them. There, in the quiet coolness they rested, waiting on the Lord.

"MIRACLE" BABY GIRL FIGHTS TO SURVIVE

Jackson County Floridian August 3, 1978

Mr. and Mrs. Horace (Bubba) Braxton, Jr. of Rt. 1, Cottondale, call four-month old Janaya their "miracle baby."

It's a miracle she has lived this long, doctors tell them, and every day they pray that a miracle will make her normal. So strong is their faith that they are traveling to Greenwood, S.C. Aug. 13 to have the Rev. Leroy Jenkins, a well-known evangelist with a television program, pray for her healing.

To look at her one would think Janaya (pronounced Ja-ná-ya) was a normal, healthy baby; she is plump, rosy-cheeked, dark-haired, weighs 12 1/2 pounds and is 22 inches long. Then you see the tube in her nose - it stays there all the time and is her lifeline. Her mother, Annette, feeds her and gives her medicine through it 15 times per day.

Janaya can neither suck nor cry; the part of the brain that controls these functions was affected when a blood vessel burst in her brain during one of her many stays in the hospital since she was born with a lower bowel obstruction.

Mrs. Braxton had a normal pregnancy, and when Janaya was born, she weighed 7 lbs. 9 ozs. She was their second child, joining a sister, Jo Anna, 3.

While in the hospital Janaya spit up a lot, and doctors' X-rays revealed that the valves in her upper stomach were immature. They told the Braxtons they'd have trouble keeping her food down, but thought it would clear up by itself by the time she reached nine months of age.

Once home, however, Janaya spit up more and more. She gained eight ounces the first week, and then started losing, and the Braxtons became even more concerned when she began spitting up a greenish bile substance. She was hospitalized again in Dothan, and x-rays then revealed a lower bowel obstruction. Doctors told the worried parents her intestines hadn't twisted enough, while developing, that it was a miracle she survived, and that surgery was imperative.

The operation was performed on a Sunday, and physicians corrected the obstruction and moved her appendix from the right side to the left. She began improving and continued to do so until Wednesday, when her temperature shot up and she was transferred to a Montgomery, Ala., hospital by ambulance with a serious infection.

"Before we left Dothan, she was having seizures," Mrs. Braxton said.

A baby specialist in the Neonatal Intensive Care Unit got the seizures under control, and she remained in Intensive Care for eight weeks, after which she was moved to Pediatrics. Once there she began seizuring again and was taken to Medical Intensive Care, where she remained for three weeks.

She was put on medicine to control the seizures and the Braxtons were called to come after her and carry her home; however when they arrived, tragic news awaited them: a blood vessel had burst in her brain. The physicians said she couldn't go home, that they'd have to do a spinal tap to keep the blood from building up inside her head.

It was at this time that Janaya quit sucking her bottle. The nurse told them that when a blood vessel bursts, it causes most babies to lose control of their tongues. "It would take two hours to get her to take three ounces of milk," Mrs. Braxton said. So she learned to tube-feed the baby through her nose.

"It was a constant battle to keep her from having seizures," Mrs. Braxton went on. "The medication they gave her to control them relaxed her so much that she'd quit breathing. She was placed in an isolette with a sensitivity monitor attached to the bed and a heart monitor on her. That way they'd know when her breathing slowed, and would pinch her, slap her foot, or pull her hair."

When she hadn't had a seizure for a week, she was sent to Pediatrics, where she stayed one day before the seizures started again. "Then the doctors gave up, said there was nothing they could do, that we'd have to get used to her quitting breathing and having seizures," Mrs. Braxton said.

So they carried her home. Janaya has scared them several times. "She seizured all night one night," Mrs. Braxton said, and she has days when all she does is spit up. Day before yesterday, every time I touched her, her milk would come up through her nose and mouth."

A neurologist in Gainesville told them that her brain is deteriorating and that her eyesight has been affected.

Janaya is on three kinds of medication which keep her practically in a stupor to prevent seizures: Dilantin, Phenobarbital and Depakene. Occasionally she opens her eyes and will move her hands slightly but that is the extent of her mobility.

"I know you think I'm calm when I speak of all this," Mrs. Braxton said, "but I've heard it so much....my husband and I have talked it out, and we have faith that God will heal her. We have bad days, but we try to look to the future."

Copyright © Jackson County Floridian

FAITH WORKS, AND JESUS NEVER FAILS

So severely brain damaged she could neither eat nor cry, see nor hear, baby Janaya lay perfectly still in her mother's arms, seemingly oblivious to the noise and chatter all around as the civic center auditorium filled with people.

Musicians appeared on stage, entertaining and inspiring the audience with gospel favorites. Finally, the band broke into the hymn that signaled the Rev. Jenkins' entrance: "How Great Thou Art."

The striking-looking evangelist, wearing a rich-red coat and black tuxedo slacks, strode onto the platform with a microphone in his hand, singing his favorite hymn with every ounce of praise within him. After the song, rather than launching into his sermon, he told the standing-room-only crowd of the Braxtons' presence at the crusade, of their baby's illness, and of their great faith.

"They even brought with them a baby bottle full of milk," he said. "That is how great their faith that when I pray for this baby, God will heal her."

He called Mrs. Braxton up onto the stage. There, he placed his hands on the motionless baby. As he prayed, Janaya jerked, threw up her hands, and kicked her little feet as though an electrical current had gone through her body.

"It will take awhile," the evangelist said, "but she will start to recover at once, and it will get better and better."

Weeping with joy, Mrs. Braxton carried her baby back to her seat in the front row. She took the tube out of Janaya's nose and offered her the bottle of milk she had brought with her. Janaya began to suck the milk from the bottle, swallowing it like any other four-month-old infant.

Many eyes filled with tears as the crowd praised God for the baby's healing and clapped their hands in approval. It was a great miracle indeed.

PARENTS BELIEVE THEIR BABY WAS HEALED

Jackson County Floridian, August 24, 1978

Joyce M. James

COTTONDALE - *"People are looking for something to draw them closer to God, and they're looking to our little girl to prove that He is alive and that He's real."*

Those words spoken by Horace (Bubba) Braxton, Jr. of Rt. 1, Gordon, Alabama, are the way he and his wife, Annette feel following the alleged "faith healing" of their five-month old daughter, Janaya Lois, in Greenwood, S.C. on Aug. 13.

Janaya, who was born with an obstruction in her lower intestine, has been in and out of hospitals since she was born and before last Sunday, was on three kinds of medication 15 times a day to keep her from having seizures. She was also tube-fed because she was unable to suck after a blood vessel burst in her brain during one of her periods of hospitalization. She was also unable to cry or move any part of her body except to move her hands feebly.

Now, since she appeared on a televised crusade in a huge civic auditorium in Greenwood, S.C. and was prayed for by the Rev. Leroy Jenkins, she is on only one type of medication, can suck a bottle, and is on a steady diet of baby food, something she had never had before. She can also move her arms and legs freely.

She has no problem with her breathing and her food is going down and staying there, her father said.

Before going, they prayed fervently for a miracle. As one grandmother said, "Miracles happen, and one might happen here."

Here is the story of their experience on the Jenkins show and the aftermath.

"We left Saturday morning, and spent the night up there, and were at the Civic Center by 8 a.m. Sunday to make sure we'd get in.

"They let us go into the lobby since it was so hot, and about 15 minutes later, the door opened, and a woman who introduced herself as Rev. Jenkins' secretary came out. She said, "Mr. and Mrs. Braxton? We want you to go with us."

"She said they had been looking for us, that Mr. Scott had sent the article. They wanted to make sure we got in.

"Well, they carried us right up and seated us in a front row. They were so nice to us.

"When he started preaching, he started telling about me and my wife, about our faith – he couldn't believe our newspaper had printed the article because most papers ridicule evangelists, he said. I'm kind of an emotional person, and when he called my wife up on the stage with the baby, I just went to pieces.

"He put his hands on the baby's head and prayed, and she jumped just like somebody had put an electric shock to her. He told Annette the baby would be healed but that it would be slow coming; that God works in His own way. He said she would eat like a normal baby and asked my wife if she had a bottle with her. She said yes, so he told her to carry her back to her chair, remove the tube from her nose, and offer her the bottle. So she did, and the baby began to suck. They kept the TV monitor on us constantly. It was amazing to watch the baby – it was like she was waking up from a deep sleep, and it's been that way ever since.

"After the program was over, people in the audience rushed up to see our "miracle baby" – that's what they called her. We like to never got out of that place. We stopped about 26 miles out of town to get some sandwich meat, and some people had seen us leave in the car and stopped there to see the baby. It surprised us that they were so concerned.

"On Friday night, Saturday and Sunday before we went on the show, we had so much trouble with the baby - she couldn't keep her milk down. Jenkins said she would eat like a normal baby, so we started feeding her baby food Monday, after we got back. The first thing we offered her was apple-sauce, and she commenced to eating it. Now she eats cereal, applesauce, bananas, etc., and it all stays down. She never strangled the first time, and has had just normal spitting up.

"Doctors told us her hearing was impaired, but clapping one's hands nearby will stimulate her. Her eyes were supposed to have been affected, too, but when we put her in her bed, she watches her mobile, something she never noticed before.

"So many people tell us, 'We know just how you feel,' but nobody does. To see her just lying there like she used to, and now in a week's time to see her do a complete turn-around... it's wonderful. We're living a normal, relaxed life now.

"Whatever happens is God's will, and we've just turned it over to Him," Braxton said. "We'll take care of little Janaya and love her, but she's His little young'un."

Copyright © Jackson County Floridian

THE DOCTORS ARE AMAZED

After the Greenwood crusade, Mr. Braxton wrote a letter to the Rev. Jenkins' office saying,

> Janaya is doing so much better. She is eating baby food now. She started making baby sounds, and squeals out when she gets upset. The doctors can't believe how she eats, and all the growing she has done.

A call to the Braxton residence a year later, on August 29, 1979, revealed that little Janaya was doing fine. Her father said she was eating, gaining weight, and trying to stand.

Janaya's healing had been an auspicious start to the Rev. Jenkins' new life in Greenwood. Thanks to a televised religious service, a child had been healed, a family's faith rekindled, and thousands of people brought to the Lord.

But the remarkable healing of Janaya Braxton and the dozens of others who were prayed for at the civic center that August 13, 1978, went unreported by the local newspapers. There was no mention of the fact that the civic center was filled to capacity for the first time since it was built a year earlier. Nor was there mention of the hundreds of young people who came to the front of the auditorium, tears filling their eyes, as they prayed for deliverance from drugs.

It was a shame that, while negative news makes headlines, the good news of God's saving grace did not even merit an inch of a newspaper column.

FIRE

There are many mansions in heaven, the Bible promises, but Rev was determined to have one on earth as well, just as he had promised his childhood playmates. With the renovation of the Stockman Street homes well under way, (see photo on page 258) he purchased a stately home on Calhoun Street, one of the main streets in town, next to a Presbyterian church that had been closed down. The lovely Victorian home once belonged to Mrs. Cooner, a piano teacher who had been kind to the Rev. Jenkins when he was a boy and had given him several piano lessons free of charge.

Like many people whose early lives were scarred by want and hardship, the reverend loved beautiful things. He filled the mansion with antique furniture from his home in Ohio and with crystal and china he found browsing through area shops.

The Rev. Jenkins was proud of his home and his antiques and delighted in inviting friends and acquaintances over to show them his latest acquisition. Hilton and Viola Dodgen, local auctioneers and appraisers specializing in antiques, visited the Calhoun Street home to view the Rev. Jenkins' extensive and growing collection. Glass-fronted cabinets and a long fruit wood dining table and sideboard displayed exquisite antique silver pieces, cut glass, and china. Carved walnut settees and chairs, covered in crimson velvet, were arranged in conversational groupings around the home.

The Dodgens expressed the opinion that the antiques were worth many thousands of dollars. Some were irreplaceable. Their professional opinion would soon prove vital.

A DANGEROUS DRIFTER

Not all visitors were as welcome. One day, a tall, skinny drifter wandered up to the Calhoun Street house. Peering through thick glasses, he knocked on the door and asked for work or a handout. This in itself was not unusual. People approached the reverend all the time asking for favors. Rev let him do some yard work and paid him at the end of the day. He also assured the drifter that he would pray for the young man's sister who was ill.

Despite the reverend's kindness to him, the drifter, who called himself Ernie Proctor, began to behave oddly. In the ensuing days, he was seen skulking around the Calhoun Street home, staring into the windows, and frightening the reverend's children.

One day, June Buckingham, the reverend's office manager, spotted Ernie peeking out from behind one of the Stockman Street houses. (see photo on page 259)

"What do you want, Ernie?" she called out.

"I want Leroy," he said.

Rev, who was working nearby, glanced up and saw the man advancing toward him, his hand concealed inside his jacket.

"Get out of my yard," the reverend said. "And you better keep that knife in your jacket."

Instead of backing off, Ernie kept coming, pulling out a large knife that had been hidden under his jacket. He muttered incoherently as he approached the reverend.

Trinka, a trained German shepherd dog, was in the yard behind one of the houses. When Trinka saw the man wielding the knife, she sprang into action, pouncing on Ernie and seizing his knife arm with her teeth, just as she had been trained to do. She held onto his knife arm until commanded to let go.

Police arrested Ernie for the attempted assault, but the Rev. Jenkins refused to press charges. Ernie was released and went to the hospital to have his arm bandaged and treated for minor lacerations. Though his wounds were minimal, in his mind they festered deeply. He vowed revenge in the presence of Greenwood businessman Jim Owens, who owned a gas station near the Stockman Street property.

"I am going to get Leroy Jenkins. I am going to burn his house down," Owens quoted Ernie as saying.

A DREAM UP IN SMOKE

People had made threats against the Rev. Jenkins before, and nothing had come of them. It is an unfortunate fact of life for people in the limelight. The reverend ignored the threats.

When he was not in residence at his new home, the reverend continued his nationwide crusades. As they had for years, the faithful crowded into auditoriums and civic centers across the country. Many arrived as early in the morning for the afternoon revivals.

In Chicago, at the Auditorium Theatre on Michigan Avenue, believers filled the main floor and all four balconies to the brim. The Rev. Jenkins had to hire a security firm to control the crowds so that he could enter and leave the theater in safety.

The Atlanta crusade, on April 2, 1978, at the Boisfeuillet Jones Atlanta Civic Center, was jammed with those seeking to be touched by the "Man with the Miracle Arm."

Meanwhile, back in Greenwood, the problem with the drifter, Ernie, grew worse. Police were concerned about some new threats he had made against the evangelist. On April 24, 1978, a police lieutenant came to the Rev's office with the following message, which was recorded and stapled in the day book kept in the office:

To Leroy:

Lt. Partridge stopped by. They received a 3-page report on Ernie. He has served time for assault and other serious crimes. They are very concerned about getting him either in jail, or out of town, as they feel he is a real threat to your safety. They are going to see the judge now about getting him locked up.

All shifts of police have been alerted to keep a close eye on your property, and pick up Ernie if they see him near the house. Lt. Partridge will check back with you later today.

Also, they say Ernie has been threatening to harm you if you do not pay him $1,500. Later he said he wanted $3,000.

In addition, I have noticed a dozen azaleas have been pulled up and stolen at the end of the street in front of #43 (one of the homes on Stockman Street.)

June

A SHATTERED PEACE

The Rev. Jenkins was scheduled to hold a crusade in Buffalo on Sunday, April 30, 1978. A few days earlier, the Chicago-based security team headed by Howard Kaufman came to Greenwood to accompany the evangelist on the plane ride to Upstate New York.

The day before the Buffalo crusade dawned beautiful and clear. Dogwoods and azaleas were already in bloom in Greenwood, and leaves were appearing on the bare branches of the pecan trees in the backyard of the Calhoun Street mansion.

In the yard, members of the security team were tossing a football around with the Rev and his sons.

Lou Jenkins, and his wife, Linnie, had come to spend a few days with their father, bringing with them their little girl, April.

The Rev.'s oldest daughter, Theresa; her husband, Ricky; and their children, Candy and baby Ricky, came up from Florida for an extended visit. Also present were daughters Candy and Sharon, who lived with their father in Greenwood, and son Dennis.

The house was bursting at the seams with visiting children and grandchildren.

The little ones toddled about the yard, getting in the way of the ball game and having a wonderful time. It was a peaceful afternoon. God was in his heaven, and all was right with the world.

In the office next door, Mrs. Buckingham made final arrangements for the Rev. Jenkins' appearance at the Atlanta Braves' farm team opening game. The Masonic lodge was sponsoring the night's festivities and had asked the reverend to deliver the blessing and throw out the first ball.

It was a gala occasion in Greenwood, and the entire Jenkins family dressed in their finest and set off for the game. Afterward, the party planned to dine at a local steak house. One of the security men drove the reverend in his limousine, and the other drove the rest of the family in another car.

Rev's infant grandchild, Ricky, remained at the mansion in the care of Viola Carmen, the reverend's housekeeper. As the cars pulled out of the driveway, Mrs. Carmen, holding baby Ricky in her arms, waved them off.

Finishing the day's work, Mrs. Buckingham locked up the office and, on the spur of the moment, invited Mrs. Carmen to bring the baby and come to her Stockman Street home for a visit.

A TOTAL LOSS

Not long after Mrs. Carmen, Mrs. Buckingham, and baby Ricky arrived at Stockman Street, sirens broke the still of the afternoon. Fire trucks raced through town and pulled up in front of the Rev. Jenkins' home, which the family had left only an hour before. As witnesses looked on in horror, black smoke poured from the windows. Before the firemen could extinguish the blaze, the house was gutted, the interior a wasteland of sooty, smoking rubble.

At the ball park, Rev had given the invocation and thrown out the first ball when several police officers threaded their way through the crowd and came to him with the news of the fire.

His first thought was for baby Ricky and Mrs. Carmen, whom he had left at the house. The officers had seen no one at the home. Newly alarmed, they all rushed to the cruiser and drove, sirens screaming, back to the house.

After a search, police discovered that Mrs. Carmen and baby Ricky were safe at Mrs. Buckingham's home. It was such a relief to know they were unharmed that for a moment the impact of the disaster did not hit the family.

But it would soon hit them hard. The Rev. Jenkins was shocked to learn that the firemen were certain the fire had been deliberately started with an accelerant and the mattresses upstairs had been slashed open with a knife. Rev immediately thought of Ernie and the threats he made just a few days earlier.

Destroyed were all the children's luggage and the clothes they had brought with them. Rev's clothing was ruined. He did not even have a suit to wear to his next crusade.

Charred photo albums lay in smoldering heaps on the floor near the bookcases. The beautiful crimson settees and chairs, of which the Rev. Jenkins had been so proud, were smoking skeletons. The china cupboards that held the cut glass and fine china were overturned on the floor, and their contents shattered beyond salvage.

Over all lay the sickening smell of burnt wood and cloth—a smell that, once experienced, can never be forgotten. Even the beds had burned, and the reverend and his family, who such a short time ago had enjoyed a carefree ball game in the back yard, suddenly found they had nowhere to sleep.

Distraught and in tears, the children and grandchildren found food, clothing, and shelter in the homes on Stockman Street. As if things couldn't get worse, the next day the Rev discovered that his tiny toy poodle had lost a litter of puppies. Apparently, the noise and confusion of the fire had been too much for the creature to bear.

A security man guarded the house through the night to see that the fire did not start up again and that no one tried to bother the ruins. The next day the salvaging began. What could be saved found its way to the lawn, where it was put up for sale. The sale netted little but served to clear the wreckage as people carted away what they wanted. Many things were given away.

The house was boarded up and remained so until the day the property was sold.

The police tracked down Ernie in Augusta, Georgia, and brought him in for questioning. Even though Ernie had admitted to several people, including June Buckingham, that he had started the fire, police suddenly bought Ernie a bus ticket and sent him out of town. Arson is one of the most difficult crimes to prove, and the police said there was not enough evidence to hold him. Ernie may not have been responsible for the fire, but his release so soon after it happened was nevertheless frustrating. Surely, it merited an investigation.

The Rev. Jenkins moved into the tiny home on Stockman Street (see photo on page 259) where he had lived as a child and which he had intended to turn into a museum. There was room enough for his youngest child, Scotty, and for twelve-year-old David. The other children doubled up and moved into the other homes on Stockman Street.

The matter of who set the fire remained unsolved. Yet in a series of articles published by a local newspaper several months later, reporters implied that the reverend may have burned his own house down. It was as if nearly losing his grandchild, Mrs. Carmen, his dream mansion, his photographs, mementoes, and all of his exquisite antiques wasn't horrifying enough.

With the suspicion of arson hanging in the air, the Aetna insurance company dragged its feet in paying the claim. The Leroy Jenkins Evangelistic Association sued the insurance company, and after a jury ruled in the reverend's favor, Aetna paid the claim.

FIGHTING CITY HALL

At first, Rev. enjoyed good relations with the mayor and town officials. A colorful, charismatic person, people enjoyed being around him. As he began to acquire and renovate property in Greenwood, he also grew in stature in the community. Everything he did wound up on the front page of the local newspaper, the *Index-Journal*. But as time went by, it seemed, the stories became increasingly negative in tone.

That's not surprising. Sensational stories sell the most papers. "Controversial" people—those who are not inclined to accept the status quo—often draw fire. The Rev. Jenkins did things some people didn't think a preacher should do.

He wore diamond rings and rode in limousines. He wore finely tailored suits and silk shirts. No more the poor child from a shabby neighborhood, he maintained that God's people should not be denied the good things in life, often quoting one of his favorite Bible verses: "Beloved, I wish above all things that thou mayest prosper and be in health, even as thy soul prospereth" 3 John 1:2 (KJV).

His customary outspokenness often landed him in hot water. As he became more involved in the community and in the lives of the people, he began to hear rumors about some of the town's officials. Many townspeople were afraid to go to anyone else with their stories. There was talk of gambling by some city officials and of working second jobs while on the city payroll.

If the Rev. Jenkins had kept quiet about what people told him, he probably could have enjoyed a peaceful existence in Greenwood. But with characteristic boldness, he talked openly about the things he had heard.

He held a press conference in which he accused two city officials of working second jobs on city time, a charge they denied. He also leveled charges against the police department and, in the process, made some powerful enemies.

GREENWOOD PANEL REFUTES EVANGELIST

Anderson Independent, July 18, 1978

Yvonne Williams

GREENWOOD—City council cleared the city manager, city engineer and police department of any wrong doing Monday in connection with allegations of harassment by evangelist Leroy Jenkins.

The results of the investigation were aired at a council meeting just after Jenkins made further charges against the city and asked that a street be renamed for him.

Mayor Thomas Wingard, announcing the results of an investigation launched by city council, said his confidence in city officials had been "substantially fortified."

The investigation by council also showed that Jenkins or "his agents or contractors had failed to obtain permits to construct, alter, repair or demolish buildings or structures as required by the Standard Building Code."

Jenkins made the allegations at a press conference in his Greenwood home. He said the city manager and city engineer were holding side jobs and working on them on the "taxpayers' time."

Wingard dismissed Jenkins' charges as a bid for "cheap and free publicity."

But in the regular scheduled council meeting Monday night, Jenkins reiterated his charges of harassment, saying he will hire private detectives to "follow through with my investigation."

Jenkins said at his press conference he had been hassled by city and state police in connection with their investigation of the fire at one of his Greenwood homes.

He also announced he plans to run against Wingard for mayor in 1980.

In a heated, terse debate Monday between Jenkins and Wingard, the evangelist said he would not allow city officials "to slap me around any more."

About 20 persons who work with Jenkins sat silent in the back of council's chambers as Jenkins debated with Wingard. No other councilman entered the discussion.

Saying he is the only resident who has "had enough guts to stand up" to city officials, Jenkins reaffirmed his belief that city police have been "snooping around my house" and city officials have "hassled" him.

Jenkins charged that Greenwood City Manager Travis Higginbotham and City Engineer T.A. Adams have impeded his renovation of Old Abby Mall and other previously condemned buildings near his home.

Jenkins said he had purchased every building permit necessary for the renovations, but Higginbotham and Adams have kept demanding he purchase unnecessary permits before he can start construction.

"I didn't ask for any of this trouble," Jenkins argued.

"You have been begging for it by not complying with the law," said Wingard adding that Jenkins had "assumed you were above the law."

Jenkins hotly responded, "That's an outright lie."

"It's your word against mine," said Wingard.

Jenkins said his appearance at the city council meeting was not only to discuss his charges of harassment, but that he had "a couple of things on my mind" to discuss with council.

He complained that a city garbage truck was passing by his house on Stockman Street. Beside the fact that the truck was noisy, it also creates a traffic hazard, Jenkins said.

"There's another street that they could go around on. There is not adequate room on my street, because there are parked cars on both sides of the road," he said.

Jenkins also asked that city council reconsider his proposal to change the name of Stockman Street to Leroy Jenkins Boulevard.

As to the garbage truck problem, Wingard responded that the Sanitation Department would have to make that decision.

"We can ask for their consideration to route trucks in the least disruptive way, but I would not dictate to a man how to do his job," said Wingard.

EX-POLICEMEN ALIGN WITH EVANGELIST JENKINS

Anderson Independent, August 2, 1978

Rick Ricks

GREENWOOD—*Two former Greenwood policemen who say they were harassed into resigning by Chief John Young have gone to evangelist Leroy Jenkins for help.*

The two former officers are Stephen Patrick Dixon who resigned July 25, and H.L. Butch Gunnells, who resigned May 12.

Young refused to discuss specifics of the former officers' complaints but said he asked one of the men not to work for Jenkins because Jenkins was too controversial.

Jenkins' alliance with the two officers comes less than a month after Greenwood City Council rejected the evangelist's charges that several city employees, including City Manager Travis Higginbotham, were guilty of conflict of interests.

In an interview with the two men in his home Monday, Jenkins said he is making their complaints part of a private investigation of the police department. Jenkins initiated the investigation conducted by Chicago private detective Howard Kaplan.

Young said he believes Jenkins had not initiated a legitimate investigation and so therefore sees no need to comment on it. Young refused to discuss specifics regarding Dixon and Gunnells, calling their resignations "an internal matter."

Jenkins said he will announce the results of the investigation Aug. 13 during his Greenwood crusade at Braves Stadium.

Dixon meanwhile has been hired by Jenkins as security chief for the Leroy Jenkins Evangelistic Association and Gunnells has applied for a similar job.

Dixon said he left the Greenwood Police Department after Young told him to stay away from Jenkins.

Young refused to allow Dixon to work part-time for the Association, Dixon said.

Dixon also said he was reprimanded by the chief for accompanying Jenkins to a recent Greenwood City Council meeting.

"He (Young) told me that I could work for the city or Leroy, but not both," Dixon said. He added that Young also suspended regular police rounds on Stockman Street where Jenkins lives after originally ordering regular watches there, Dixon contended.

"I just felt like I was being harassed...I think the reverend was being harassed too and I think the chief was going too far," Dixon commented on his resignation.

Dixon also questions a reprimand he received shortly before resigning. He said Young criticized him for driving too fast to a scene of a serious crime.

Gunnells attributed his resignation to Young's criticism of him for living with his girlfriend.

He said the chief continually "picked at me" about the living arrangement because of a neighbor's complaints. "I just didn't think it was any of the police department or the chief's business," Gunnells said.

Gunnells also complained that Young suspended him from the force for several days beginning Jan. 23 without proper investigation.

"I was accused of slapping a girl in the face at a local bar," Gunnells said, "But she wasn't even in town when it happened. The chief didn't check. He just took somebody's word."

There is no police report on the incident.

Both officers also criticized Young for threatening them with loss of pay for time they spent in the hospital.

They charged that Young encouraged officers of the department to inform on each other and Dixon said he was asked to inform on Jenkins.

Both Gunnels and Dixon said that while working as patrolmen they had observed a few officers stealing merchandise such as farm produce and milk from local businesses.

Although several businesses called to complain about missing merchandise, no action had been taken against any police officers, Dixon said.

Dixon said he was on the police force for 5½ months. Gunnells was employed there for almost two years.

The meeting Monday was Gunnells' first formal introduction to Jenkins.

"These young men just tried to do their jobs, but they ended up being harassed for knowing me or for other reasons," Jenkins said. "I just feel everything is not right at the police department."

When contacted about the charges, Young confirmed that he ordered Dixon not to work for Jenkins, "because he is too controversial."

"But I didn't say he couldn't hang around with the reverend. I never told him that," Young said.

It is not unusual for any policeman to have a second job, including security work. But police chiefs normally monitor the work to make sure the men are not doing something they consider offensive to the community.

The chief discounted Jenkins' promise to tell all at the crusade, saying, "I think he has told all he knows."

Copyright © Anderson Independent

EVANGELIST ASKS FOR PROBE OF POLICE

Greenville News, August 3, 1978

Kay Lapp

GREENWOOD—*Evangelist Leroy Jenkins has asked the State Law Enforcement Division to investigate the Greenwood City Police Department, which he says, "is so rotten you can't believe it."*

Kathy Littlejohn, a SLED representative, said the agency has received the request but is still "weighing the situation" before accepting or refusing. A decision probably will be made by next week.

Jenkins was joined by ex-policeman Stephen Patrick Dixon in making the allegations against the department. Dixon will be working for Jenkins as a security officer.

Dixon resigned from the police force July 25 after serving since March and had not completed a six-month probationary period at the time. Dixon was one of two city officers who were working part time for Jenkins. The two were asked to resign their part-time jobs by Police Chief John Young. The second officer is still working for the police department.

Dixon said officers on the force take fruit, vegetables and ice cream from the stores they patrol.

Jenkins said officers are drinking, "whoring" and gambling. The police are so rotten you can't believe it," the evangelist said.

Chief Young, who refused to give credence to the allegations, said he had not heard such complaints until brought forth by Jenkins and Dixon. Anyone who knew of officers taking merchandise but did not report it could also be considered guilty, Young said.

Jenkins had also been complaining of police harassment over building permits for improvements on his property.

He carried his charges of harassment to the city council, but its investigation found no evidence to substantiate the charges.

"You play ball in their park or not at all, so what good would it have done to tell the chief?" asked Dixon. Dixon also said he has been harassed by the chief and will go to the council to complain of the treatment he has received.

Dixon said he resigned rather than be fired when his probationary period was over. Dixon said he was "treated like the plague" for being friendly with Jenkins after being forced to quit the part-time job. He said he was transferred to another shift and given foot patrol duty.

Chief Young said he could not comment on Dixon's resignation because it was "an internal matter. "But he said he is ready to produce Dixon's personnel files if the matter were taken to court or to a labor board—"the proper place" for a hearing on the resignation.

Jenkins said he is going to continue making allegations against the department until a "full investigation" is completed.

The allegations are not a way to gain "cheap publicity" as Mayor Thomas Wingard has charged, Jenkins said. "It wasn't cheap. I spent $80,000 in Greenwood and that doesn't include the mall," said the evangelist, who moved to Greenwood in 1977 from Delaware, Ohio.

Jenkins was referring to a shopping mall he is creating inside the church building he owns in Greenwood.

THE ANIMOSITY DEEPENS

The Rev. Leroy Jenkins' battles with city hall, including his request for a name change for Stockman Street and rerouting of the garbage trucks, were big news in the South Carolina foothills. The story of his battle with city hall made headlines not only in the Greenwood *Index-Journal* but also in the *Anderson Independent*, a town twenty-five miles away, and in the *Greenville News*, which served a large urban area some fifty-seven miles north of Greenwood.

The newspapers couldn't seem to get enough of the outspoken evangelist who dared to challenge the "good old boys," including the police, city council, and even the mayor. He accused public officials of malfeasance and moral turpitude. He called upon the state's law enforcement agency to investigate the entire Greenwood Police Department.

Instead of looking within themselves for the moral infection that many suspected was at the heart of this small community's leadership, Greenwood officials closed ranks against the Rev. Jenkins. Something had to be done to silence him.

He made a daring request that the Greenwood Police Department be investigated by an "impartial" state agency, the State Law Enforcement Division (SLED), hoping such an investigation would bring to light things he had deliberately kept from the media in order not to embarrass the people involved.

One such case involved the sexual violation of a local woman in the back of a police car. The frightened young woman had approached the Rev. Jenkins with her story because she was afraid to tell the police. She wept as she recounted having been coerced into having sex with a policeman in the backseat of his patrol car. She became pregnant, but the patrolman refused to acknowledge her, or the child. When the Rev. Jenkins requested that SLED institute a probe of the Greenwood Police Department, he met with their representative, bringing the young woman with him. Astonishingly, nothing was ever done about the woman's charges.

Another potential headache for town leaders was the Rev. Jenkins' purchase of a downtown property where he said he intended to install a newspaper, one that would "tell the truth."

Finally, there was the question of race. Some small towns had missed the social changes taking place in larger cities. Greenwood was one of them. The town hierarchy was white. For the most part, whites stayed on their side of town, and blacks stayed on theirs.

The Rev. Jenkins filled the Greenwood Civic Center to capacity with crusades in which blacks and whites worshiped side by side. He was the first evangelist in memory to mix races in religious services. Earlier in his ministry, he incurred the wrath of the Ku Klux Klan by baptizing blacks and whites together in Snapfinger Creek near Atlanta. Then the KKK had warned his mother she would find him hanging from a tree. His "color blindness" was unacceptable to many, so when the Rev. Jenkins announced he was thinking of running for mayor to replace Thomas Wingard in 1980, his potential for drawing votes from Greenwood residents of all backgrounds was a dangerous indication that he might easily win the election. If he did, blacks would surely be encouraged to participate in local politics.

THE SPECTER OF ARSON

The motives for wanting the Rev. Jenkins out of the way were fairly obvious. It was only the means that need be devised. A local newspaper report provided the perfect opportunity.

The *Anderson Independent* mistakenly reported that the Holy Hill Cathedral in Ohio had "burned to the ground." The newspaper also said the Calhoun Street home had been burned by an "unknown" arsonist.

From the articles, no one could know that Ernie Proctor was a suspect in the Calhoun Street fire. Proctor had threatened to burn the reverend's house down and had even called the Association office to tell June Buckingham he had been the one to set the fire. But he was never charged with a crime by police.

By raising the specter of two arson-caused fires associated with the Rev. Jenkins, the newspaper gave local and state authorities the excuse they needed to call upon the Bureau of Alcohol, Tobacco and Firearms (ATF) to begin an "investigation" into the reverend's activities. Later, the solicitor[1] for Greenwood County, William T. Jones,[2] was heard to say, "Get Leroy Jenkins off the streets!" Those who worked for the Rev. Jenkins were shocked at that. Here was a man who was teaching people about the value of faith, who was encouraging young people to get off drugs and lead a good life, who had refurbished a blighted neighborhood and an abandoned church at his own expense—this was someone the top local law enforcement officer wanted off the streets!

A longtime supporter of the ministry, June Dunlevy, shared an experience in Greenwood that illustrated the feeling of ill will some people had for the Rev. Jenkins. After the reverend's conviction, she prepared a notarized statement to his lawyer,

---

[1]   In South Carolina the district attorney is known as the solicitor.

[2]   Not to be confused with his son, Eighth Judicial Circuit William "Townes" Jones IV.

telling of her experience, hoping to show that a plot had been in the making for some time:

TO THE SUPREME COURT OF SOUTH CAROLINA

Justice Bruce Littlejohn
Justice J.B. Ness
Justice George Gregory
Justice David W. Harwell

In the interest of truth and justice, I do respectfully submit for your appraisal and consideration, the following incident and conversation which occurred in Greenwood, S.C. six months prior to the arrest and incarceration of Rev. Leroy Jenkins, now being held at Walden Correctional Institute, Columbia, S.C.

On the morning of Nov. 6, 1978, I stopped for gas on the outskirts of Greenwood, S.C. The attendant, who seemed to be the owner, was very friendly and we engaged in conversation.

I said, "We are from Boone, N.C., and are on our way home. I can tell you that nothing has ever happened to me like happened here yesterday. We have been attending the two day Leroy Jenkins crusade at the Civic Center. A little Baptist lady from Monroe, N.C. received her sight after being blind for five years."

He said, "Is that right? We stay awfully busy here and I have never been to one of his crusades, but I'm going to watch him on television some time."

I answered that I hoped he would.

He then remarked, "Rev. Jenkins has been down here for about a year. He has stirred up a lot of things down here and I don't doubt that a lot of it is true, but THEY ARE OUT TO GET HIM."

I was deeply troubled, on the way back to Boone, by the attendant's remarks, as we had visited Rev. Jenkins' boyhood home and having seen his high exposure there in Greenwood, feared the WORST. I later realized the true import of the attendant's words when I read in the Greenwood Index-Journal that agent Bruce Mirkin infiltrated the Leroy Jenkins Evangelistic Association on Sept. 5, 1978.Rev. Jenkins was arrested on April 17, 1979, a period of approximately 8 months.

I, the understated, do solemnly swear and affirm that the above account is true and correct and is given voluntarily and without the knowledge of anyone connected with the case of Rev. Jenkins.

(signed) June Dunlevy (Mrs. William. J. Dunlevy)

SLED TURNS DOWN JENKINS' PROBE REQUEST

Index-Journal, September 7, 1978

Duncan Mansfield

Evangelist Leroy Jenkins' request for an investigation by the State Law Enforcement Division (SLED) into alleged corruption in the Greenwood Police Department has been denied, a SLED spokesman confirmed today.

SLED assistant director Leon Gasque made the decision last week after a meeting in Anderson with local agent Eddie Clark, said Hugh Munn, SLED public information officer. Clark made a pre-investigation into the Evangelist's charges filed with SLED more than a month ago.

Munn said Capt. Gasque sent Jenkins "a personal letter" concerning the results of the pre-investigation. While the SLED spokesman said he hadn't seen a copy of the letter, Gasque told him that he felt Jenkins had not exhausted all remedies on a local level.

Munn said he did not know what other "local remedies" Gasque had referred to, if any, in his letter to Jenkins. After completing its own investigation into the charges last month, Greenwood City Council determined the allegations were without foundation.

Concerning the evangelist's failure to obtain building permits before beginning construction on his property, Mayor Thomas Wingard told Jenkins at the July council meeting, "It has been explained to you that you have to have a permit before beginning construction .If you continue to assume that you're above the law, you will continue to be harassed."

At the meeting, Jenkins said he had the proper permits in possession. City officials, however, contend they were obtained after construction was started. The majority of alleged harassment has come from the Greenwood Police Department, according to Jenkins, who has said the department is fraught with "drinking, whoring and gambling."

Copyright © Index-Journal

CITY ADMITS TO HARASSMENT

The State Law Enforcement Division's announcement that the Rev. Jenkins "had not exhausted all remedies on a local level" in his efforts to investigate the police department was ludicrous. Even SLED spokesman Hugh Munn admitted he didn't know what these "local remedies" would be.

The Greenwood City Council said they had investigated the police department and pronounced the charges without foundation. What else would they say? For years there had been rumors that some of the top town officials had a regular poker game going and often engaged in other immoral activities. From their perspective, it was "stick together or fall apart."

Why the newspapers were reluctant to conduct their own investigations of the Rev. Jenkins' charges is anyone's guess.

Mayor Wingard admitted at the meeting that Leroy's charges of "harassment" were valid, and that the council considered harassment a legitimate way to conduct city business. The mayor added the police department would continue to harass building contractors hired by the Rev. Jenkins.

"Harassment" is not a legitimate tool to enforce building codes. Even if the evangelist was tardy in acquiring his permits, the fact that he did have permits indicated that his work was within the building codes, making harassment totally inexcusable.

The Rev. Jenkins had complied with all legal requirements and never felt he was "above the law" but rather that the law was above him and other ordinary citizens of Greenwood.

In addition to the ongoing harassment, the city was allowing enormous garbage trucks to trundle up and down the two-block-long, narrow street where the newly remodeled houses were located when they had no business there at all.

The decision by SLED not to investigate the charges the Rev. Jenkins made against the police department was amazing. It was unlikely the Greenwood police department's internal investigation would shed light on anything.

It appeared that the two agencies had decided the preacher was a threat and closed ranks against him.

Meanwhile, the reverend continued to move more of his operations to Greenwood.

JENKINS BITTER ON EVE OF DEPARTURE

Columbus Dispatch, August 31, 1978

Ron Rovtar

Delaware, Ohio—Delaware won't have Leroy Jenkins to kick around anymore.

This is part of what the controversial evangelist had to say when contacted at his Greenwood, S.C. offices Tuesday after the Dispatch learned he had been quietly moving his offices from Holy Hill Cathedral here to a location near his new home in the South.

"It (Delaware) is the most unappreciative little city I've ever seen in my life," said the bitter evangelist. As in the past he contended his cathedral has brought a great deal of money into the city north of Columbus.

"I despise it," he declared.

Jenkins in the past repeatedly threatened to leave central Ohio when angered by outspoken critics of his church. This time he apparently means it.

Although he says he intends to return to Holy Hill to conduct services on most weekends, the self-styled minister admitted he has been silently moving office equipment to a location in Greenwood he purchased about a year ago. He said plans have already been made to move computer equipment to South Carolina this weekend. When the evangelist announced the purchase of property in Greenwood a year ago, he said he would spend a good deal of time there, but claimed he couldn't move his offices because of the expense involved in transferring the computer gear.

Jenkins says he plans to keep Holy Hill cathedral open at least temporarily, but left the long-range future of the structure an open question. He said it is possible the Leroy Jenkins Evangelistic Association would eventually sell the facility and other property, including the Pollack Road mansion the evangelist has called home since he came to Delaware.

Jenkins moved to Delaware about 10 years ago when given property in the area. Besides Holy Hill Cathedral, a restaurant and a health food store in Delaware, Jenkins also had plans to open a boys ranch south of the city. These plans fell through.

Holy Hill Cathedral ran into difficulty last year when state building inspectors found the structure, much of it built by church members, unsafe. After several weeks of litigation, Jenkins agreed to make building changes and the structure was later reopened.

Partly as a result of this battle with the state, the angered evangelist made an abortive attempt to run for governor of Ohio, but pulled out of the race in March. He said he felt he could not serve two masters.

Since purchasing many of the buildings on a Greenwood street where he grew up, Jenkins has continued his crusades throughout the country. Among other crusades, he expects to be at the Washington Monument Sept. 23 as part of a three day crusade in the nation's capital.

He said he has also opened a restaurant in Greenwood and is going to publish a newspaper in his home town. Political plans again are on the evangelists agenda. He said he is going to run for mayor of Greenwood when the position comes up for election in three years.

"I'm very content here," Jenkins said of his new home. "I'm trying to quiet down and live as normal a life as I can. I like it here better because of the climate, and – I don't know – I just get tired of the winters up there."

There has been one break in the quiet however. The house Jenkins was living in recently caught fire. He claims it was an apparent case of arson.

Jenkins isn't sure if he will build a cathedral in South Carolina. "The people down here want me to. It depends on how the economy goes."

As for visits to Ohio, Jenkins says Holy Hill is not too far out of the way for him to make frequent stops for Sunday services. Many of his recent crusades have been in Chicago, Detroit, and Indiana. He has been in Delaware five of the past seven weekends.

"I guess I feel obligated," said Jenkins. "I have a lot of friends in Ohio. They're like a family. We worked together and laid bricks together, (during construction of Holy Hill Cathedral.)"

When he is not in Delaware his long-time friend and associate, the Rev. Richard Diamond of Mansfield, handles the service.

Jenkins says he will probably lease the offices at Holy Hill and that he is offering Ohio Wesleyan University here the use of the cathedral during the week because the university doesn't have an auditorium as big.

Still, there are a lot of Ohioans Jenkins doesn't appreciate. "I can't really understand a lot of people," he lamented. "You go to one church and they go to another one and they can act real snobbish. It hasn't been the people in general, it's the officials. They don't want honesty in government."

ENTERS THE SERPENT

Despite the Rev. Jenkins' differences with city officials, there were many happy times on Stockman Street. Greenwood was a good place for the Rev. Jenkins to gather himself together after the tension and excitement of the crusades. No one attending the huge revivals could understand the physical and mental energy such a ministry demands. The meetings lasted an average of three and one half hours, with the evangelist on his feet the entire time, pacing the stage, passionately preaching the old-time religion.

These revivals were as entertaining as they were inspirational. The reverend loved to sing, and, with his rich baritone, he put all his heart and soul into such classics as "How Great Thou Art" and "Amazing Grace." As God gave him the gift of knowledge, he moved off the stage and out into the audience, where hundreds of people received physical and spiritual healing.

At these times, he was unstoppable. Even when stage crews flashed the lights off and on to let him know his time was up, he went on with his work. As long as he was under the anointing, his eyes shone, and he radiated strength and purpose, as he stayed on to shake a few more hands, and pray another prayer.

When he was finally spent, he had to be rushed from the auditorium, protected from the frenzy of the people who tugged and pulled at his clothing. By the time he reached the waiting limousine, his clothing might be torn, his cufflinks missing, even his tie.

After the meetings, fatigue set in. The Rev. Jenkins was often too exhausted to speak. At these times, the relative peace and quiet of his Greenwood home was the perfect tonic. There, he didn't have to be "on stage" all the time. He could laugh and joke with his employees, let his hair down a little.

Unfortunately, these recuperative periods were not to last. He had made too many enemies. And they were not about to let him rest.

THE LITTLE HOUSE ON THE PRAIRIE

Like many dynamic, high-energy people, the reverend was always the most content when involved in a new project.

As soon as workmen finished transforming the run-down Stockman Street houses into charming cottages for the evangelist's friends and employees, the Rev. Jenkins turned the last house in the street into a restaurant, which he hoped would attract the downtown lunch crowd and where he could occasionally demonstrate his considerable cooking skills.

The Little House on the Prairie was a hit from the day it opened. The menu included mouth-watering Southern dishes such as turnip greens, crumbly corn bread, crusty-brown pork chops, Rev. Jenkins' special cloud-soft mashed potatoes, and delicious pale-pink pinto beans cooked with fatback.

He hired Lillie Drake, famous for the other restaurants she had operated in Greenwood, and together they prided themselves on operating one of the town's popular breakfast and lunch spots.

Electric and gas company workers, businesspeople, bankers, secretaries, shopkeepers—all came for the food and the camaraderie. The Rev. Jenkins was in his glory, supervising the buying of fresh vegetables, cooking favorite dishes, and occasionally serving food as he laughed and mingled with diners.

THE DECEIVER APPEARS

It was during the Stockman Street renovations that Billy Murphy first appeared. His clothes were ragged and worn, his black hair curled over his forehead, and his blue eyes shone with sincerity, as he told the Rev. Jenkins of the string of bad luck he had suffered. He said he had no home, because he had been kicked out by his wife.

He had recently secured a job as a laborer for Don Cantrell, one of the reverend's contractors, who was remodeling the homes on Stockman Street. Cantrell introduced Murphy to the reverend as a longtime friend, down on his luck. A trusting man with a sympathetic heart, the Rev. Jenkins was always eager to help when asked.

But Murphy had lied about his troubles. He had even lied about his name. Billy Murphy was in fact Bruce Mirkin, an undercover agent for the Bureau of Alcohol, Tobacco and Firearms (ATF),[3] who had been brought in by the South Carolina Law Enforcement Division (SLED) to presumably investigate the fire at the Calhoun Street residence.[4]

Don Cantrell, the contractor who had introduced Murphy as a longtime friend, did not even know Mirkin. Embroiled in his

---

[3]   In addition to the Waco massacre, the ATF is the same agency responsible for the Ruby Ridge, Idaho, tragedy. Around December 1990, ATF agents had cornered Randy Weaver, a fugitive on a weapons charge, at this remote cabin. When the shooting stopped, Weaver's 14-year-old son lay dead along with Weaver's wife, shot by a sniper's bullet as she held her child in her arms.

[4]   Several of Jenkins' employees had already been subjected to intensive questioning by SLED immediately after the fire. There was no evidence that the fire had been set by anyone within the Association. Although the insurance company dragged its feet in paying the reverend for his losses, a court decision in the Rev. Jenkins' favor forced them to do so.

own trouble with the IRS, he was threatened with prison if he did not become a part of the deception.

So Bruce Mirkin, alias Billy Murphy, came on the scene, with a tape recorder fastened to his body under his clothes, posing as a friend, while collecting whatever information he could against the Rev. Jenkins, for whatever reason the ATF wanted it.

Mirkin latched on to the Rev. Jenkins, making himself available to assist the reverend in any way he could. He ran errands, befriended the reverend's children, and tried to become indispensable to the Association.

At first, the Rev. Jenkins was glad for such a willing and enthusiastic helper and took Mirkin along with him on some of the crusades to help with crowd control. Later, the man began to trouble him, though he could not say why. Suspecting he might be a plant from the IRS, he allowed Mirkin to hang around for a while to see what he was up to. (see photo on page 277) Afterall, He knew he didn't have anything to hide.

Mirkin, alias Murphy, liked to go to area clubs for a good time, and occasionally the Rev. Jenkins went with him. He soon tired of this, preferring to stay home with his family and close associates, cooking his favorite recipes, relaxing in his yard, and just savoring being alone.

When the reverend didn't accompany him, Mirkin escorted his daughter, Candy, around to some of the local clubs. After one such evening, Candy said Mirkin plied her with drinks and attempted to take advantage of her. She broke free and escaped, but the Rev. Jenkins' relationship with Mirkin had been dealt a lethal blow.

His assignment was not faring much better. Although Mirkin kept his tape recorder running during the months of October, November, and December of 1978, he found nothing amiss with the evangelist or his operation. The surveillance had been a waste of taxpayers' money.

The ATF called Mirkin back to Marietta, Georgia, where he was put on other assignments. Apparently the bureau had decided not to spend any more time on surveillance of the Rev. Jenkins.

By this time, the reverend had found a more suitable dwelling than the little home where he had been raised. It was a lovely Southern mansion, surrounded with acres of virgin timber, a perfect place for him and his children to live. Sons David and Scotty were still in school, and they had been living with relatives and friends since the fire drove them out of the big Calhoun Street house. Now it was time to gather his family into one place, and the mansion on New Market Street seemed ideal.

He dove into the project of renovating the mansion. Work also progressed on Abby Mall, the old vacant Presbyterian Church the Rev. Jenkins was turning into a shopping mall. Several of the shops in the mall were already leased, and prospects looked good for the remaining space. Work crews rushed to complete work on a supper club in the mall before its New Year's Eve opening. The event was a huge success. The Rev. Jenkins went from table to table greeting his friends and acquaintances.

The years of hard work in Greenwood had borne fruit. Stockman Street and the office on Magnolia Street were well established. The Little House on the Prairie was going strong. The Rev. Jenkins had a lovely, spacious home on New Market Street, and the Abby Mall was almost fully leased.

Despite troubles with a few local officials, the reverend was making a place for himself, his family, and his employees in Greenwood. There was even some positive press coverage from time to time.

A BIRD IN THE HAND
WHO CAN'T BE PUSHED

Anderson Independent, April 5, 1978

Karen Pettit

Greenwood—Bobby was in a foul mood Tuesday. He wouldn't sing the religious hymn, "How Great Thou Art." And he refused to wave good-bye to his visitors.

But Bobby, pet parrot of the Rev. Leroy Jenkins, (see photo on page 257) did tuck his head under his bright green wing with deep red coloring underneath and cry like a baby. He wailed, "Waa-a-a-h."

Bobby wasn't unhappy. He was just mimicking the sounds he had heard of a baby crying. His cries came at the chiding of Jenkins, "The baby wants a bottle, huh? The baby want a bottle? "Later Bobby warbled, "The baby wants a bottle."

Bobby, 2 1/2 years old, was purchased by Jenkins, a faith healing evangelist, about two years ago in Tampa, Fl., from a pet shop. Jenkins says he is teaching religious songs to Bobby so that the parrot can sing at Jenkins' faith healing crusades.

Although Jenkins has planned a crusade Sunday in Greenwood at the Civic Center, Bobby isn't on the program yet.

As Jenkins moved Bobby's cage from the house to the back porch, Bobby clenched his claws around the metal bars, and hung upside down. On the porch table, Jenkins arranged a green and yellow tablecloth which matched Bobby's feather colors.

The table was to be used as a rest for Bobby's cage. Jenkins said, "We might as well give Bobby some class or he might not like it." But Bobby must not have liked the added touch of class. Tuesday he was unwilling to join in singing with Jenkins' soul-stirring version of the religious hymn, "How Great Thou Art," as he had performed on an earlier occasion for an Independent reporter.

At that time, as Jenkins walked down the hall singing "then sings my soul, my Savior God to Thee," Bobby echoed in with Jenkins on the chorus, "how Great Thou art." Then, as Jenkins sat in his living room, Bobby called, "Rev, someone's at the door."

Jenkins said Bobby frequently will call out announcing a visitor even when there is no one at the door. "He does that to get you to come to see him. He's lonely."

But Bobby did demonstrate a new talent Tuesday as Jenkins tried to get his parrot to sing. He danced.

"Hi, Bobby, what a pretty bird," cooed Jenkins as he leaned over to get Bobby from his cage. Bobby remained speechless.

"Do you want to sing for us?" asked Jenkins, dressed in white slacks and white jacket. Still no answer from Bobby.

"Come on Bobby, let's sing," said Jenkins, a flamboyant minister who has residency in Ohio but maintains a vacation home in Greenwood.

Jenkins tried again with the song, "Then sings my soul, my Saviour God to Thee." This time, in the part where Bobby was to sing, there was silence. But Bobby began stretching his neck, ruffling his wing feathers and lifting one foot over the other again and again on top of his cage. He tilted his head from side to side in time with the hymn.

"He's dancing for you," Jenkins said. Jenkins leaned on the cage to talk to Bobby. Bobby tilted his head as Jenkins pleaded, "Don't you want to sing for Rev.?"

Bobby continued to dance but his movements were interrupted as sirens from a nearby ambulance distracted him. He strained his neck as if to hear the sounds better and then watched closely and carefully as a photographer took his picture.

"He's had so many stories done on him," Jenkins said, "He's used to having his picture made. He knows exactly what you are doing."

Jenkins tried for a final time to get Bobby to sing. "If you are going to sing, go ahead." Still no warbles. "Give me a kiss, Bobby," Jenkins pleaded as he leaned towards Bobby and puckered his lips. Bobby leaned his beak over to the minister.

"Hi, Bobby," the minister said softly. Bobby answered, "Bye,"

"Bobby, wave good-bye," said Jenkins in an effort to get the bird to wave his claws to his visitors.

"Bye, Bobby," said Jenkins. "Wave bye-bye."

"No," answered Bobby.

Copyright © Anderson Independent

THE TRAP IS SET

Entrapment is defined as "the act of officers or agents of the government in inducing a person to commit a crime *not contemplated by him*, for the purpose of instituting a criminal prosecution against him."[5] (emphasis added)

An undercover agent is guilty of entrapment when, to obtain evidence against someone, "he originates the idea of the crime and then induces another person to engage in conduct constituting such a crime when the other person *is not otherwise disposed to do so*."[6] (emphasis added)

The case of the *State of South Carolina v. Leroy Jenkins* certainly appears to fit that description. From the moment he insinuated himself into the Rev. Jenkins' life, Bruce Mirkin, alias Billy Murphy, did everything he could to try to poison the reverend's mind, to induce him to do something completely against his character.

He gained the reverend's confidence by flattery and cajolery, telling the preacher what he wanted to hear. He pretended to be a confidante, when he was in truth a confidence man by profession. The Rev. Jenkins, being human, was as susceptible to

---

[5]   Black's Law Dictionary, West Publishing Co. (1991)

[6]   *Ibid.*

these manipulations as anyone else would be under the same set of circumstances.

Mirkin had returned to Atlanta after failing to find anything amiss regarding the fire at the Calhoun Street house. But something happened that would bring Mirkin back to Greenwood and back into the reverend's life.

EVANGELIST'S DAUGHTER ARRESTED

Anderson Independent, December 6, 1978

GREENWOOD—The 19-year-old daughter of Evangelist Leroy Jenkins was arrested on four charges Monday evening after an incident with a State Highway Patrolman, a Patrol spokesman said.

Candace Elaine Jenkins, of 46 Stockman Street, was arrested just north of Greenwood and charged with speeding, no driver's license in possession, disorderly conduct and resisting arrest, Patrol Capt. M.G. King said.

King said Patrolman C.R. Keasler signed warrants in the case before Greenwood Magistrate Charles Henderson Tuesday morning. Miss Jenkins was released into the custody of her father a few hours after the incident.

King said the Patrol would not comment further on the incident, which occurred on S.C. 25 at 7:25 p.m. until a final disposition.

In a telephone interview from his home, Leroy Jenkins accused officers of treating his daughter roughly, claiming she had suffered bruises on her hands from being handcuffed.

Henderson said the charges against Miss Jenkins will be heard January 3 in Greenwood Magistrate's Court, except for the resisting arrest charge, which will be heard during the Jan. 8 term of General Sessions Court.

BILLY MURPHY BACK ON THE JOB

On the night of her arrest, Candy, just nineteen years old, had been babysitting her sister Theresa's children and Scotty, her youngest brother. Suppertime came, and she decided to leave the little ones with Scotty while she drove to McDonald's for some hamburgers.

Slipping into her truck, with a few dollars in her jeans, she rushed to McDonald's. Just as she reached the fast-food restaurant, a state trooper pulled her over, and the officer asked to see her driver's license. In her haste, Candy had left the purse with her driver's license in it at home.

After she told the officer who she was, Candy said his attitude became hostile. He demanded she get out of the truck and shouted at her, "Don't you try to get away."

He then walked around to the back of the truck, presumably to run a check on her license tag. Candy panicked and ran into the restaurant to call her father to ask him to bring her license over.

Patrolman Keasler rushed in behind her, knocking her down. He pushed her to the floor with his knee in her back and twisted her arms behind her to put her in handcuffs. According to Candy, Patrolman Keasler continued to yell at her not to try to run away, even after she was on the ground.

Candy had no intention of running from the patrolman. If she had, she would have run *away* from McDonald's, not into it. Brutally slapping cuffs on her, the patrolman dragged the teenager to his patrol car, shoved her inside and took her to jail where she was booked and fingerprinted. Painful bruises, from where the steel handcuffs had been forced on her, were already discoloring her arms. Her jailers took away her shoes, replacing them with paper slippers. To this day, she remembers how cold her feet were.

The Rev. Jenkins was shocked to hear that Candy was in jail. When he heard her side of the story, he was enraged, as any parent would be. She could hardly have been speeding as she turned into the McDonald's parking lot. While she should have had her license with her, this innocent omission did not warrant the patrolman's knocking her down, handcuffing her, and dragging her into the patrol car.

MIRKIN/MURPHY STRIKES AGAIN

Hearing of Candy's arrest, Bruce Mirkin, alias Billy Murphy, was soon on the telephone from Atlanta, looking for the Rev. Jenkins. But the reverend had left instructions that he did not want to talk to Murphy. Unable to reach him by phone, Mirkin came to Greenwood and found the reverend in his backyard.

The reverend was not thrilled to see Murphy again. But Murphy was a practiced manipulator and knew how to ingratiate himself. He pretended to care about what had happened to Candy and to share the evangelist's outrage.

Murphy goaded the pastor, playing on his instincts as a father and urging the reverend to let him "get even" with Patrolman Keasler by burning his house down.

The reverend wanted no part of such a plot.

"I couldn't believe that he was serious," the Rev. Jenkins said later, admitting that he had thought about "punching the trooper in the nose."

However, Mirkin was determined in his task and eventually gained the reverend's confidence once again. He had finally found a way to bring the troublesome, muckraking reverend to his knees. While the reverend expressed his fury at what the patrolman had done, Murphy gathered every embittered word onto his tape recorder.

He also played upon the Rev. Jenkins' resentment toward *Anderson Independent* newspaper reporter Rick Ricks, who had written a series of negative articles about the reverend just weeks earlier. And, for good measure, he tried to talk the preacher into getting revenge against a local businessman he felt had cheated another friend out of some money. After his failed attempt to get incriminating information about the Calhoun Street fire, Mirkin appeared determined to get the Rev. Jenkins one way or the other, no matter what.

The ATF agent persuaded Frank Minor, a painter who was working on the Rev. Jenkins' new home, to accompany him to a gas station where he purchased several cans of gas. He then drove to Keasler's home. As he pulled into the driveway, policemen swarmed out of the bushes and arrested them both.

At the police station, Mirkin was booked for attempted arson along with Frank Minor. He told the police that the Rev. Jenkins had hired him to torch Patrolman Keasler's house.

It was a sham, of course. Mirkin's arrest was a ruse to get Frank Minor and Scott Shirley, another Association employee who had been recruited by Mirkin, into jail. Once there, they were in the hands of Greenwood solicitor William Jones, who visited them daily. Later, in a sworn statement given to the Rev. Jenkins' lawyers, Frank Minor said Jones coached them on their testimony.[7]

Capitalizing on the perception in some minds that the Rev. Jenkins had been guilty of burning down his own house and the inaccurate report by the *Anderson Independent* that the Ohio church had been bombed,[8] the ATF agent had successfully planted the seeds of the Rev. Jenkins' betrayal at the hands of Greenwood justice.

Scott Shirley, who had been recruited by Mirkin in a plan to assault the newspaper reporter, was released on bond after a few days. Shirley claimed Solicitor Jones made a deal with him, promising him that he would not do time if he would implicate the Rev. Jenkins as a conspirator. Shirley went along with the plan, testifying that the reverend had planned the arson attempt.

---

[7] See chapter, "A Witness Recants – Too Late."

[8] See chapter, "Setting the Stage for Accusations of Arson."

Frank Minor was held until trial, because his family could not afford to post the $150,000 bond. Minor was terrified and intimidated by the police. He agreed to cooperate with the solicitor.

And so, a man who had never conspired to hurt anybody before in his life was indicted for conspiracy to commit arson and assault.

After the trial, when the Rev. Jenkins was sent to prison, (see photo on page 265) Frank Minor came to the reverend's attorneys and volunteered to tell the truth about what went on in the jail and the many nights the solicitor came to him and the sessions that ensued.

In a sworn statement, he said that he and Scott Shirley were taken out of their cells and taken into rooms where Jones sat and talked to them for hours each night. Minor said Jones told them the Rev. Jenkins was going to be "off the streets" and would be sentenced to twelve years on four counts of conspiracy to commit arson and conspiracy to commit assault and battery. The reverend had to be sentenced to more than ten years, Minor quoted Jones as saying, because state law mandated that anyone sentenced to more than ten years could not be released on bond pending his appeal.

The young men testified as they were instructed, and Jones achieved his desired result: the Rev. Jenkins was sentenced to twenty years, reduced to twelve years. As a comparison, a convicted murderer in the United States serves an average sentence of six years.[9]

It is important to remember this: there was no arson, and there was no assault.

"I wanted to give Keasler a black eye," the Rev. Jenkins said later. "If I had wanted anything to happen to him, I would have done it myself."

---

[9]   Bureau of Justice Statistics, Prison Sentences and Time Served for Violence, 1995

THE ANDERSON
INDEPENDENT ARTICLES

A Reputation Destroyed

Before the plot to sideline the Rev. Jenkins unfolded, believers came by the busload to the crusades, which were often as entertaining as they were edifying. Gospel songs shook the rafters as the faithful raised their hands in praise. Often, celebrities and movie stars thrilled the crowd with their testimonies. The Rev. Jenkins' dynamic message of God's healing power held audiences spellbound.

Thousands were made physically and spiritually whole in civic centers, theaters, and auditoriums from Chicago to Miami, and Baltimore to Los Angeles. Often, those vast halls could not hold the believers who sought to be a part of this great outpouring of

God's Spirit, where miracles happened just as they had in the days when Jesus walked the earth.

If the faithful could not come to the crusades, the crusades came to them via one of the eighty-seven television stations across the nation that aired the *Revival of America* television program. In the Association's files are hundreds of testimonials from people who were blessed, delivered, saved, and healed.

As the Lord promised, "He that believeth in me, the works that I do shall he do also; and greater works than these shall he do; because I go to my Father" John 14:12 (KJV).

INACCURATE AND CARELESS

Not everyone appreciated the ministry. One Sunday in early spring, the Rev. Jenkins woke to find his face splashed in full color on the front page of the *Anderson Independent*[10] newspaper. Anderson is a community of approximately thirty thousand people some forty miles northwest of Greenwood.

It is customary when a newspaper targets an individual, to offer that individual an opportunity to tell his side of the story. Without warning, the *Anderson Independent* hit the newsstands promising a weeklong series of articles purporting to be an "insightful and interesting look into the life of a fifth-grade dropout who has become one of the nation's leading evangelists."

The articles were inaccurate and careless. The pejorative tone of the articles was disturbing. Incredulous and hurt, the Rev. Jenkins read each issue in disbelief. Could a small-town paper be so desperate for increased circulation that it would publish sensationalist stories at the expense of a man's reputation? Or could the reason be far more troubling?

---

[10] In 1981, the *Anderson Independent* became the *Anderson Independent-Mail*.

Later events would make it seem that there may have been a well-orchestrated plot to turn public opinion against the Rev. Jenkins. By criticizing some of the members of the Greenwood establishment, the Rev. Jenkins alienated some powerful people.

Throughout the tabloidlike onslaught by the *Anderson Independent*, friends and family rallied around their beleaguered pastor, including new pal Billy Murphy, a.k.a. Bruce Mirkin, the ATF agent who was instrumental in the Rev. Jenkins' arrest. (See chapter "The Arrest.") Mirkin murmured his sympathy while stoking the fires of the reverend's anger toward the *Independent* reporters. Mirkin even offered—not one time but many times— to "beat up" Rick Ricks, one of the reporters. It must have been tempting. The Rev. Jenkins was outraged that his life's work had been reduced to a few articles filled with innuendo, warmed-over gossip, and out-and-out lies.

Even so, the reverend had no intention of allowing Billy Murphy to hurt Rick Ricks. The evangelist is a strong man. He faced down the Ku Klux Klan years before when they poured acid on his tent and tried to run him out of town for baptizing blacks and whites together. Many times through the years, people tried to disrupt his services only to find themselves facing his righteous anger. He has been confronted by kooks and stalkers of the most sinister kind, and he has stood up against attack and criticism from all quarters without flinching. He did not need Mirkin or anyone else to do his fighting for him.

He did, however, vent his ire in language unbecoming a man of God. Most people say things they don't mean when they are angry. Even preachers. They blow off steam, and then it is forgotten. Not this time. This time the Rev. Jenkins' angry words went right into the tape recorder strapped to Mirkin's body.

These emotionally charged remarks, uttered in the privacy of his own home, were the basis for a conspiracy charge against the preacher that would result in a terrible miscarriage of justice. These tapes were introduced as evidence that the Rev. Jenkins entered into a conspiracy to beat up Rick Ricks. When the reverend heard the tapes, he was convinced they had been doctored. He was furious with the reporter, certainly, but he had not conspired with anyone to beat him up.

If there was a conspiracy, it was concocted by the ATF and others to entrap the outspoken preacher and put him out of business.

This and the following chapters include a series of articles published by the *Anderson Independent* that helped to create a climate of hostility toward the Rev. Jenkins and make it that much easier to seal his doom.

WHO IS REV. LEROY JENKINS?

EDITOR'S NOTE: More than a year ago the Rev. Leroy Jenkins established his evangelistic forces in Greenwood and began appearing with some regularity on the front page of the Independent.

Controversy seemed to mark his path wherever he trod.

He bought an Associate Reform Presbyterian church in Greenwood and converted it into a shopping mall. A mansion he purchased burned. He became embroiled in arguments with the Greenwood establishment.

Then he began to project himself into the political life of that city and this state. He has announced his intention of becoming mayor of Greenwood and governor of South Carolina. He made a brief try at becoming the chief executive of Ohio when his evangelistic team was centered in Delaware, Ohio.

Whether or not Leroy Jenkins ever becomes governor of South Carolina, he certainly qualifies as one of the more interesting persons to land in our midst.

As a result, two Independent reporters, Rick Ricks and Jim Galloway, have spent a great deal of their time over the past nine months gathering information for this series. Galloway has been assigned almost full time to the story.

We think their efforts have produced an insightful and interesting look into the life of a fifth-grade dropout who has become one of the nation's leading evangelists.

GREENWOOD—The Rev. Leroy Jenkins comes from South Carolina, where he was adopted and raised.

He comes from California, where he tried to kill a man, and from Atlanta, where he discovered the profession of faith healing.

He comes from Dallas, where he first called himself Reverend. It was also the place where, in his early 20's, he met a lonely, rich widow who he claimed as his natural mother.

She gave him her name, and the financial backing to enter the evangelistic business. He later left the widow and her name, but took his modest beginning and built it into a small empire that attracted $3 million in tax free donations in 1977.

His charismatic style, caustic preaching and reputation as a faith-healer drew thousands of the faithful to crusades throughout the nation.

More than 10 times as many watch him every Sunday morning on television: his television ministry is the financial backbone of the Leroy Jenkins Evangelistic Association, Inc.

He wants to be more than an evangelist. He ran a half-hearted race for the governorship of Ohio in 1977, and has visions of becoming the governor of South Carolina–after he is elected mayor of his hometown.

Jenkins began his hike to fame in Atlanta in 1960, when his arm–supposedly sheared off in an accident–was miraculously re-attached during a tent meeting.

It was Jenkins introduction to faith healing, and faith healing's introduction to the youthful fireball with "the power."

But the evangelist's story began in the small town of Greenwood and is likely to end there. Jenkins moved back home a year-and-a-half ago, and says it is where he would like to finish his career.

Copyright © Anderson Independent

THE BEGINNING

Though he has no first-hand knowledge of his birth, Jenkins says he was born on a North Carolina Indian reservation, the illegitimate son of a Cherokee woman. Jenkins claims his grandmother found him cast away in a field to die, and gave him to his adopted mother, Willamae Jenkins.

Willamae and her husband, Amos Jenkins, lived in York County, S.C., but moved to Greenwood when their new son was only a few years old.

The family was poor and lived in one of several bungalows on Stockman Street—it was something Jenkins could never get used to, though he had never known anything else.

"I was meant to be a rich man's son, and I hated a patch worse than anything," Jenkins once wrote.

His mother was a woman once obsessed with religion, and she later followed her son's footsteps, conducting faith-healings of her own.

One of his first recollections was of his mother being taken away to a state mental hospital in Columbia when he was only 5 years old. She had allowed herself to almost starve to death, wasting away to 80 or 90 pounds.

"And I saw the doctors comin' out of the house with my mother, and I looked up, and I could tell she was leaving," Jenkins said in a four hour interview with Independent reporters.

And I started crying, and just out of nowhere I heard something—'Don't worry, I'll take care of you.' This is the first time I realized I had a calling on my life."

Jenkins described his father, usually absent, as an alcoholic who did not share his mother's beliefs until late in his life.

His childhood was heavily laced with religion. Jenkins says boyhood friends called him "Prophet Jenkins" when he began preaching to them. He spent a great deal of time at a local Church of God, singing and playing the guitar. (see photo on page 256)

Little emphasis was placed on education. Jenkins was passed on to the fifth grade before he dropped out of school, though he admits he never went beyond the second grade in learning.

Jenkins once wrote that he was asked to leave because his mind, obsessed with religion, was never on his school work. "My teacher was a real b____ I threw a brick through the schoolroom window and ran out laughing," he told one reporter.

Because of his adoption and Indian heritage, Jenkins says he was treated as an outsider, which probably, more than anything else added to his drive to succeed. After he was laughed at by a particularly spiteful woman, he made a vow that was to affect the rest of his life.

I said, 'You old b___! One day I am going to be rich and come back and buy this d___ street. And I'm going to run everybody off.' And that's what I did," he said.

He ran away from home with a friend when he was about 15 years old, using money stolen from a jukebox for a grubstake.

They drifted through small towns in the south, spending much of their time in Tampa, Florida, where Jenkins was later to make his headquarters. Despite his religious upbringing, Jenkins was torn between piety and a disregard for any rules but his own.

"I was a–I guess, a good thief. I could steal with never you watching me, 'Cause I did when I was a kid–that's how I survived," Jenkins said.

The pair later split, with his friend going back home and Jenkins continuing on to Texas. He met a Christian family that took him in.

After two years he returned home to Greenwood in a green 1940 Ford with one gear–no reverse. But things were too quiet in Greenwood, and he moved on to Atlanta, where he took a job as a theater usher.

He eventually quit the job after deciding that movies were sinful. But before he quit he met his first wife, "a beautiful girl with long black hair."

MARRIAGE, MOVING, AND A GUN

Anderson Independent, April 8, 1979

Jim Galloway and Rick Ricks

One month later they were married, Jenkins borrowing 50 cents from Ruby Garrett's mother for the marriage license, then traded away Ruby's piano for some furniture. Jenkins says he was 13 years old, as was Ruby–her mother signed the license for both of them.

(On the advice of his business manager, Jenkins later wrote that he was 17 years old when he got married, and Ruby was 15. This places his age at 43–if he were married at 13, he would be a more unlikely 39.)

They were married on their lunch hour, and that night drove to Greenwood, where soon after Jenkins tried to find work.

According to Jenkins' autobiography, an often rambling work entitled, "How I Met the Master":

> I worked at a number of jobs in Greenwood. Once I got a job at the city water works. When asked if I could read water meters, I said, "Sure, I have some college experience."
>
> They gave me a job and I found a friend to teach me how to read water meters over the weekend. I felt that I would love this job if I could work inside in the office. I bought a typewriter, charged it to the company and got fired.

I started working for the S.H. Kresge Company. I told them I had a college diploma and would bring it in to them. I always forgot it, though. I decorated my car with little gadgets without paying for them. I got fired there, too.

From Greenwood, Jenkins and his wife moved back to Atlanta and began raising a family. They would have seven children before the marriage would survive on paper for nine years more.

After living five months in Atlanta, Jenkins, his wife, his two sisters and their husbands packed up and moved to San Jose, California, where they shared a rented house.

Jenkins and the two husbands were working as house painters when Jenkins showed a penchant for guns and violence. He pulled a pistol on an unarmed fellow employee and shot three times.

"One day a painter who was working with us got fired. He was mad because I didn't get fired. He had been there longer than I had. I told him he was just too old to paint. This made him so mad he threw paint on me. In return I poured a gallon of paint on his car. When I got off from work that night I went downtown and bought a pistol."

In his autobiography, Jenkins said he fired five times, but that each bullet exploded in mid-air before it found its intended mark, 40-year-old Ray Bullock. "I knew God had spared his life," Jenkins wrote.

A San Jose Mercury account of the incident, dated Sept. 14, 1956 differs slightly:

"We were painting the gable of a house," officers quoted Bullock as saying. "I stepped off a ladder to get some putty, then he (Jenkins) took my paint bucket and was pouring his paint into my bucket.

Then I grabbed my bucket. He had his bucket. The two buckets hit together in the gravel. There was a little paint spilled on myself too."

At 12 noon (Thursday) I stopped work for lunch and started to Leroy and told him I did not like it for putting paint on my car, and me and him would fight it out. He left and picked up a rock and a stick. I said you just as well be a man and come on and take it.

"*I was going after my lunch from my car and he said, 'Come on up to my car.' I started, but I thought that he might have a gun in the car as I knew he had one for I'd heard him bragging about it.*

"*So I turned back, got my lunch went into the house where the other fellows were eating...He came to the window and said, 'You ———, come out here now.' I walked out the door and he began shooting.*

"*So when I heard the gun snap I then made towards him. He turned to run and I ran after him. He fell on some rocks.*

"*When I took the gun away from him, my hand and his came down with the gun and hit him in the stomach. Then the gun came loose from his hand and he began to beg me not to hit him."*

Bullock told officers he then returned to the house to finish his lunch.

Jenkins was hospitalized for head cuts and a bruised hand, but was only fined $25 for assault in a Sunnyvale, Calif. Court. The report is not specific about the charge of which Jenkins was convicted.

"*They got me. I don't remember–assault with attempt to kill. I was standing as close to us, from here to you, and I took that pistol, I pulled it, and I pulled the trigger, 'cause I intended to blow him in two," Jenkins said of the incident.*

The three shots fired–not five–did not explode in mid-air, but went wild, the result of a shaky hand and an "ancient Iver Johnson .32 caliber pistol," police said in the news report.

A few months later, Jenkins says he, his wife and the two
other couples returned to Atlanta, where Jenkins operated a
business selling antique furniture and pianos, and dabbled in
real estate. It was in Atlanta that Jenkins would find his call-
ing and begin a career as a struggling tent preacher.

Copyright © Anderson Independent

THE TRUTH SHALL SET YOU FREE

What the *Anderson* Independent editor referred to as an
"interesting and insightful" series of articles written by two
reporters who had spent months "gathering information" was in
truth nothing more than a mishmash of old stories, half-truths,
rumors, and lies.

Newspaper "exposés" operate on the assumption that their
subjects have hidden—or tried to hide—certain aspects of their
lives from the public.

In the Rev. Jenkins' case, this was not possible. First, he has a
habit of telling all about himself in his crusades, the good and the
bad. Additionally, the reverend has written several books about
his life, so there is nothing to expose about him.

The *Independent* articles included elements that would make a
seasoned journalist blanche: innuendo and hearsay, mistakes and
inaccuracies, and manipulation of the facts to promote a specific
point of view.

Where the reporters had a choice between taking the Rev.
Jenkins' word for something, or someone else's, they invariably
chose the latter.

Perhaps the *Independent's* greatest sin was creating an atmosphere
in which a jury might find it easy to send a man to prison for some
angry words inadvertently spoken into a hidden tape recorder.
Ultimately, the Rev. Jenkins spent more time in prison than the
average murderer. Prominent South Carolina lawyers practicing in
the state capital shook their heads at the length of the sentence. "He
was set up," said one, "and everybody knows it."

TWISTING THE MIRACLE ARM

"FAITH HEALING" MADE JENKINS A FAITH HEALER

Anderson Independent, April 9, 1979
Jim Galloway and Rick Ricks

EDITOR'S NOTE: This is the second in a series of articles on the career of Rev. Leroy Jenkins.

The faith healing career of Leroy Jenkins began in Atlanta on Mothers' Day in 1960, the result of an accident that injured his right arm.

The injury is as much the subject of controversy as the rest of his career—Jenkins says his arm was healed by a miracle. His doctor says the arm healed itself.

"I certainly wouldn't quarrel about God healing him—but putting it back together had something to do with it," said the surgeon who stitched the cut together 18 years ago.

As Jenkins tells it, he was at his home in North Atlanta, removing a 250-pound section of plate glass when it slipped.

The glass cut Jenkins' right arm, to be sure—the ragged scar is still there. But the size of the cut is the subject of dispute.

According to Jenkins' version, the glass severed muscle, tendons, bone and all, leaving his arm hanging on by only a shred of flesh.

He was taken to the hospital, where the doctors begged him to let them amputate the arm. Jenkins offered a "high reward"—the amount has never been made public — to 32 physicians if they could save it.

Despite their alleged reluctance, doctors put the arm in a cast and Jenkins walked out. The arm had already begun to turn black with rot.

A few days later, Jenkins was at a tent meeting held by the late evangelist A.A. Allen. A tent filled of people saw Jenkins raise both arms and throw off the partial cast.

"I stretched it out and looked at my fingers. They were like those of a baby's hands. They were a different color and a different temperature. When I touched something with one finger I felt it in all of the other fingers. It was so helpless, yet it was still alive.

"This hand and arm are a constant amazement to me. I had to learn to use it all over again. I often dropped things that I picked up with my right hand until I got used to the touch of it. The fingers of this hand cannot be finger printed. There are only two lines in the palm of my hand."

The event was considered remarkable enough to put Jenkins on the cover of Allen's religious magazine, with two articles and more pictures inside.

But the medical side of the story differs somewhat.

Dr. Albert L. Evans was on call at Georgia Baptist Hospital when Jenkins was brought into the emergency room. "It was a right serious injury," the doctor admitted, although the cut did not sever the bone or any tendons.

The two largest arteries to the hand had been sliced, along with one of three nerves, also leading to the hand. Jenkins was admitted to the hospital for observation, but "I had never thought of amputating," Evans said.

Only one other surgeon—not 32—was consulted over the accident, and only because Evans happened to meet him in the hall. Jenkins never offered any "high reward", Evans maintains.

In addition, Jenkins claims his brothers had to threaten a team of surgeons in the operating room to prevent them from amputating the arm. Evans says there was no such argument, and Jenkins' cut was stitched up in the emergency room.

Evans still has records noting Jenkins' visits after the accident, which occurred May 8, 1960. He stayed in the hospital about eight days and left with his arm in a cast.

On May 17, Jenkins returned to Evans to have the cast changed to a splint. (According to a witness and his own literature Jenkins experienced his healing the next day.)

On May 21, Jenkins came back. Evans was "worried about the use of his hand."

On May 28, "the incision had healed over" and Jenkins was told he could move his arm.

Evans hasn't examined the evangelist since that last visit in 1960. But he said Jenkins' right hand is probably atrophied because of the severed nerve. Otherwise, both the arm and the hand are perfectly normal.

"All I can say is—I see him on television every now and then. I'm proud of the d____ good job I did," Evans said.

Whether or not the miraculous healing of the arm ever occurred, the accident was indeed the beginning of the Rev. Jenkins and his $3 million-a-year business.

For not only was he the subject of a miracle, but Jenkins also had assumed the "power" to conduct other healings in the name of God.

According to his autobiography, Jenkins said he begged a tent and an organ from a retiring preacher and slowly began crossing the country, spreading the miracle of his arm.

He actually joined Allen as an assistant, offering the testimony of his healing to the large crowds Allen drew, and providing healing to those "in need of a miraculous touch," Allen's magazine stated.

Twenty-year-old Jenkins was at a Dallas tent meeting four months after his healing when he attracted the attention of an elderly, well-to-do woman. The woman's name was Maudie Bartz.[11]

"He looked out on the audience and saw me and he come walkin' off that platform and come just as straight to me as a duck to water." She paused, then added, "And he said, 'Mamma, there you are, I've been looking all over for you," she said 18 years later.

Mrs. Bartz, the lonely and wealthy widow of an Odessa, Texas trucking contractor, gave Jenkins the financial support he needed to make his start. She provided the tent, the organ, a home in Dallas, a checking account and a car.

In a four-hour interview with the Independent reporters, Jenkins said he believed—and still believes—the woman to be his natural Cherokee mother. With long, braided hair, Mrs. Bartz admits.

There is no mention of Maudie Bartz in his autobiography.

With this new backing, Jenkins and two other Texas associates founded Miracle Arm Revivals, Inc. a forerunner of his current association.

It was a small operation, similar to a thousand others run by traveling evangelists and consisting of little more than the tent, and organ paid for by the widow Bartz. Its headquarters was Jenkins' home in Dallas.

But the Association had the evangelist's own personal touch.

"He'd lay his hands on anybody and they'd pass out. He really had the power," Mrs. Bartz fondly remembered.

---

[11]   The story of Maudie Bartz's contributions to the ministry will be discussed in the chapter, "Maudie" on page 124.

Three months after Miracle Arm Revivals was formed, Jenkins' relationship with the widow, then in her 70's, became more than financial.

Maudie's husband, Gust, had been dead for three years. He had left her without any children of her own, so she "adopted" Jenkins, along with his wife and four children.

The Rev. Leroy Jenkins became the Rev. Leroy Jenkins Bartz. His wife, Ruby, and the children–Danny, Theresa, Dennis and Candy–also had their last names legally changed to Bartz, Odessa court records show.

Mrs. Bartz, who is now in her mid-90's, doesn't remember how much money she spent on her new family, though her accountant says it amounted to "thousands" of dollars.

Neither does she remember how long Jenkins stayed with her, although it wasn't more than a year and a half.

She says she does remember that he left the home she provided him in Dallas without saying good-bye.

Records show that by 1962 Jenkins had formed a new corporation in Tampa, Fl.

The break with the widow Bartz was a boost for his career–The Leroy Jenkins Evangelistic Association; Inc. had a much broader appeal than a migrant organization named after a healed arm.

The name Bartz only stayed on Jenkins' posters and magazines for a short time. Jenkins says it still remains on some of his property.

Faith healing became the mainstay of his ministry, although a more popular concern was given an emphasis equal to the legend of his miracle arm.

Jenkins became an outspoken enemy of the forces of "satanic communism" in an area where the Cuban missile crisis and the Bay of Pigs invasion had already sparked great concern.

The most popular of his targets was of course, premier Fidel Castro, "a creeping beast from the bottomless pit pouring its poisonous anesthesia upon the heedless, lukewarm, pleasure-occupied Christian."

In the five years he was in Tampa he was able to solidify and expand his ministry. In addition to a church, he opened a nursing home, a retirement home and a faith healing clinic. (see photos on page 263)

But along with his growth came the critical attention of outside agencies, including the local office of the Better Business Bureau wherever Jenkins held his crusades, and various Chambers of Commerce.

His nursing home was "the former Sulphur Springs Motel and was opened around March 1964," the office reported.

Jenkins advertised his convalescent home for those "who do not develop enough faith in God to receive their healing at one crusade, or who could not maintain their faith long enough for a protracted recovery."

Jenkins became more and more the target of criticism, but a hot temper combined with the passion inherent in his profession often turned the tables on his critics.

He learned to return blow for blow, the bureaucratic slings and arrows thrown by the local governments who tried to force him to hold his crusade meetings in line with local ordinances. Government officials who thought him troublesome often provoked the fight, but sometimes it was Jenkins who threw the first punch.

After making an unannounced visit to the Bahamas for a series of crusades in 1963, Jenkins was ordered deported by Nassau officials.

No reason for the deportation was given, but if it was not for faith healing it might have been because of his early reputation as an integrationist. One of his first tent meetings in Atlanta was harassed by the Ku Klux Klan when he refused to segregate.

Jenkins regularly passes out a reprint of the account by The Nassau Daily Tribune:

"A crowd of 200 demonstrators waited outside the Supreme Court during the hearing of the habeas corpus application, and when Jenkins left the court he was engulfed by a cheering disorderly crowd as he made his way to a Bay Street restaurant for lunch.

"At a similar demonstration at the airport a disorderly crowd surrounded the entrance to the U.S. Immigration Service office and sang hymns. People in the crowd shouted threats, most of them against the editor of The Nassau Daily Tribune and his family.

"His children and his children's children shall perish,' one demonstrator shouted."

Both of Nassau's newspapers were apparently critical of Jenkins. The Nassau Times examined one of those "cured" by Jenkins. "The unfortunate man was seen a few weeks ago. He is still a cripple confined to bed. What is more ... we never heard of the Greek people taking a holiday to celebrate his "cure" (as Jenkins reported) because he was never cured."[12]

Jenkins was jailed in a similar controversy in Fort Pierce, Florida, for refusing to comply with city ordinances hurriedly enacted by the local city council when his crusade tent arrived.

The crowd that demonstrated for his release also raised the $1,500 bond to set him free. Jenkins filed suit against the city, but after he left both parties agreed to let the matter drop.

---

[12] This is a serious charge since it attacks the very core of the ministry. The Independent had an obligation to ask the Rev. Jenkins to comment on this incident. As it happens, not everyone who receives prayer is healed. On the other hand, there is ample documentation of healings through personal testimony as well as physicians' reports. Had the reporters conducted a thorough investigation of the thousands of people who have been healed and blessed through the ministry, the article may have been more balanced

As his following grew, Jenkins became more bold and let it known that God did not approve of those who stood in his way. A youth caused a disturbance at one of his crusades in Tampa:

"That boy left the tent yelling, 'That is not of God. That man is a fake.' Before he got in his car he fought one of my tent boys ... A few days later the evening news carried his picture on the front page of the paper. He had been killed in an accident.

"There were others who put their hand against the crusade. Several people in the furniture factory across the street signed a petition, complaining that our loud speakers were turned up too loud. They turned it in to police headquarters. One day later a fire swept through the building.

"I learned the meaning of the scripture "touch not mine anointed, and do my prophets no harm..."

Claims that God was behind the sometimes fatal accidents befalling critics came often from Jenkins. It became a tactic used repeatedly in both Delaware, Ohio and Greenwood.

Copyright © Anderson Independent

THE MIRACLE ARM
AND THE PROPHECY

Either you believe in God or you don't. And if you believe in God—an all-powerful, all-knowing entity—you must surely believe that he can do a little thing like heal a man's arm.

Jesus was in the miracle business. He spent his entire ministry healing the sick, delivering souls from bondage, and teaching his disciples to do the same. "He who believes in Me, the works that I do he will do also: and greater works than these will he do, because I go to my Father," John 14:12 (KJV).

The Rev. Jenkins' ministry began with the healing of his arm. If someone wants to discredit his ministry, casting doubt on the healing is a good place to start.

Although there were many witnesses to the severity of the injuries to twenty-year-old Leroy Jenkins' arm, *Anderson Independent* reporters did not consult these witnesses but relied only on the recollection of one man, the reverend's treating physician, who, at the time of the *Independent* interview was in his nineties. Having presumably treated thousands of patients in the intervening years, Dr. Evans should not have been expected to remember with perfect clarity events that happened years before.

At the time of the accident, the *Atlanta Constitution* reported the incident under the headline "Young Atlanta Business Man Faces Death Because He Refuses Amputation." The story of the Rev. Jenkins' miracle arm has been told in books and magazines many times and has never been challenged by anyone.

The *Independent* quotes Dr. Evans as saying he never considered amputating the arm. Unfortunately, his memory does not serve him well in this instance.

In his autobiography, *How I Met the Master*, the Rev. Jenkins recalls a different scenario.

> I remember Dr. Evans coming to my bedside. On the ninth day he came in and said, "If you are not going to co-operate with us, we are going to send you home. There is nothing left for us to do."

Among the many witnesses to these events were the reverend's two brothers, Harold and Wallace Jenkins, as well as other family members and neighbors. To the day she died, Rev's sister, Polly, recalls the blackened hand, the fingers vile with infection and so swollen they were splitting open. She even remembers the putrid stench.

Hundreds of people were present in the Rev. A. A. Allen's tent when Leroy Jenkins came there to be healed. They heard the Rev. Allen call out for him in that crowded tent.

"Where is that young man that cut off his arm? Come up here," the Rev. Allen said.

They saw the young Leroy Jenkins, trembling with fear and pain, walk up the aisle to the platform.

A number of young evangelists stood on A. A. Allen's platform that day. Among them were the Rev. Don Stewart; the late Rev. Nelson Patterson, of Zanesville, Ohio; and the Rev. Franklin Walden, of Atlanta. Neither one of these fine evangelists ever challenged the story of the Rev. Jenkins' healing. The Rev. Don Stewart, who inherited the Rev. Allen's ministry upon the latter's death, was also present and captured the healing on audiotape.

When he was healed, the Rev. Jenkins raised his arms to the heavens and began to wiggle his fingers. They began to lose their swollen and blackened appearance and to resume their normal shape.

"Whether or not the miraculous healing of the arm ever occurred...," the *Anderson Independent* states with a note of skepticism, "the accident was indeed the beginning of the Rev. Jenkins and his $3 million-a-year business."

The *Independent* reporters may not believe in miracles, but if we are to believe the words of Dr. Evans—that the reverend's right hand is "probably atrophied because of the severed nerve," the fact that it is not—is a miracle in itself.

The Rev. Jenkins uses his perfectly shaped and functional right hand to garden, write letters, beat corn bread batter, pray for the afflicted, and, in the first days of his ministry, to fight those who came to the tent crusades to challenge the validity of his ministry. In other words, his hand is normal.

The Rev. Jenkins is the first to recognize the skill and care of men of medicine. But he gives God the credit for his "miracle arm."

HOW TO TOPPLE A GOVERNMENT

The *Anderson* Independent *mentions* the Rev. Jenkins' order of deportation from Nassau in 1963. But it neglects to tell the fascinating story behind the order.

On October 23, 1963, during a revival before an enormous crowd of supporters, the Rev. Jenkins made a prophecy that the esteemed attorney L. O. Pindling would be the next prime minister of the Bahamas.

The prophecy, delivered innocently enough, threw the government into an uproar, because, unknown to the Rev. Jenkins, the established government did not want Pindling to become prime minister. They viewed the reverend's prophecy as interference in the internal affairs of the islands.

The government arrested the young preacher and sought a deportation order against him. It would not have been politic to reveal the real reason for the expulsion order, so therefore they labeled the Rev. Jenkins "undesirable according to a reliable source."

A storm broke over his arrest, as hundreds of protestors filled the public square. The shops closed, and the cabs quit running, paralyzing the city.

Front-page stories about the case dominated the newspapers for three days running.

The case went all the way to the Bahamian Supreme Court, which reversed the expulsion order and rewarded the Rev. Jenkins his court costs.

God's word was true. The prophecy He had given the Rev. Jenkins came to pass with a vengeance when Sir L.O. Pindling became the first black prime minister of the Bahamas. Ten years later, in 1973, he led his country in its successful bid for independence from Britain. Throughout his twenty-five years as prime minister, the nation prospered as never before.

The deportation proceeding against the Rev. Jenkins was so outrageous, so contrary to the spirit of democracy, that English law was changed to prevent anything like it from happening again. But you didn't read this in the *Anderson Independent*.

STOP PRESS—JUDGE ORDERS THE RELEASE OF LEROY JENKINS

Bahamian Times, November 1, 1963

Acting Chief Justice Mr. Justice Scarr this morning ordered the release of U.S. faith healer Rev. Leroy Jenkins on the grounds that a deportation order against him was not validly executed.

"Governor-in-Council had the power to make a valid order but exercised that power in an invalid manner so far as the arrest of Mr. Jenkins was concerned," Mr. Scarr said.

He ordered that Mr. Jenkins be released and awarded him costs for the court action. Crowds inside and outside the court cheered the decision.

A crowd of over a thousand thronged the Public Square just outside the Supreme Court building on Wednesday morning to witness what turned out to be one of the greatest public interest proceedings in the history of the country.

Copyright © Bahamian Times

L.O. Pindling appeared for the Rev. Jenkins at the hearing. The lawyer was so incensed by the Rev. Jenkins' arrest, he wrote a stirring article for the *Bahamian Times* that appeared the same day.

ON NAKED BACKSIDES

Bahamian Times, November 1, 1963

L. O. Pindling

When freedom loving people and God-fearing citizens see the naked backsides of their Government exposed to the winds of shame like our Government's was exposed this week it is time for the citizens to move and the Government to go.

Pindling continued to lambast the government's classification of the reverend as "undesirable" based on the word of an unnamed "reliable source."

There is apparently a person or group of persons in this country who are so powerful that they can pass on information to the Government and the Government will act upon it - will order the arrest of a man upon it - without even letting the man know what the charge is or who his accusers are...

In the years to come this country will realize the great service that Rev. Jenkins has done it. He has proved the incapacity and maliciousness of this Government in a way that perhaps few could. As of this minute, Rev. Jenkins, Mr. Addersley nor I have no idea as to why the minister was being deported. The Court seemed surprised to hear this, but that was and is the position.

Copyright © Bahamian Times

GET THE FACTS

Did the *Anderson Independent* deliberately withhold this fascinating story from the public, reporting only that the Rev. Jenkins was deported from Nassau as undesirable? Surely, if they read the articles provided them, they would have had all the facts necessary for a balanced story.

CHARACTER ASSASSINATION CONTINUES

JENKINS IN THE LIMELIGHT

ROAD TO GREENWOOD WOUND THROUGH OHIO

The evangelism business was good in Florida, but by 1966 business opportunities and a rocky marriage gave the Rev. Jenkins reason to move on.

The narrow "spirit filled Presbyterian" rediscovered southern California during some crusade tours - he had lived there less than 10 years before as a house painter. But in the midst of a successful career, he was now in a position to enjoy the California sun and the lifestyle that went with it.

Jenkins packed up and moved to San Bernardino[13] in Feb. 1967. His wife stayed behind, and she would never

---

[13]   A rural desert community, San Bernardino in 1967 was hardly representative of the "California lifestyle" as it is used in this context.

rejoin him. They were finally divorced in 1975, when Jenkins charged her with "gross neglect of duty".

His wife issued a counter complaint, also charging neglect but adding accusations of extreme cruelty. She later refused to participate in the divorce proceedings, and even had the telephone removed from her home.

Custody of the two small children - David, 10 and Sharon, 12 - was awarded to Ruby[14]. Even before he was permanently settled in California, he ran into trouble with authorities. On Feb. 3, 1966, Jenkins was driving a white Cadillac with Florida tags when he was pulled over by a Los Angeles patrolman. A resultant search uncovered both prescription and non-prescription drugs - and a large amount of cash. Jenkins told the officers that he had received the money at a crusade, but the evangelist was arrested on charges of possession of dangerous drugs without a prescription, and possession of dangerous drugs, according to Los Angeles court records.

Jenkins pleaded guilty to the charge of possession of dangerous drugs and was sentenced to 30 days in jail, court records indicate. But he was given a summary probation on the condition that he pay $75 or spend 15 days in the county jail. The conviction was dismissed April 29, 1968.[15]

Jenkins does not deny that the event occurred, but said the drugs in the car were for a gospel singer in the same car with him who was going through "the change of life."

---

[14] While Ruby Jenkins retained custody of several of the children, Danny, Dennis, Lou, Candy and Scotty lived with their father in Delaware, Ohio.

[15] The "illegal drugs" were a commonly prescribed tranquilizer, and the charges against the Rev. Jenkins were dismissed.

It was not a prestigious welcome for Jenkins, and he was not long for California.[16] The main reason for the short stay was the 80-acre farm given to him by an elderly Ohio couple in 1966.

BORN AGAIN—AGAIN

But before Jenkins arrived in Delaware, Ohio, the Leroy Jenkins Evangelistic Association, Inc. had to be legally "born-again" - this time in the state of Georgia. Former associates say the lack of accurate record-keeping prevented him from getting his tax-exempt status from the federal government while he was in Florida.

The status is important in the evangelism business. With it a religious organization can accumulate a large amount of non-taxable property, as long as the property is used for religious purposes.

Donors to the organization can also deduct their offerings from their own income tax returns, assuring a greater income for the religious organization.

Although he had no intention of moving to Georgia, the state where the miraculous healing of his arm occurred, a new, properly drawn charter would assure that his church would receive the recognition of the federal government.

---

[16] The Rev. Jenkins' California crusades attracted thousands to the tent cathedral and the auditoriums where he held his meetings. He became the favorite of many Hollywood celebrities, who appreciated his colorful style, his relaxed way of relating to them, and the fact that he did not sit in judgment of them the way many religious folk did. However, he felt a stronger calling in the Midwest. His reception in Ohio when crowds packed his tent at the fairgrounds, along with the gift of the farm, convinced him that he should establish his headquarters there.

In September, 1966, the Association received its Georgia corporation papers. Two months later the Association filed for its sought after tax status, proclaiming that it had only $16,463 to its name.[17]

And in answer to the inquiry, "Are you an outgrowth or continuation or any form of predecessor," the Association answered, "no."

The Jenkins Association was not as poor as it sounded. The Jenkins Association may have had only $16,463 in a savings account Nov. 15, 1966, but only two days passed before it received more than 80 acres of Ohio farmland – later valued at $250,000.

Jenkins took a piece of California with him, and entered Ohio with a flourish. (He had an unsuccessful hair transplant in 1966, and now wears a toupee.)

He acquired a taste for the limelight that showered the Hollywood stars and cultivated his friendship with them. He began to spend time at the homes of Mae West and Liberace.

His church became known locally as "The Church of What's Happening Now,"[18] although he retained the name of his evangelistic corporation. In addition, he now had the assets to push him to the fringe of national recognition.

In 1967, he reported the corporation's total assets at $16,463. By the end of 1968 he had received $678,000 in

---

[17]   The Leroy Jenkins Evangelistic Association, Inc. received tax-free status in August 1966 when it was incorporated, and was never denied that status.

[18]   Comedian Flip Wilson created an entire comedy routine for his 1970s television show that was inspired by the Rev. Jenkins. His popular sketches about "Rev. Leroy," his wife, "Ruby," and "The Church of What's Happening Now," were a tremendous hit. The Rev. Jenkins took it in stride as part of the price of success.

contributions, and the first $250,000 phase of a boy's ranch was under construction.

Supposed to house 32 boys when it was completed, the boys ranch existed for only a few months and had only five or six boys when it was closed by the state.

Jenkins also bought a small hotel in Daytona Beach, Fla. for $300,000 to create the Leroy Jenkins Palace Inn, according to a report from The Daytona Beach News. He later sold it for $750,000.

Although he received strong support from local Midwestern followers, Jenkins' entrance into Ohio was not viewed without concern.

As he did in Florida, Jenkins attracted the attention of local authorities when he began holding numerous healing crusades on his Delaware, Ohio farm property and in a Columbus, Ohio auditorium.

In 1968, shortly after Jenkins arrived in the state the Ohio attorney general's office began an investigation into Jenkins and his crusades, The Independent has learned. The investigation was conducted by the office's consumer fraud and crime section, a source says.

An official of the Ohio state medical authority confirmed that the investigation took place. No case was ever made.

Contributions to his growing television ministry amounted to $754,243 in 1972. He reached the million dollar mark in 1975, attracting $1,278,701 in gifts and contributions.

The Association's earnings doubled in 1976, and the ministry received almost $3 million in 1977, according to a copy of the Association's tax return, provided by Jenkins.

The Association's 1977 tax returns are not available from the Internal Revenue Service. The tax returns of tax-exempt organizations are public record according to federal law.

Jenkins' years in Delaware, Ohio, were not quiet. On Feb. 3, 1971, a Lincoln Continental owned by Jenkins burned outside his barn on his Pollock Road property.

One year later, Feb. 19, 1972, the dormitory for Jenkins' boys ranch burned. (see photo on page 264) Damages including the cameras and related equipment inside, were listed at $250,000. The dormitory had been used as a storehouse since the state closed it down, and officials listed the cause of the fire as a faulty oil furnace.[19]

Jenkins was frustrated by his inability to develop his Pollock Road property. Local zoning officials refused to allow the farmland, located on the edge of the river, to be used in any of the several ways Jenkins considered.

Jenkins had planned to build a shopping center on the land, along with a religious subdivision. Permission to construct the projects was refused because of the poor quality of the roads leading to the area - the township couldn't afford to improve them, city officials said.

A SECOND MARRIAGE

Anderson Independent, April 10, 1979

Jim Galloway and Rick Ricks

Socially, Jenkins became a man-about-town, although his divorce to Ruby Jenkins was not complete until 1975. For thirteen years Jenkins said he had been dating a gospel singer named Linda Peck, and April 16, 1977, they were finally married.

According to Jenkins' Revival of America magazine, "the bride wore a candlelight satin gown in the Victorian style, with a ruffle of handmade imported princess lace around the neck and sleeves....

"The groom descended from the balcony of the front of the church accompanied by a fanfare from the band." It was

[19] If officials ruled the fire had been caused by a faulty furnace, what purpose would the Independent have for bringing it up?

for Jenkins - not the bride - that the audience stood for and clapped, the magazine noted.

More than 1,500 followers attended the wedding. Guests were charged $1 per car to park in the lot behind Holy Hill Cathedral.

His marriage to Linda Peck did not last long - a special "wedding edition" of his magazine was printed, but never distributed. The marriage ended in June 1977 when Jenkins says his wife refused to follow him to Greenwood.

But it was Mrs. Jenkins who filed for the California divorce, citing irreconcilable differences. She refuses to talk about the divorce.

Jenkins' venture with his Holy Hill Cathedral ended badly.[20] The evangelist regularly held meetings in a tent on his 250-acre farm, and in an auditorium in Columbus.

But after local authorities refused to allow him to do what he wanted with his land in 1972, Jenkins announced he would pull out of Delaware and build a $5 million cathedral in Columbus.

"If God doesn't smite the people here, the ones who have done me wrong, He'll have to resurrect Sodom and Gomorrah and apologize to them," Jenkins was quoted as saying.

He sold the Pollock Road property to a Columbus firm for $250,000, and likewise arranged for the sale of his home, which he purchased in 1971 for $350,000.[21] However, both sales fell through and Jenkins did not move.

---

[20] This comment couldn't be more off the mark. Holy Hill Cathedral was a smashing success, a beacon for Christians throughout the country where the gifts of the Holy Spirit were in abundance. The *Independent* itself admits the ministry was a financial success during this period.

[21] The Rev. Jenkins purchased the home at 470 S. Sandusky St. for $75,000, not $350,000 as reported in The Anderson Independent. One telephone call to the Association office could have prevented such a needless error.

And he remained to build his church, which he added to his Sandusky Street home inside the city limits.

According to 1976 tax returns, the Holy Hill Cathedral in Delaware, Ohio was completed at a cost of $654,000. The auditorium included a health food store and a restaurant.

For his personal use, a combination greenhouse and tree house was also constructed, which cost the Association $14,000. Jenkins did not follow guidelines set down by the Ohio State Building Code in constructing the cathedral, which would later cost him thousands of dollars in repairs.

Although the state inspected the religious building, memos on problems in construction were not received in Columbus, 30 miles away.

A state building official said it is possible the memos were intercepted before they got to the proper desk in Columbus.[22]

Jenkins sent small tokens, including autographed pictures of himself, to the family of the local building inspector.

His supervisors later judged the inspector to be enamored with Jenkins, and he was relieved of inspecting any construction sponsored by the evangelist.

The building authority came under such pressure from Jenkins that it issued an order that no employee would be allowed to set foot on Jenkins' property alone.

Jenkins' violations were many, according to Gerald Bruce, a supervisor in the state building authority's industrial relations department.

The main concern was a huge central truss, about 150-feet long, that held up the roof and connected the auditorium to the three-story parsonage. The truss was constructed of "old sections of railroad beams," Bruce said.[23]

---

[22] The *Independent* offered no facts or evidence to back up this claim.

[23] This statement is false. Steel beams and trusses were given to the church by a Columbus steel firm, Lowendeck Steel.

The cathedral's original plan called for inside columns, but the beams replaced them – Jenkins would not provide revised plans showing the beam in place, the supervisor said.

Jenkins had also built stands for his television cameras and two balconies capable of seating 85 to 100 persons all supported by the main beam, Bruce said. The balconies were ordered taken down.

Stairs coming down from the balcony resembled "ship's ladders" and Jenkins decorated the front of his pulpit with "non-fire-rated carpet," Bruce said.[24] The church had no sprinkler system, and the church's seating capacity of 1,500 exceeded state limits for an area that size. Fire walls installed later reduced the Cathedral's capacity to 900,[25] Bruce said.

Jenkins has since repaired most of the deficiencies cited, strengthening the main truss and rewiring the building, but not before the state took him to court. Jenkins carried the numerous decisions against him to the supreme court and lost.

During the court test, state attorneys and employees say they were besieged by telephone calls from Jenkins' followers, and even threatened by Jenkins.

The evangelist called up one supervisor of the Ohio state building inspection department as recently as February to inform him a curse had been placed on him.

Jenkins told the supervisor that something tragic would happen to him or to his family within four months, "or he's not a man of God," the supervisor said.

Jenkins hired a contractor to make the repairs on the Cathedral in December 1977 and four months later the

---

[24]   This, too, is false. Mr. Buchanan of C.E. Buchanan Carpets in Westerville, Ohio, provided the fire-rated carpets that covered the floors of the cathedral.

[25]   Seating capacity was never reduced to 900 but remained at 1,200.

building was dynamited.[26] Three weeks after the bombing, Jenkins' house in Greenwood was burned, and police determined the cause to be arson.[27]

Interpreted as another act of antagonism by the state, the controversy over the Cathedral was probably one of the reasons he left for Greenwood.

"I tell you, if you gave me the whole state I wouldn't have it. They are a cold, heartless bunch of hypocrites that I never in my life want to see again," Jenkins said of Ohio.

Jenkins moved to Greenwood in the summer of 1977 to find a warmer climate and a warmer people. He moved in with a style equal to his stature, purchasing not only his boyhood home, but almost the entire street it stood on.

"Prophet Jenkins" had come home to show his neighbors that he had finally made good. He left behind in Ohio enemies and admirers, but hardly anyone in between.

And though they knew his hatred was not aimed at them, followers in Ohio are still bewildered by his leaving.

"There are a lot of lost people here, because their God moved to South Carolina,"[28] said one follower.

Copyright © Anderson Independent

---

[26]   Fire inspectors ruled there was no "bombing." The Rev. Jenkins' confusion about the event was understandable considering the fact that threats against him had been made in the past.

[27]   It should be noted here that Ernie Proctor, the drifter who had threatened to burn down the Rev. Jenkins' house, was questioned by the Greenwood police but never arrested or charged with the crime.

[28]   This comment cannot be attributed to a member of the church since no one in his right mind would make such a blasphemous remark.

TEARING DOWN A CHURCH

There are so many inaccuracies in the series of articles by the *Anderson Independent* that the mind reels.

The *Independent's* assertion that the cathedral was not properly constructed is inexcusable. Photos of the cathedral under construction show the immense steel beams that support the roof. Certified welders were used when any welding had to be done. The beams were strong and so well placed that the roof didn't move a fraction of an inch when the supporting beams were cut out from underneath it.

The State of Ohio brought out a stress machine that put thousands of pounds of pressure and motion on the beam, to see if it would budge or tremble. It did neither, but stood solid.

Contrary to the article, there were no "old sections of railroad beams" used in construction. No secondhand materials were used at all.

The *Anderson Independent* charged that "Jenkins decorated his pulpit with non-fire rated carpet" is another out-and-out lie. Mr. Buchanan of C. E. Buchanan Carpets in Westerville, Ohio, provided the fire-rated carpets that cover the floors of the cathedral to this day. (see photo on page 256)

When the additional fire walls that the state required were installed, the auditorium still seated 1,200 people, not 900, as reported by the *Independent*.

If the *Anderson Independent* could make so many errors in reporting about Holy Hill Cathedral alone, can they be trusted to report anything else?

People trust the newspapers. When they read an article, they assume the reporter has done his homework. People quote newspaper articles as sources of fact. Such formidable power and influence ought to be tempered by extreme care and caution on the part of journalists and their editors.

No one supports—or exercises—freedom of speech more than the Rev. Jenkins. But most readers don't know that this very freedom creates a virtual shooting gallery for journalists who have an axe to grind, who wish to build a career on the back of a well-known personality, or who are just too lazy to check the facts.

The Rev. Jenkins is a prophet of God, and just like Jesus Christ and his followers, he inspires enmity in the hearts of those who are stung by the truth.

"Blessed are ye, when men shall revile you, and persecute you, and shall say all manner of evil against you falsely, for my sake" Matthew 5:11 (KJV).

OHIO MINISTRY AN OVERWHELMING SUCCESS

Despite the remark by *Independent* reporters that "Jenkins' entrance into Ohio was not viewed without concern," the Rev. Jenkins was welcomed in Ohio. The mayor of Delaware spoke at the dedication of Holy Hill Cathedral and led a march of two thousand people to the lake on the ranch property where a baptismal service was held. It was said to be the largest group to be baptized at one time in Ohio.

For several years before he built Holy Hill Cathedral, Rev held services in the Ohio Theatre, just across from the state capital building in Columbus, thirty miles south of Delaware. At that time, the historic theater was run-down and neglected, its plush seats threadbare. If it hadn't been leased by the church for those few years, it most likely would have been demolished.

Eventually, historic preservationists realized what a treasure they had in the theater with its decorative moldings, its high ceilings strung with chandeliers, and its grand hardwood stage where actors and actresses of note brought the outside world to the heartland. The Ohio Theatre has been restored to its original glory and is now considered a historic treasure.[29]

---

[29]   The early days of the Ohio ministry are further chronicled in the book, "*As the Wind Blows over the Life of Leroy Jenkins vol. 1.*"

A BEACON IN A WORLD OF DARKNESS

The charge that the Rev. Jenkins' venture with Holy Hill Cathedral ended badly is outrageous. Holy Hill Cathedral was a beacon for the believing faithful ever since its construction. Television programs filmed there were beamed over eighty-seven stations throughout the United States, ministering to 440,000 families. The church enjoyed a regular Sunday attendance of 1,200.

The Rev. Jenkins' innate wisdom and the guidance of the Holy Spirit led to the creation of the attractive complex on South Sandusky Street in Delaware (later renamed Healing Waters Cathedral[30]). The addition of the church and office complex and a seven-acre blacktop driveway increased the value to nearly two million dollars, benefiting the Association financially as well as spiritually.

WHO ARE THESE PEOPLE?

Reputable newspapers generally won't run a story without confirmation from at least two reliable sources, and they are hesitant to print quotes or opinions repeated by people unwilling to "go on record."

The *Independent* articles are laced with phrases such as "crusade sources confirmed," "officials confirmed," "sources who were formerly in Jenkins' organization," or "sources say."

Who are these "sources"? Let them come forward with their accusations. The fact that everyone's word but the Rev. Jenkins or his supporters was taken as gospel is highly suspect.

---

[30] The name change was inspired by the pure, clean water flowing from a well God directed the Rev. Jenkins to drill on the church property.

DYNAMITE STORY FIZZLES OUT

The newspaper's claim that the church building was dynamited is false. The fire department in Delaware determined that the burns found on the main beam were most likely caused by a riveting gun used in construction and not a bomb or any other incendiary device. One call to the church office or to the Delaware City Fire Department would have cleared that up.

A PRIVATE LIFE

With the help of his housekeeper Nell Heard, the reverend kept his children Lou, Danny, Dennis, Scotty, and Candy well dressed, well fed, in school, and enjoying every advantage he could give them. The children lived an almost-idyllic life. In a large pasture behind the house, the Rev. Jenkins kept miniature goats, a calf named Mickey, and a herd of deer. A rooster named Buggy patrolled the yard like a watchdog, flying up, spurs at the ready when anyone ventured onto the property.

Two tiny white poodles, Faith and Hercules, added to the cacophony, racing madly about and yapping ferociously at an unperturbed Buggy.

A belligerent turkey made his home in a backyard coop. The Rev. Jenkins was the only one who could come near him. Together they put on a great show. While the reverend performed a ceremonial Indian dance complete with a feathered headdress, the turkey joined in, spreading his enormous tail, bowing his head, stamping his feet, and spinning in circles. Supposed to have served as a featured guest at the Thanksgiving table, he danced around that issue with ease.

In these pastoral environs, the Rev. Jenkins spent many happy hours with his children. The days of the traveling tent meetings were over, now that the weekend crusades and church services provided for the needs of the ministry.

THE BOYS' RANCH

In its brief existence, the Leroy Jenkins Boys' Ranch touched the lives of a number of youngsters. The ranch had a spring-fed lake stocked with fish, a big pole barn, and acres of grassy knolls and hardwood trees. Deer peeked from the copses, while raccoon and squirrels foraged about.

The boys who sought refuge there were treated with love and concern by the young preacher. Many returned later to tell how the experience changed their lives and gave them something to hang on to when the going got rough.

Mark Colvin, who spent time at the ranch during the summer of his seventh year, returned to visit the Rev. Jenkins at Healing Hill Cathedral in June 1991.

"I was just a little kid," Mark recalled, "and when I saw a cancer fall off a man's face into Rev. Jenkins handkerchief, I didn't know if I was looking at Leroy Jenkins or at God himself!

"Then he turned and looked at me and said, 'The Lord just told me that you have a deformed heart. The valves in your heart are too small, and you are not getting enough blood.'

"He went on to explain just what I was going through. He told me how I would try to run and play with the other children and this pain would come, you know, and I wouldn't be able to join in the activities as the other kids would.

"I'm there lookin' at him, and he's telling me everything about me.

"Then he said to me, 'As I lay hands on you, the Lord is going to give you a new heart!' and he prayed for me. I remember, as he prayed for me I started crying, I didn't know why then, but I realize now that I was in the presence of the Lord. My heart was healed then, and it is still fine. I can do anything I want to."

Through the years, other boys came by the church in Delaware to see the Rev. Jenkins and to tell how the Boys' Ranch helped them.

Such was the reputation of the Boys' Ranch that one day a prominent woman—a sheriff from a neighboring state—brought a baby boy to the ranch and laid him in the Rev. Jenkins' arms. The child had suffered severe burns on his body.

"Here," she said, "take him. His parents don't deserve to have him."

The Rev. Jenkins took the child, whose name was Scotty, and raised him as his own beloved son.

The Boys' Ranch caught fire on a cold winter night while the Rev. Jenkins was having dinner with friends. Alerted by a church member, Rev and his guests rushed to the Boys' Ranch where they could see the fire was already blazing out of control. Despite all the firemen could do in the freezing weather, everything was destroyed. Luckily, there were no boys in residence at the time. (see photo on page 264)

As noted in the *Anderson Independent* article, fire inspectors blamed the fire on an oil furnace.

The Rev. Jenkins decided not to rebuild the Boys' Ranch. For some time, he had felt the calling of the Lord to reach out to the nation through television, a medium that would reach many thousands more people every day. He turned his focus to this endeavor.

SUPERSTAR FOR GOD

ON THE STREET
WHERE HE LIVED

Anderson Independent, April 11, 1979

Jim Galloway and Rick Ricks

When Evangelist Leroy Jenkins steps before a crowd of anxious followers, dressed meticulously in brightly colored clothing and sporting flashy jewelry, he often sings, "I Did It Thy Way."

Although a casual observer might find the evangelist's rendition - complete with his mock Elvis tone - a bit corny, the song and the way Jenkins delivers it say a lot about what he is and what he stands for.

Critics have leveled every imaginable jibe at Jenkins during his career but even his bitterest enemies seldom deny that the man possesses a style unparalleled in the history of modern evangelism.

On Stockman Street, the street he owns, Jenkins often roams about, giving orders to his underlings and telling those who challenge him exactly what he thinks about them, using language that is seldom heard in any church.

Inside the Jenkins compound,[31] a 6-foot-tall statue of Jesus can be found standing near the evangelist's white Cadillac limousine. The statue stands in Jenkins' driveway, near a patio furnished with white metal furniture.

To the left is a heated swimming pool with a blue and white winter top. To the right is a small chapel Jenkins made from the remains of an old tenement shack.

On one end of the compound is a one-story brick building - larger than the other buildings - which has served as a temporary home of the Leroy Jenkins Evangelistic Association.

On the same street there are many small brick houses, and The Little House on the Prairie operates a restaurant Jenkins built for a local couple.

A few blocks north is Old Abby Mall, an Associate Reformed Presbyterian Church Jenkins bought and converted into a shopping center.

Stockman Street and Old Abby Mall represent Jenkins' Greenwood realm, the niche[32] he has carved out for himself in his hometown.

Jenkins decided last year that what he'd accomplished in Greenwood this far was good. After resting a few months he began trying to get Stockman Street renamed to Leroy Jenkins Street or Leroy Jenkins Boulevard.

So far the prominence of the Stockman family has weighed more heavily in the minds of city planning and zoning officials than the prominence of Leroy Jenkins. The street has kept the Stockman Street name.

---

[31] The word "compound" implies a fortress or enclosure. This is misleading. Stockman Street was simply a small neighborhood.

[32] The *Independent* neglected to mention the large furniture store and warehouse downtown and the warehouse on Maxwell Street where the Rev. Jenkins intended to install a newspaper. His "niche" was growing every day.

*Although Jenkins normally lashes out at government offi-
cials who stand in the way of what he believes to be his mission, he has remained relatively calm about the street issue.*

*But the issue is a relatively small one, since passing motor-
ists have little difficulty spotting the flags, signs and other
paraphernalia which the reverend has used to make his personal mark on the street where he lives.[33]*

*In February, Jenkins crowned his Greenwood acquisitions
by purchasing a $230,000 home on New Market Street, a
bastion of the town's wealthier residents. It is the finest home
Jenkins has ever owned, and he acquired it from J. Richard
Abney, Jr., a member of one of Greenwood's leading families.*

*The purchase may bear out the contentions of one former
Jenkins employee, who says Jenkins has been torn between
his desire to be a part of the Greenwood establishment and
his natural impulse to say what he thinks about any given
situation.[34]*

*The opinion is further supported by Jenkins' changing
demeanor; one minute he is quiet and reverent, the next
minute outspoken and angry.*

*One minute he talks about his duty as a min-
ister, the next minute he jokes about sex.*

Copyright © Anderson Independent

---

[33]   Stockman Street is not a major thoroughfare. Many Greenwood
residents didn't even know where it was until Leroy Jenkins
moved back. If they passed by the homes and saw the changes, it
was because they made an effort to. Additionally, the reverend was
living in his New Market Street home—not at Stockman Street
as reported in this article.

[34]   Who is this former employee? How do we know this person
exists? Reliable newspapers don't normally print hearsay from
unnamed sources. The *Anderson Independent*'s stories are filled
with anecdotes from "former employees" or "crusade sources,"
leading one to question the newspaper's intent.

JENKINS, AN EVANGELIST WHO'S A STUDY IN STYLE

In an interview he unblushingly told a trio of newspapermen that he is "a great lover." And he has spoken frankly of getting back at those who go against him.[35]

Yet he is capable of sudden, overwhelming gesture of charity, such as the Christmas party he held last December for Greenwood's disadvantaged children. At that party, Jenkins passed out dollar bills to the youngsters attending.

And in another demonstration last year, a poor black man came to Jenkins complaining that he had no money and could not feed his family.

Jenkins suspected that the man only wanted a few dollars for a trip to the liquor store, but he sent one of his employees home with the man anyway.

When the employee returned he certified that the man had a houseful of hungry children, but nothing to feed them. Soon Jenkins' employees were filling the house's pantry with groceries.

Such are the contrasts of Jenkins' multi-faceted personality.

An unexpected visit to Jenkins' home can find him embroiled in a hot rage over something that happened between him and the visitor months ago.

But as time goes by, Jenkins will calm down into a quiet, friendly tone.

Dressed in shorts and a t-shirt or other casual attire, Jenkins putters around in his yard like more of an employee

---

[35] If the Rev. Jenkins truly wanted to "get back at" people by hurting them, why would he speak of it openly? Perhaps the reverend was referring to plans to continue the fight with City Hall over the roadblocks thrown in front of him whenever he tried to improve his property. This point should have been clarified for the reader.

than an employer, and is usually outwardly friendly to passers-by.

He can talk of cars, lawn mowers, and other unimportant things, as though he were just another Greenwood businessman at his leisure.

But the slightest thing can set him off; as he wanders along Stockman Street, most of which he owns, he can spot a workman goofing off and immediately launch a tirade that will not cool for hours.

Jenkins himself gave what is perhaps the best description of his temper, if not his entire method of operation: "If you make me mad, I'll fight you...And I will in a minute, whether it's right or whether it's wrong.

"I don't stop to think whether it's right or wrong. If you make me mad I'm going to fight you. If you hit me I'm gonna hit you back. If you love me, I'm gonna love you back."

One quiet evening last August, one of the many families who visit Stockman Street each day drove through the Jenkins compound, only to be forced to the side of the road, "in an abrupt and reckless manner."

According to a city police report, the offending vehicle was a black truck driven by Jenkins himself. Although Jenkins remained in the truck, his then chief of security, Patrick Dixon, got out and talked to the Clinton couple inside the car.

Police soon arrived and Dixon told police he had "been having trouble" with a car of the same description as the Clinton couple's.

Police advised the agitated couple, who were taking advantage of Jenkins' constant public invitations to visit the street, that they would have to see the Greenwood magistrate in order to press charges against Jenkins.

But no charges were filed.

That sort of quick-tempered flamboyance has typified Jenkins' life ever since he was a child.

During a July 29 interview, Jenkins described his expulsion from the fifth grade many years ago. At the time, he attended what is now the Greenwood District 50 school office, and was growing tired of the classroom.

"My teacher was a real b____," he remembered. "I threw a brick through the classroom window and ran away laughing."

In that interview, Jenkins also told with relish his promise to a disrespectful local woman to one day become famous and return to buy the street he had grown up on.

"A lady down the street laughed at me once. You know I was adopted and got a lot of grief because my skin is darker than my adopted family's.

"Well, that lady down the street laughed at me, and I said, 'You old b____! One day I am going to be rich and come back and buy this whole d___ street. And I'm going to run everybody off'...and that's what I did."

Money is a key factor in the style of Leroy Jenkins.

Jenkins brags to crusade audiences about buying up the street in Greenwood, and about his other acquisitions. In his magazine, Revival of America, Jenkins has in the past flaunted his relationships with Liberace and Jimmy Carter, although research has shown these relationships to be much more superficial than Jenkins claims.

Jenkins constantly boasts of his friendships with celebrities and movie stars, and visitors to his home and office are often shown pictures of the reverend and various stars.

He often refers to himself as a "superstar" and supports that contention by dressing in flashy clothing and jewelry.

And he insists he is only 41.

But documents left behind in Jenkins' past show varying birth dates for ages up to 44. In a December interview, Jenkins told The Independent he was unsure how old he is, claiming he was born to an unmarried woman on a Cherokee Indian reservation near Fort Mill, S.C.

When Jenkins first arrived in the Greenwood area, he flashed large amounts of cash regularly, including one instance where he bought out a local store impulsively.

Sources close to the reverend say he still keeps large amounts of cash in his home because he dislikes the inconvenience of checks and credit cards when making purchases around town.

Former LJEA employees have said Jenkins often will bring creditors into the Association's office and order them paid by check on the spot.

But usually, it is Jenkins who does the buying and his secretary, June Buckingham, who keeps the Association books balanced.

In 1976 he was quoted by the Cleveland (Ohio) Plain Dealer Sunday Magazine as saying LJEA is run by "a four man board; the Father, the Son, the Holy Spirit and me."

And in an interview with the Independent, Jenkins clearly demonstrated that he controlled the Association fettered only by divine intervention.

But Jenkins has told other outsiders the opposite is true.

"I have a board of directors over me," Jenkins said." Anything I do has to be approved by them."

Interviews with former staffers indicate that both statements are partially true. While what Jenkins does usually goes unchallenged, Mrs. Buckingham's influence on Jenkins is sometimes extensive.

Mrs. Buckingham, widow of a wealthy Dayton, Ohio attorney, has actually provided substantial financial backing for Jenkins during lean periods.

"Around the office we used to call June mother superior," one staffer recalled. "We started that in front of the reverend's mother one time, and she told us to watch out, that June was a lot more powerful than we thought."[36]

---

[36] Once again, an unnamed source.

Mrs. Buckingham, who claims to have been healed of skin cancer by the evangelist, has remained a mysterious element in Jenkins' life, however.[37]

But actual control of the organization seems to worry Jenkins little. Instead, he often grapples with problems over the image he is projecting as an evangelist and public person.

When he first began his move to Greenwood, Jenkins would stay at the Thunderbird Motel in town. He was frequently seen in the motel's bar, and has since been seen often at several other of the town's watering holes.

"You have to go where the sinners are if you're going to preach the word of the Lord," Jenkins has said.

A one-time confidant described the reverend's dilemma over his image; "You've got to realize that basically, Leroy Jenkins is a very lonely man. He wants to go out and party and have fun just like any one else, but occasionally he becomes really conscious of what people think of him."

In a Jan. 15 telephone conversation with The Independent, signs of Jenkins' growing restlessness with the problem of his popularity showed itself.

"This is the last time I am ever going to give an interview with a newspaper," Jenkins said. "And I'm thinking of dropping off television, too.

---

[37] It is unclear what the Independent means by the author's "mysterious role" within the Leroy Jenkins Evangelistic Association. It is no mystery that Mrs. Buckingham served the Association as secretary-treasurer for almost 40 years. Additionally, the co-author believes the Rev. Jenkins was instrumental in her healing, and she gives the credit to God. Had she been asked, the co-author would have been happy to clear up any mystery about her role in the Association. Further, it is laughable to think that *anyone* had much influence over the strong-willed and independent evangelist.

"People are after you all the time, they want this and they want that. I guess the only reason I've stayed in this business is because people are always asking me to help."

Regardless of Jenkins' image consciousness, his presence in both Greenwood and Delaware became such a political issue that most were forced to choose sides.

In Delaware, Jenkins sought to make extensive additions to his Pollock Road property, including a shopping center and subdivision. When the Tri-Township Council met to consider the change, Jenkins swamped the meeting with his supporters.

According to Tri-Township Fire Chief Rex Scott, the firehouse where council was scheduled to meet was surrounded early by Jenkins' supporters. Scott managed to get Jenkins' neighbors in through the back door so they could speak to council on the possible zoning change.

But the meeting was held during extremely cold weather, and Scott feared a fire call would create utter chaos, since Jenkins' supporters had blocked the fire station's garage doors.

"I asked him to get them to move several times; it was a real hassle," Scott said.*"Finally, without saying anything, he just motioned to the people in front of the doors with his out-stretched arms. They parted like the Red Sea."*

The council turned down Jenkins' proposal that night, and things quieted down for a while, but the remainder of Jenkins' stay in Delaware was punctuated with similar incidents.

When he arrived in Greenwood, Jenkins quickly established a friendship with the city's young mayor, Thomas Wingard, who the reverend took on several crusades.

But once again, city inspectors and police began discovering alleged violations by Jenkins of various ordinances and the stage was set for confrontation.

Last summer, Jenkins accused Greenwood City Manager Travis Higginbotham, City Engineer Shorty Adams and Police Chief John Young of misconduct ranging from conflicts of interest to acute alcoholism.

He soon dragged the city police force into the argument, accusing them of illicit sex and theft from the city's merchants.

A former LJEA office worker told The Independent she was sent out by Jenkins to inquire about Higginbotham's sex life.

The evangelist said he also sent private investigators out to ask about Higginbotham's sex life.

City council called a meeting to air the charges against the various officials, then rebuked the evangelist's allegations in open session.

The meeting, again well attended by Jenkins' supporters, erupted when Wingard accused Jenkins of promulgating the charges as a publicity stunt.

Jenkins stalked off in a rage, later telling a reporter his friendship with Wingard had ended.

Shortly thereafter, Jenkins announced his intention to run for Wingard's job, although it would not be up for election again for three and a half years.

Many Greenwood residents believe Jenkins could make a successful bid for the mayor's job if he wanted to, certainly a more serious bid than his recent abortive attempt to be elected governor of Ohio.

An elective office could offer Jenkins a new outlet for energies, since he has expressed some desire to move away from the hectic pace of his religious activities.

Doubtless, the Jenkins image would remain the same whether he were to remain in religion or chance a foray into politics. And there is a strong possibility he might do both. The image of Jenkins as an outspoken evangelist and even as a politician is one with which the public is familiar.

Copyright © Anderson Independent

GOOD JOURNALISM
VERSUS TABLOID TACTICS

The preceding article is a perfect example of supermarket tabloid journalism. Instead of using named, reliable sources for its story, the *Independent* reporters interviewed "a former LJEA office worker," a "one-time confidant," "one staffer," "former staffers," "former LJEA employees," "one former Jenkins employee," and "sources close to the reverend."

How do we the readers know if these sources even exist? How do we know that all of these sources are not one person? How can we expect a former employee, possibly one who was fired, to tell the truth?

Precious few current or longstanding employees were interviewed for this article.

Worse, the Rev. Jenkins never had a chance to be heard and to defend himself against claims made in the article. It seemed more like a smear campaign than an effort to inform.

Perhaps the series of articles were punishment for daring to challenge the established order of things in a small Southern town. There had long been rumored to be shenanigans going on in Greenwood. People whispered about public officials engaging in unsavory and illegal activities, including gambling and prostitution. Ordinary citizens repeated these things to the Rev. Jenkins, hoping he could do something. The only thing he knew how to do was preach. So he preached fire and brimstone down on the sinners, and they couldn't take the heat.

The *Independent*'s characterization of the evangelist is interesting if slightly superficial. The warmhearted, colorful preacher has never been shy about expressing his feelings. Honest and open by nature, he is eager to amuse and to entertain. He sees his jewelry and clothing as proof of God's investiture. He doesn't believe preachers should live dismal, downtrodden lives. He is grateful for his success and for his spiritual gifts as well. He is no longer that little boy in secondhand clothes, peering into the back of a church, wanting to go in but afraid the ushers would shoo him away.

If the Rev. Jenkins is emotional or temperamental on occasion, he is only human. Among other things, he lost two beloved children in their youth. He suffered two failed marriages. He knew all about fans who stalk celebrities long before they became a Hollywood cliché. His life has been threatened many times. He is under constant spiritual attack. Responsibility for a ministry with hundreds of thousands of members takes a heavy toll.

If it were a crime to be temperamental, the jails would be full of celebrities, opera divas, ball players, and just about everyone else at one time or another.

Truthful and open by nature, the Rev. Jenkins' innocent expressions would have made interesting reading, if that had been the intention of the newspaper articles. The fact that so many people support his ministry indicates his own words were of greater interest than gossip by ex-employees.

As the Rev. Jenkins often answers his critics, he has more people in the restrooms than most preachers have sitting in their congregations. Some people may not like his style, but he is reaching a lot of people who are not reached by others.

CITY COUNCIL WHITEWASH

The *Independent* reports that " Greenwood City Council called a meeting to air the charges against the various officials, then rebuked the evangelist's allegations in open session."

It should be noted the city council investigated itself. Naturally, they would deny the allegations against them. If a fraction of the time and money spent on the series of articles devoted to the Rev. Jenkins had been used to look into the activities of some city officials, this sad tale might have ended differently.

JENKINS' POPULARITY PUTS HIM AT RISK

The Rev. Jenkins' popularity in Greenwood at this time was very high. Many had attended his crusades held at the new civic center and were supporters of the ministry. Others had heard of his interest and concern for the common man and felt that he wanted to right the wrongs down at the city hall.

His interest in running for mayor of Greenwood to see justice and righteousness prevail made him a real threat. It was in the interest of the "powers-that-be" that the *Independent* ran the series of articles that destroyed the Rev. Jenkins' reputation in the community. Could the *Independent's* editors and reporters have been willing participants in this plot? Or were they mere pawns in the solicitor's plan to "get the Rev. Jenkins off the streets"?

What they did not do, whether they intended to or not, was to present the truth to the people of Greenwood so that they could make up their own minds about this gifted evangelist.

MAUDIE

MAUDIE'S SAVINGS WENT TO ADOPTED SON'S CAUSE

Anderson Independent, Thursday, April 12, 1979

By Jim Galloway and Rick Ricks

She had an eye for hot canvas tents, sawdust floors and sweaty cries of passion.

She feasted on preachers who shouted themselves hoarse with the word of God and audiences that jerked and convulsed to a wild frenzy.

And she was delighted when the healing began. To watch the exorcism of the demon responsible for a backache, high blood pressure, or even cancer was to watch the hand of God at work.

Maudie Bartz is a tough, domineering woman who just turned 99, a recluse hidden in the faraway oil town of Odessa, Texas. She is a pioneer in the original sense of the word, an uneducated woman with a fierce sense of religion.

She came to Odessa when it was a gathering of 800 persons connected to the rest of Texas by a wagon trail. It's now a booming town of 81,000.

Maudie was a strong girl, with long dark hair that hung past her knees. She never went to school, but taught herself how to read and write.

She pens religious poems:

"If I could catch that old owl, I would silence his hoot.

Every time I am ready to do something I want to do, there is that warning hoot. That pesky buggar."

In 1913 Maudie married Gust Bartz, an independent trucking contractor who hauled drilling equipment for the companies in search of black gold.

In the first years of their marriage, Maudie would climb into a pair of trousers - a very unladylike thing to do at the time - to join her husband at the wheel of one of their trucks.

Gust Bartz died in 1958, leaving Maudie without children or close relatives. He left her wealthy, though for a time she insisted on making her own way by running a flower shop next to her home.

She grew her own flowers so she could sell them cheaper. One frequent customer remembered her working in a pair of dirty overalls, with diamond rings shining on her fingers.

One by one, she gave all the rings away, except for her wedding ring.

...... 'IT WAS ALL PLANNED AHEAD'

Religion was always the focus of her life - even now she considers herself a "spiritual" woman. She never went to church, but she loved a good tent meeting.

It was a "spiritual nudge" from God that took her 250 miles away to a tent meeting in Dallas, Texas, in the fall of 1960, where she met a young man named Leroy Jenkins.

"It was all planned ahead. It was 'specially planned,' she said, 18 years later. "I'm an old lady and I'm in my middle 90's, and I'd worked hard all my life and saved my money, and I didn't have nowhere to put it, so I put it in the ministry.

"And I financed all his first ministry," she said.

At the tent meeting in Dallas, Jenkins was an assistant for the late A. A. Allen, testifying to the miracle healing of his arm that had occurred only months earlier.

She wasn't sure what she was looking for, but when she saw Jenkins she knew she had found something.

"He looked out on the audience and saw me, and he come walkin' off that platform and come just as straight to me as a duck to water," she paused, then added, "And he said to me, 'Mamma, there you are. I've looked all over for you.'"

Jenkins tells the story in the reverse, saying that Mrs. Bartz first called him her son. "Well, I don't know how it was, but anyways, I saw her and something clicked and then later on she told me that she was my mother," Jenkins said.

Mrs. Bartz, who was born in Louisiana, says she never had any children and chuckles at the suggestion that she might be the evangelist's real mother.

She is, however, one-quarter Cherokee. Though he has no first hand knowledge of his birth[38], Jenkins says he is the illegitimate son of a Cherokee woman on a North Carolina reservation.

Copyright © Anderson Independent

A STRANGE PROPHESY

Anderson Independent, April 12, 1979

Jim Galloway and Rick Ricks

In any case, it was a strange prophecy, but one that Mrs. Bartz fulfilled shortly after their meeting by "adopting" Leroy - who was then in his early 20's - and promising him the financial backing to begin his career as the head of Miracle Arm Revivals, Inc.

---

[38] Does anyone have "first-hand" knowledge of his birth?

"He didn't have no clothes of his own. He was wearing Brother Allen's clothes. So I took him down to a men's shop, and I told the man at the shop, 'Now you dress him up, from head to foot. And you send me the bill,'" she said.

The organization was a small one, the forerunner of the present Leroy Jenkins Evangelistic Association. It was formed in December 1960, only a few months after their meeting.

Tightening the bond, Jenkins had his name legally changed to Leroy Jenkins Bartz - on March 14, 1961, according to court documents.

His wife Ruby Lee and their four children also had their last names changed to Bartz.

"I didn't just adopt him, I adopted the whole family," Mrs. Bartz proudly remembered. She saw Ruby Jenkins and the children only once, when they came to visit for "three or four days."

Though available court records verify only Jenkins' name change, Mrs. Bartz contends the Jenkins' were actually adopted. And years later, a copy of the evangelist's birth certificate, with the name Leroy Jenkins Bartz, was spotted by an employee in the Association's files.

Mrs. Bartz says the adoption was her idea, that she went so far as to get the permission of Jenkins' adopted mother in Greenwood.

People would talk if they saw "an old woman runnin' around after a young man." They wouldn't talk if he called her "mother."

Mrs. Bartz had never met Jenkins before the Dallas tent meeting, but she suspected that Jenkins had a stormy past by the way he reacted to questions. "There must have been a dark streak somewhere...He'd look at the ceiling and shut up."

Jenkins used Maudie's name for at least a few months in his magazines and his promotion bills. But when he suddenly left Texas, he also left the name.

"They just dropped it. 'Course I didn't say nothin' about that. I done what I was supposed to do - I put him in the business. And then I was through," she said.

The young man that she adopted was almost fanatical about his calling. According to his autobiography, Jenkins had already determined that movies were evil (though he later changed his mind) and former associates said he had the same feeling about television.

"He was a young man, and he was really sold on the ministry...He was scared to death about everything. He was afraid of doing something wrong that wouldn't please the Lord," she said.

Jenkins was a ball of energy under the tent - the faithful would pass out at the touch of his "healed" arm. There were times you couldn't walk across the sawdust floor because of the exhausted bodies lying on the ground, Maudie Bartz remembered, still greatly impressed.

It is the reverence that she holds for those times that keeps her from condemning Jenkins. She hopes he will someday go back to the old way.

"His first ministry was a good ministry....But you know, money as a rule will ruin a lot of people. And I think it tarnished Leroy. I think that when the money started comin' in from his preachin', it gave him a different feelin'. Now that's just the way I feel. I might be wrong," she said.

She can't remember exactly how much money she spent on Jenkins and his family. "When you start to buy an organ, and paying $5,000 for an organ, and buyin' a tent..."

Her accountant places the figure in the "thousands."

"He had a checking account, and everything he needed for a tent revival - organ and chairs and tent and everything," she said. Another pause. "So that's where my labor went all my life."

She was anxious to please Jenkins, and gave the family a car and a home in Dallas. But her experience with her adopted child was bittersweet. When she finished building a cement-block church on a 10-acre lot in Odessa that would seat 500 people, she took the young Rev. Jenkins-Bartz to see his gift.

"He just stood and looked at that church and give it a good horse laugh. And he never did hold a meetin' in it," she said.

Mrs. Bartz says Jenkins and his family left Texas without a word to their adopted mother. "He just figured he'd milked this ol' cow dry, and was goin' on," she said coolly.

"He don't need me anymore, he's got a good footin' now. I give him a bank account, he knew there wasn't none left. He didn't need me."

Jenkins says he gave the house and the church back to Maudie when he left. She in turn gave the house to a Houston evangelist, and the church to one in Dallas. She has supported other preachers since, but none has received the attention Jenkins did.

She now spends her time in her house alone - she hasn't left her property in two years, and she hasn't seen a doctor in 20.

Though she is almost blind, she paints four or five hours every day, sending the oils to ministers, who in turn sell them to raise money for their churches.

She is not poor, but neither is she rich - she lives on the rent from her flower shop and a trailer park she owns. She is lonely.

Though obviously stung, Maudie still talks to Jenkins from time to time. She was named a temporary officer of the Leroy Jenkins Evangelistic Association, Inc. when it was first formed in Florida in 1962.

Jenkins calls her once every five or six months.

"I still consider myself his adopted mother, but when I get ready to do something with the property, you know, I'll not leave it in his name.

"Because he's got no business with it, he's got plenty."

Copyright © Anderson Independent

MAUDIE'S LEGACY OF LOVE

Maudie Bartz loved the Lord, and she knew a man of God when she saw him. When she met the Rev. Jenkins, she wanted to help the fiery, young evangelist get off to a good start. Her financial help was a beautiful expression of love and generosity. (see photo on page 260)

In the preceding article, *Anderson Independent* reporters claim that Maudie told them she was ninety-nine years old at the time of the 1979 interview. Yet when Maudie died four years after the interview, the court determined she was ninety-three years old. That would have made her only eighty-nine at the time of the interview. Was Maudie putting one over on the reporters? Had she become confused in her later years? Or were the reporters simply sloppy?

At the time Maudie claimed Leroy Jenkins as her natural child, she was firmly convinced of the truth of the statement. In 1936, when the Rev. Jenkins was born (if indeed that is his actual birth date; he has no birth certificate), it was not wise to admit to having Indian blood, especially out on the Texas plains.

Likewise, it is understandable that, in fear and embarrassment, a respectable married woman might wish to conceal an Indian child from her husband.

Whatever the truth is, Maudie is gone, taking her secrets with her.

Maudie did everything she could to tie the Rev. Jenkins to her. She not only adopted him but also his entire family. She gave him a home and a car to use. She built him a church to use. She set up a bank account for him, which, at the time of her death, still had the $10,000 in it that she had deposited for him. She wanted him by her side.

Eventually, the ministry to which the evangelist had been called beckoned, and he packed up his little family and moved on to new endeavors, leaving behind the house, the car, and the bank account with $10,000 in it.

Maudie, true to her desire to dedicate her life work to the ministry, then gave the house in Dallas and the church to other preachers.

Maudie was truly blessed by God for what she did for the Rev. Jenkins. The scripture says that if you give so much as a cup of water to a prophet in the name of a prophet, you will receive a prophet's reward. Maudie enjoyed good health and financial security, until the end of her life.

Shortly after Maudie gave her interview to the *Independent* reporter, her health failed her. She was declared incompetent and died in 1983.

Maudie's estate amounted to hundreds of thousands of dollars, which she gave to several religious organizations.

She entrusted her adopted son, the Rev. Jenkins, to serve as her executor, and he made sure that her bequests were carried out. He saw to her funeral and disposed of her property for the court. He received only the $10,000 that she had put in the bank for him.

How sad that almost at the end of her life, when her mind was failing her, she turned on the one that was dearest to her. Out of her desire to have him and his family near her, she made some injudicious remarks to a careless reporter, who used a lonely old woman's feelings to hurt the very person she loved.

MYSTERIOUS POWER OF FAITH

A JENKINS CRUSADE: "MONEY....MIRACLES"

Anderson Independent, April 13, 1979

Jim Galloway and Rick Ricks

In Greenwood on Aug.13, 1978 - In a reserved front row seat is the couple with their 5-month-old baby.

Janaya Braxton has the movements of a 3-week-old infant and can't be fed through her mouth - a special mixture of food must be forced down the tubes stuck through her nostrils.

Janaya's parents are hopeful. They took the baby off her prescribed medication when they started the long drive to the Greenwood auditorium 24 hours before.

There is Curley Waters, a tired black man from Charlotte who walks down the center aisle with his legs caged by the frame of an aluminum walker.

Guided by a polite and courteous usher, his wife and grown daughters help him into a seat in the "healing" section apparently reserved for those with canes and crutches.

There is the boy in the blue shirt, with glasses and long hair and a slight scowl on his face. He came from North Carolina, too, mainly because his parents brought him.

There is the father who walks through the auditorium doors with his son cradled in his arms, the boy wrapped in an old winter coat to keep him warm on a hot afternoon.

His son is as pale as a skeleton. His hairless head is simply a skull with a blue-white layer of skin stretched tightly over it. Saucer like (sic) eyes and an occasional guttural sound are the only obvious signs that the boy lives.

And there is Candy Jenkins, the daughter of the main attraction and more properly Candace. She sits high in the stands with her two girlfriends, both willowy blondes.

Hanging somewhere in the background is a local law enforcement representative, keeping tabs on what Jenkins does and says in order to make an informal report on Monday.

In Asheville on Sept. 10, 1978 - the tuxedo-clad members of the small band begin a medley of bluesy religious tunes, waiting for the appearance of the man they call "the Rev."

They move from a lively rendition of "Amazing Grace" to a more curious selection, "Oh Danny Boy."[39]

Most of those who have not taken their seats mill around the souvenir table, others reserve plastic gallon jugs of "miracle water" drawn from Jenkins' blessed well in Delaware, Ohio. It's the biggest seller at every crusade.

The water has been used for a variety of purposes - from stopping heart attacks to starting cars to selling apartments for disheartened landlords, according to promotional literature.

Using miracle water "as a point of contact" also cured Candy Jenkins of "high cholesterol, ulcers, possible gall bladder trouble, etc." - again according to promotional literature.

The water is selling at the low price of $2.70 for one gallon.

---

[39] The song "Danny Boy" is one of more than 100 songs composed to the same tune, an ancient Irish melody first recorded in the 1700s.

There are 8 x 10 glossies of Jenkins in an Elvis-like pose, his wide white-collar shirt unbuttoned to the middle of his chest and his lip curled in a slight sneer; pendants with Jenkins' picture for $6; "dial-a-verse" machines for $5; free Leroy Jenkins Songbooks, Leroy Jenkins bumper stickers and calendars; books of all kinds, including Bibles.

Souvenir attendants gather wads of money in their hands.

In Greenwood on Nov. 5, 1978 - The conductor of the band walks to the center of the platform with the microphone in his hand.

"I have some water here," he calls out to the restless crowd, holding up the familiar gallon jug of Miracle Water.

"How many people know about this water?" The hands of half the audience shoot up in the air.

"How many people have experienced healing as a point of contact with this water?" he calls out. A third keep their hands high, and the conductor points to the tables where the product can be had.

"Now, how many of you have seen these?" It is a new item, a white T-shirt with a head and shoulders photograph of a humble Leroy Jenkins on the front.

In the crowd a lady and her small children, all wearing the same T-shirt, proudly raise their hands and beam.

"We have - how many?" (He looks to the attendants at the souvenir table)"Five sizes?

"How many of you women have children? Come on, more of you have children than that. That's more like it. Take some home to the kids."

In Greenwood on Aug. 13, 1978 - Suddenly a dark-skinned man in his mid-40's moves across the stage and launches into song, reaching deep for each note and carrying it loudly to the microphone in his hand.

The crusade has begun - this is the Reverend Leroy Jenkins.

He wears black pants and a fire-red coat and waves a diamond studded hand.

He is happy and healthy, the epitome of success – in sharp contrast to his audience. And three television cameras are taking it all in.

The organization does not make a great deal of money from the crusades themselves. Videotapes are edited and then distributed to the 34 stations that carry Jenkins' half-hour programs on Sunday mornings.

Mail-order advertisements on the television shows and in his magazines attract most of the money that comes into Jenkins' Greenwood offices.

The orchestra and Jenkins move through several gospel standards, but soon the reverend halts the music and gets right down to business.

"I think I am going to take the offering early in case you get mad and go home," Jenkins jokes.

He is referring to his promise of a few weeks earlier that he would "tell all" about alleged corruption in the Greenwood city government and police department.

After assuring the audience that he has "the respect of most of the citizens of my hometown," Jenkins launches into a tirade in which he accuses city officials of conflict of interest and alleges that certain city policemen are guilty of theft and illicit sex (in the back seat of patrol cars).

The evangelist's charges fall on appreciative ears; he receives ovations with each stinging barb. But the charges have been aired by Jenkins before, each time with little elaboration.

He draws the loudest outburst yet from the audience of 3,000 when he vows that "things are going to change" because he plans to run for mayor in three years.[40] It is not the first time he has mixed religion and politics. He ran for governor

---

[40] It was because of this kind of popular response that the Rev. Jenkins' announcement that he might run for mayor of Greenwood posed a real threat to the city government.

of Ohio in 1977, but withdrew from the race well before the state primary.

Jenkins' attack on the Greenwood establishment flattens out into a general sermon on hypocrisy, as he rambles from local examples to more universal events, then back again.

Half of his sermon is spent defending his own flamboyant lifestyle. He is protective of his wealth and personal habits, and makes no bones about the control he has over the Leroy Jenkins Evangelistic Association, Inc.

While he was in Ohio, The Cleveland Plain Dealer quoted him as saying that his organization is controlled by a "four-man board. The Father, the Son, the Holy Spirit and me."

He rails against those who believe that he lives too well – he drew $89,000 from the organization in 1976, not including a $50,000 loan the organization made to him. The allowance is far above Billy Graham's yearly take-home pay. In 1977 Jenkins' salary dropped to $31,000.

"Anything of God prospers and anything that prospers is of God," is his standard reply to critics.[41] *His wealth is a sign of God's approval, and he doesn't care who disagrees.*

"I was hired by God and He's the only one who can fire me." Jenkins drives a white Cadillac limousine, paid for by the Association, and a car his 19-year-old daughter drives is also registered as being owned by the Association.

---

[41] The Rev. Jenkins does not believe that everything that prospers is of God. He does believe that God wants His people to "prosper and be in health, even as your soul prospers." He believes the scripture that says God will cause men to give unto your bosom, and he has gladly received gifts of clothes, diamond rings, and cars, which he accepts as a fulfillment of Scripture. It is also important to remember that it takes a great deal of money to operate an organization as large as the Rev. Jenkins'. Television alone gobbles up a huge percentage of the annual budget.

"When they were walking, He was riding a jackass. If they'd been Cadillacs back then I'm sure he'd have one because he was first class," he told a crowd at another crusade.

Officially he doesn't approve of smoking or drinking, though he privately admits that he does drink socially. But he likes even less those who are critical of his appearance at local bars and lounges.

"The Bible says 'a little wine for the stomach's sake," Jenkins admonishes the crowd, though he admits the scripture was not intended to include scotch and water.

His Ohio lawyer claims Jenkins drinks wine - but only for medicinal purposes. A bartender in Greenwood says Jenkins' favorite drink is a Blackjack and Coke.

In Asheville on Sept. 10, 1978 - Something is wrong with the sound system, and the echoes of the auditorium obscure his words, though snatches can be caught here and there. Parents strain to hear the Greenwood prophet, and children with dirty faces run up and down the aisles.

"There is no person greater in my mind than Billy Graham. Billy Graham's with Him. He's one of the finest people that ever walked this ground and I'm with him all the way," Jenkins says trying to console those who feel torn between Jenkins and the state's native son.

It is near the end of the sermon and Jenkins gets in one last sarcastic jab at a group that generally does not sanction his work - the "college crowd."

"You know where LSD came from - acid - they made it in a college laboratory. They already taught them how to smoke pot." His audience applauds the statement.

The sermon does not last long. Jenkins is not an outstanding speaker, but the audience is not looking for flowery prose.

In the 30 minutes that he has spoken, Jenkins has made them believe that all things are not only possible, but are about to happen within the next hour. That is what they have come to hear.

There is now a small, sobering pause in the tempo of the program – it is time for the first miracle of the afternoon. Jenkins knows it and the crowd feels it.

The reverend walks down the center aisle until he meets a couple from Lexington, Ky. The wife tells Jenkins that her husband has been deaf since 1962.

Jenkins pulls the man out of his seat and into the center aisle, then yanks the plugs out of his ears. "You won't need these anymore."

He covers the ears with his own hands, and hands around the auditorium rise, palms toward the man about to be healed.

"In the name of Jesus Christ..." Leroy steps back. He snaps his fingers in the man's ears, one at a time.

"Can you hear that?" The man shakes his head. It didn't work. Jenkins quickly changes the subject.[42]

"God has told me that he's got a check in his pocket made out to me. Ma'am have I ever spoken to you before?" he asks the wife of the deaf man.

She does not understand, but stammers out a "no".

"Did you tell me he had a check in his pocket?"

"No, sir."

"Does he have a check in his pocket?"

"Yes, sir."

"How did I know that?"

"I guess God told you."

"How many people believe God told me that? God does talk to me, whether you believe it or not." And Jenkins walks on to the next person to be healed.

---

[42] The man must have heard what the Rev. Jenkins said, for he answered by shaking his head. In the face of no other evidence, it seems the man did hear the question, but did not realize that he was actually hearing. Quite often people who have been deaf for many years are confused for a bit. Hearing takes getting used to.

In Greenwood on Aug. 13, 1978 - It is again time for the first miracle of the afternoon, but this time it will work.

Annette Braxton of Gordon, Ala., and her daughter are ushered onto the stage, and Annette begins to tell the story of their faith and how it drew them to the Jenkins crusade.

Janaya's doctors don't know exactly what is wrong with her - one has diagnosed her symptoms as spinal meningitis. She had heart surgery when she was 2 weeks old, and a resulting infection brought on a series of chronic convulsions.

Before she made the trip to Greenwood she was under three types of medication to control the convulsions. One medicine paralyzed her throat muscles so she could not swallow.

Annette Braxton was taught to tube-feed her baby through the baby's nose.

Janaya does not move much, and her skull is not developing normally. She has spent two of her five months in a Montgomery, Ala., hospital. Doctors have given her parents little hope - but they also said taking Janaya to see Jenkins wouldn't hurt, if they had faith to do it.

Annette Braxton cries throughout her tale, and tears begin to choke her when Jenkins lays his hands on the baby's forehead. Jenkins calls for all the hands in the auditorium to rise in sympathy. He yelps and pulls his hands back, the baby begins to cry and the mother shrieks.

"Did you feel that?"

She nods, "Praise the Lord, thank y' Jesus. Thank y'Jesus."

The hands of the spectators remain high and a few women in the audience catch the fever and begin shaking.

Mother and child are handed down to the crowd of well-wishers on the floor. Mrs. Braxton has heard her baby cry, something she hasn't done in four months. She gives her a bottle and Janaya begins sucking. She has not done that in a long time, either.

The momentum is with Jenkins and he breaks into song, with a lone piano trailing close behind. He is soon in the crowd and works his way to an excited elderly woman.

The hand is on the forehead again. He jerks, knocking her backward and she is healed.[43] She runs - as much as an elderly woman can run - up and down the aisle, her hands held high.

First-aid workers in bright orange jumpsuits gather at the rear of the auditorium and watch closely, just in case.

Auditorium authorities require their presence.

Jenkins heals a second woman, then points out Curley Waters, the man from Charlotte with the aluminum walker.

Waters is shy and quietly remains sitting when Jenkins asks for his crutch. The wife hands it to him - miracles only work if there is nothing else to lean on. Jenkins hangs the microphone around his neck and passes the walker to an assistant. The hand is on the forehead and Curly Waters is healed. Jenkins moves on, and Water tries to stand to prove to his fellows that his afflicted leg is indeed mended.

He slowly steps up and down the row of chairs, holding them like he held the walker. He returns to his seat and will remain there the rest of the afternoon.

In Asheville on Sept. 10, 1978 - Leroy Jenkins once billed himself as the "only known Holy Ghost-filled Presbyterian

---

[43] The *Independent* reports that Rev. Jenkins "jerks, knocking her backward, and she is healed." Rev. Jenkins does not knock people backward; it is the power of God that hits them. To demonstrate this, he often touches people with his finger lightly on the forehead or doesn't touch them at all, and still people "fall out" or are "slain in the spirit." The Rev. Jenkins didn't invent faith-healing: It has been around for quite a while. Even John Wesley, the founder of Methodism, believed in and preached about the gifts of the Holy Spirit, including prophecy and speaking in tongues, and considered them alive and well in Christian churches.

in the world who tells you things about yourself which only you know."

God has just told Jenkins that 72 persons in the audience have cancer - and don't know it. Exactly 897 have already sought God for their salvation, including 12 preachers. Four atheists in the audience are left out in the cold.

He asks the 47 youngsters in the audience who have smoked pot to stand and be healed of their habit. There are no "plants" in this audience - all are genuine. First one stands, then two, five, 10 and 20.

"I know you're out there."

No. 46 stands, then Jenkins points out a reluctant 47 and announces the group's forthcoming healing. At the same instant, potsmokers No. 48 and 49 jump up in the back rows.

They are ignored by the reverend and quickly sit down, embarrassed to have spoiled his count.[44]

In Greenwood on Aug. 13, 1978 - *"God told me there are 17 young people in this auditorium who have been smoking pot. I know because God just told me so. Three of you are on this side of the room,"* Jenkins announces, pointing to stage right.

The first to stand is the boy in the blue shirt from North Carolina. The television cameras zoom in on his face, which still holds a slightly defiant scowl. His father and mother are crying.

The father will later write out a check for $20 to the Leroy Jenkins Evangelistic Association, Inc.

Two more potsmokers stand on that side of the auditorium, and Jenkins moves to the other side of the auditorium.

High in the stands, Candy Jenkins leans over and says something to the two willowy blondes next to her. The blondes

---

[44]   Here, the reporter is attempting to read minds. How did the reporter know whether the reverend ignored them or not, and how did the reporter know they were embarrassed?

nudge each other, then stand – giggling. Twelve other teenagers join them.

The boy in the blue shirt closes his eyes while Jenkins says the prayer that will release him from the grip of marijuana. The boy waits a few minutes, then walks outside.

He returns with the smell of tobacco on his breath.

Unnoticed throughout the prayer is a portly woman with pencil in hand and a clipboard pressed closely against her breast. While others are praying, she quietly approaches Curley Waters and hands him the clipboard.

Waters takes the pencil quizzically, then signs one of the pieces of paper on the clipboard. He has just agreed not to hold Jenkins or his associates responsible if he should suffer a relapse from his cure or to charge Jenkins with practicing medicine.

"Neither Leroy Jenkins nor his Association can heal me" – only God, the affidavit[45] states.

Two or three other ladies protect similar clipboards gathering the signatures of all who have received Jenkins' special attention this afternoon.

In Asheville on Sept. 10, 1978 – Using small buckets, ushers systematically collect the tithe envelopes made out to LJEA. Jenkins takes a brief, on-stage rest while the band again plays "Oh Danny Boy."

The crowd stirs and some begin to leave, but Jenkins calls them forward for one last miracle. He asks for those with tobacco habits to throw their cigarettes on the stage, never to use them again. He is immediately under a deluge of small flying boxes, smashing them with his feet as he walks across the stage.

---

[45]   The release forms for radio and television that are filled out and signed by those that the Rev. Jenkins has prayed for are not an affidavit. Their only purpose is to secure the name and address of those prayed for so that their progress can be followed, and to get their permission to use them on radio or television.

The band plays, "You Light Up My Life."

Suddenly Jenkins is off the stage and out of the reach of anxious autograph-seekers who are held back by a line of employees.

In Greenwood on Nov. 5, 1978 - As a final tribute to the crowd, Jenkins tells them to line up single file around the auditorium. The line, wrapped entirely around the inside of the civic center, slowly moves past Jenkins to allow each person to shake hands with the prophet. The crippled are carried in the arms of friends or relatives, just for a prayerful touch. No talking is allowed however, or else the line would move too slowly.

The line takes thirty minutes to pass. Jenkins climbs back on stage to say good-bye, then hurries off to his waiting limousine. Again, a line of employees protect their leader's retreat, clasping hands to prevent the curious from following him.

In Gordon, Ala. on Dec. 8, 1978 - The miracle of four months ago is still working for the Braxtons.

Their doctor refuses to talk about the incident, to explain exactly how much of their daughter's improvement might have been supernatural. But it is plain that the Braxtons attribute their daughter's progress to faith-healing.

"All her improvements have to do with Brother Jenkins praying for her and the Lord healing her," Annette Braxton says. "She hasn't had a tube in her since that day."

They waited five weeks before telling Janaya's doctor they had taken her to see Jenkins.

Janaya now tries to raise her head and move her legs and arms, and she has made enough progress to be taken to a children's institute in Philadelphia.

In Greenwood on Aug. 13, 1978 - A worker gathers up the armful of canes and crutches scattered between the chairs.

There were no discarded wheelchairs.

As the worker walks toward the center aisle he is brushed by the father with his skeleton-like son in his arms. The father has a defeated look on his face – Jenkins never even glanced the boy's way.

The worker also avoids Curley Waters, who slowly makes his way to the outside without his walker. The walker wasn't thrown away – it was picked up by one of his daughters.

Waters dips every time he steps on his right foot, but steadily makes progress until he stops to rest by one of the restrooms. His family has left him for the moment, gathering their reserved gallons of miracle water.

His wife joins him and he leans on her shoulder as they pass through the door. He is not walking – his wife is now his crutch and she can barely hold his weight.

They slowly make their way the last 20 feet to the curb.

"The kids have gone to get the car. You sit here on the curb and I'll go get them," she tells him.

Waters was not healed, but the failure was not Jenkins' nor God's. The blame lay in the heart of the black man with a near useless leg, according to what Jenkins tells his followers.[46]

In his autobiography, Jenkins tells the story of one of his first attempts at healing:

"One day our pet cat died. We gathered together for the funeral. We cried so loud we could be heard a block away....

"I told the children if they would agree in prayer for the cat it would return to life. We all laid our hands on the cat and began to pray. It didn't move. So we buried our pet with many tears. I felt that some of the children did not have faith."

Copyright © Anderson Independent

---

[46] Where the reporter got this information is anybody's guess. Healing is a mystery. Why some receive it and some do not is not always easily understood. How did the reporter know that the man was not healed and simply needed time to recover, as often happens?

THE MYSTERIOUS POWER
OF SIMPLE FAITH

Faith healing is nothing new. Old Testament prophets practiced it. Jesus was a faith healer. He gave the credit to God, saying, "It is my Father that doeth the work." His absolute simple faith that God would answer his prayers seemed to be the catalyst that made them effective.

Demonstration of the power of God to heal shows people that there is a God, that he is all-powerful, and that he hears and answers their prayers. It is entirely scriptural. If you believe in God, then it is only logical to believe that God can heal.

People are healed in many ways. Some have been healed by placing a Bible on the source of their affliction. They have been healed in prayer circles and at shrines such as the grotto at Lourdes. Others drink holy water or pour it over themselves. Some are healed by their own prayers or by the prayers of others. In all these healings, there is usually a point of contact, or a catalyst that helps the believer to release his faith.

The gospels tell of a woman with an "issue of blood." She spent all of her money on doctors, to no avail. Then one day she saw Jesus walking through her village surrounded by a crowd. She made her way through the throng and touched the hem of Jesus' garment.

"Who touched me?" Jesus said. The woman confessed that she had touched the hem of his garment, and now she was healed.

"Daughter, be of good comfort." Jesus told her, "Thy faith hath made thee whole" (Luke 8:43–48, KJV).

Why some people are healed and others are not is a heartbreaking mystery. Why some faith healers are successful, while ministers of great faith and other spiritual gifts are unable to effect healing also is an enigma.

Some people believe healing depends upon a person's faith. But there have been healings involving people who did not know they were being prayed for, and yet they were healed.

On the other hand, some people with great faith sometimes do not receive healing. It is a mistake to say that the fault lies in the heart of the afflicted. Who can know the mind of God? The important thing is to keep believing, keep praying, and keep living a life pleasing to God.

As the Rev. Jenkins often says, "Some people that I have prayed for do not get saved—and some don't get healed, but that doesn't stop me from praying."

It is significant that in the many years of the Rev. Jenkins' ministry, no one has ever proved him to be a fraud. They cannot. If they take the time to follow up on the healings, they find that they are genuine. After efforts by many skeptics, no one has ever found a "plant" in one of the crusade audiences.

True, there are some so-called faith healers who have resorted to trickery to promote their ministries. Lacking sufficient power in their prayers to get things done, they try to fake results to stimulate enough faith in the beholder to affect a miraculous cure. But a counterfeit ministry could not survive decades of scrutiny by doctors and skeptics as has that of the Rev. Jenkins.

God hears and answers his prayers. In the crusades, the Rev. Jenkins obeys the biblical command to lay hands on the afflicted and pray the prayer of faith. He prays for people over the phone, through the mail, and out in the front yard. And his prayers are answered.

The Rev. Jenkins does not claim that he has any power to heal but that it is the Father who does the work.

The Rev. Jenkins has simple, total faith. It is a faith that comes not by formal education, but is a gift that God has given him, as Paul explains in his letters to the Corinthians. He believes in Jesus' words as recorded in the Bible. He hears God's voice, and obeys.

IS GOD A BUTTONED-DOWN TYPE OF GUY?

Why did God single out someone like Leroy Jenkins—a man who is, according to the *Independent*, emotional, temperamental, flashy, flamboyant, and controversial—to preach his word? Shouldn't God pick as his prophets and preachers people who are a little more toned down?

In truth, the gifts of the Holy Spirit have been given to all manner of men and women, from bishops in brocaded robes to storefront preachers in the meanest inner-city neighborhoods. The ranks of God's anointed include biblical scholars and simple country pastors, former convicts, and a tiny Catholic nun. Each has a unique gift; together they are integral parts of the body of the church.

The lives of God's anointed are not conflict free. Martin Luther was certainly controversial, and so was his namesake, Martin Luther King. John the Baptist got into hot water when he told the Pharisees—who thought their ascent into heaven was guaranteed—they first had to repent.

No one was more controversial than Jesus Christ. People criticized him for his dress, for hanging out with sinners, for healing on the Sabbath, and so on. He was so controversial that it led to his crucifixion.

If people want a preacher in a button-down suit, there are plenty of them around. In fact, there's something for everyone out there—even preachers who sing like Elvis Presley. If one can't get you into church, then maybe the other one will. What really counts in the long run is substance, not style.

BIG BROTHER IS WATCHING

Perhaps the most disturbing part of the *Independent* article was the statement that a member of law enforcement was monitoring the church service.

"Hanging somewhere in the background is a local law enforcement representative, keeping tabs on what Jenkins does and says in order to make an informal report on Monday," the article said.

This should have been chilling news to anyone who respects the Constitution of this great nation. In this country, people are free to worship God as they please. South Carolina is the site of more Revolutionary War battles than any other state. Greenwood residents can count on both hands ancestors who fought and died for such concepts as the separation of church and state. Every church, every preacher in Greenwood should have raised an outcry when this was revealed. Spying on church services and filling out reports might happen in countries living under repressive regimes. It should never have happened here. In American churches, people shouldn't have to look over their shoulders.

SETTING THE STAGE FOR ACCUSATIONS OF ARSON

A week before the Rev. Jenkins' arrest in Greenwood on the charge of conspiracy to commit arson, the *Anderson Independent* published a front-page article headlined "Cathedral Insured Just Before Blast." The timing of this article seemed almost too perfect to be coincidence. If the reporters wanted to paint the Rev. Jenkins as an arsonist, they couldn't have done a better job of it.

It was the third day of a weeklong series of front-page articles on the Rev. Jenkins, which chipped away at his credibility little by little with each paragraph. Whether reporters Rick Ricks and Jim Galloway, intended to or not, were making it much easier for Greenwood authorities to get the outspoken minister out of their town—for good.

In the following article, the reporters' claim that the cathedral was the target of an "unsuccessful dynamite blast" is false. But Greenwood newspaper readers could not know that; they knew only what they were told.

For their authority, the *Independent* relied heavily on dismissed and disgruntled employees, recycling comments, and charges already proven false by the fire department officials of Delaware, Ohio.

The article is a tragic example of the damage an irresponsible and careless reporter can do to an innocent person, trying and convicting him not in a court of law, but in the pages of a newspaper.

CATHEDRAL INSURED JUST BEFORE BLAST

Anderson Independent, April 10, 1979

Jim Galloway and Rick Ricks

Evangelist Leroy Jenkins took out a $1.2 million insurance policy on his Ohio church a week before the building was hit by an unsuccessful dynamite blast placed in its superstructure, the Independent has learned.[47]

Sources who were formerly in Jenkins' organization also say the church, called Holy Hill Cathedral, was emptied of most of its contents only days before the weekend blast occurred.[48]

---

[47] There was never a dynamite blast. Burn marks were found in a small area of the cathedral ceiling. The Delaware City Fire Department–who was called in immediately after the fire was discovered–determined the burn marks may have been accidentally caused by welding during the renovation of the church building. The damage was so minimal no insurance claim was ever filed. The boom, in other words, was a bust.

[48] The only items that had been removed from church property and taken to South Carolina at this time were books, financial records and a computer. An explosion at the church would have been a great loss to the Evangelistic Association, and could not have been recovered through insurance.

But after almost a year of investigation, federal and state investigators are still stymied by the bombing and the burning of Jenkins' Greenwood home, which occurred three weeks after the explosion.

Law enforcement officials have not made any arrests, nor have any suspects been named in connection with either incident.

Jenkins' church in Delaware, Ohio, was struck by the dynamite blast April 8, 1978. When the evangelist's Victorian home burned three weeks later, the federal Bureau of Alcohol, Tobacco and Firearms joined the State Law Enforcement Division in looking for any possible connection between the two incidents.

Representatives of ATF and SLED have been reluctant to discuss the investigation, except to say the probe is continuing. Neither agency would say whether a connection between the Ohio and South Carolina incidents has been ruled out.[49]

Jenkins, whose crusade business attracted almost $3 million in donations in 1977, said he knows authorities have questioned some of his former and current associates, but denies involvement in either the bombing or the Greenwood fire.

The evangelist said he has volunteered to both SLED and ATF to take a lie detector test. "I told 'em I would take the polygraph test here, and I wanted them to do the same."

Neither law enforcement office has taken Jenkins up on his offer.

In a four-hour interview with Independent reporters, Jenkins confirmed that, in the name of his Association, he purchased a $1.2 million insurance policy on the Holy Hill Cathedral from a Lexington, Ky. company.

No claim on the policy was ever made, because the damage to the church was so slight, Jenkins said. The insurance was bought because his organization was considering placing

---

[49] No connection was ever established between the two incidents.

*a second mortgage on the Cathedral, the evangelist said. The
mortgage was never made.[50]*

*Sources say the policy offered coverage from four different
companies, including Lloyds of London. California Union
and Great American Surplus insurance companies provided $500,000 in coverage each, and Lloyds of London and
Employees of Warsaw supplied $100,000 of coverage each.*

*The church parsonage complex was completed in 1976 at
a cost of $654,000, according to the Association's tax returns.
More than $83,000 was spent on improvements for the
Cathedral in 1977.*

Copyright © Anderson Independent

PROPERTY CLEARED

*Several associates[51] of the Jenkins crusade organization in
Ohio have told the Independent the Cathedral was cleared of
personnel and property shortly before the explosion.*

*And all Delaware, Ohio, employees of the Association
were ordered to attend a crusade being held that weekend in
Greenwood, several sources said. Jenkins denies any order was
given, although he said two bus loads of supporters came from
Delaware to Greenwood that weekend.*

---

[50] The Rev. Jenkins was advised by some business associates to put a first mortgage on the building–not a second mortgage as the *Independent* reported–to pay an outstanding bill owed to one of the Association's creditors. The mortgage was never obtained because the creditor generously agreed to a plan by which the Association could pay off the debt.

[51] Although a number of sources are quoted throughout this article, few are named. One who is named was a contractor who had been fired by the Rev. Jenkins. A judgment was awarded the Association against the contractor but never collected because the fired contractor left the area by the time the judgment was awarded.

Crusade sources also say that only a few days before the bombing in Delaware, two of Jenkins' Delaware associates - one of them a building contractor - were asked to remove material from the cathedral.

Television film, photographic prints, and mail-order inventory located in the Cathedral were loaded in a truck and driven from Ohio to Greenwood immediately, the sources said.

The building contractor who helped remove the material, named John Conley, was suspicious enough of the request to also have his company's equipment removed from the Cathedral, sources said. Conley has since left Ohio, after giving a signed statement to investigators[52].

The contractor was officially in charge of repairing the Cathedral, which had been closed by Ohio state authorities because it did not meet building code specification.

When the two men arrived in Greenwood with the equipment, Jenkins told office workers there that he never ordered the material, and that the men had acted on their own, crusade sources confirmed.

Officials confirmed reports by witnesses who heard a small explosion in the area of the Cathedral at 2 a.m. Saturday, April 8, 1978, about an hour after two busses pulled out of the church parking lot and left for Greenwood.

A message threatening an explosion was received over the organization's prayer line on Monday morning, when it was manned by a regular worker, Delaware police said.

Quickly arriving at the scene, police began hunting for the bomb. They soon found that it had gone off. Damage to the

---

[52]   The contractor had been ordered off the job because he did not fulfill the requirements of his contract. He disappeared with the money that had been advanced to him for the work. The Association subsequently obtained a judgment against him, which they were never able to collect, as the contractor could not be found.

cathedral was so slight that tests had to be made to determine if there was an actual explosion.[53]

"I went up there and looked at it, and it didn't look like anything that couldn't have been done with a couple of M–80's,"[54] said Capt. John Gatton of the Delaware Fire Department.

The bomb was found to have been strategically placed under the building's main beam above the auditorium. A slightly larger blast would have moved the beam slightly more and sent the whole building crashing down, several official sources said.[55]

Copyright © *Anderson Independent*

POLICE GIVEN NAMES

Jenkins has given law enforcement authorities the names of two men he believes are separately responsible for the two incidents.

The evangelist claims an itinerant Georgia man[56] was behind the burning of his Victorian mansion in Greenwood, and linked a former Ohio associate to the dynamiting of the church.

The Augusta, Georgia, man had previously threatened Jenkins, after which the evangelist turned an attack dog

---

[53]   As noted earlier, officials determined there was no explosion.

[54]   M-80s are essentially firecrackers with a small amount of dynamite in their caps. No traces of M-80s or any other incendiary devices were ever found.

[55]   Once again, the *Anderson Independent* reporters play fast and loose with the truth. It would take quite a large explosion to cause a cave-in of the Cathedral ceiling.

[56]   This is a reference to the drifter who had menaced the Rev. Jenkins with a knife, and who had threatened in front of witnesses, including the police, to burn down the Calhoun Street house. He was questioned by police and released.

on him.[57] The drifter was questioned by SLED about the Greenwood fire, but released after passing three separate polygraph tests last May.[58]

Federal authorities have questioned the Ohio man, who later fled, and has since told friends he fears Jenkins.[59]

In the taped interview with Jenkins, the evangelist gave two different versions of the incident leading to the Ohio explosion.

Although he linked the associate to the bombing, Jenkins later reversed himself and said he believed there was no explosion of any kind.[60]

"We were standing out there with my security guys in the yard. And he (the associate) points out a field way out there

---

[57] The dog, Trinka, belonged to June Buckingham. She was a family pet that had been trained as a guard dog by a Florida company. No one ordered Trinka to attack Ernie. She seized Ernie's arm after he pulled his knife. She was well trained and, it turns out, was a good judge of character.

[58] It is common knowledge that polygraph tests are not admissible in court because of their unreliability. It is also a fact that the tests can be fooled by accomplished liars, sociopaths or individuals whose grasp of reality is limited.

[59] Could this fear be attributed to the fact that the Rev. Jenkins obtained a judgment against him and is legally entitled to a refund of the money paid this contractor?

[60] The *Anderson Independent* goes to great lengths to quote the Rev. Jenkins' different thoughts as he puzzled over the so-called "explosion" at his church. Although he had been threatened before, he could not conceive of anyone bombing the church. When the Delaware Fire Department investigated and told him a few charred places in a small area of the Cathedral ceiling had likely been caused by a welding tool, the reverend thought no more about it.

and says, 'There's a hit car out there with dynamite in it,'" Jenkins told reporters at one point.

That associate, he believed, had a hand in the explosion.

But after first acknowledging there was a bombing, he later told reporters no bomb was ever placed in the church.

"I don't believe it was no bomb," he said. "Cause I believe dynamite would have had to have done more than it did..... my God, dynamite's going to have to leave an impression."

Earlier in the conversation, Jenkins said he believed the explosion was caused by "powder burns" from a riveter being used to repair the Cathedral.

"....And I thought that's what it was. 'Cause I said I don't see nothing wrong with this ceiling. And I didn't believe anybody did anything to it, but they said they did, and it didn't look like it to me," Jenkins said.

"He didn't believe it from the very first, because when the call first came in, something just told him it wasn't true," echoed June Buckingham, his personal secretary and treasurer of the organization.

Despite Jenkins' disclaimers, police are convinced there was a dynamite blast in the church, although it was an ineffective one.[61]

A possible connection between the Ohio bombing and the burning of Jenkins' Greenwood home is still being investigated by the State Law Enforcement Division, SLED confirmed this week.

Jenkins had moved much of the furniture out of the house shortly before the fire, taking it to his childhood home on Stockman Street. Jenkins says, however, that he intended to continue living in the mansion, and use the Stockman Street home as a museum.

---

[61] The Delaware City Fire Department—experts in such matters—came to a different conclusion.

A day after the fire, a spokesman for the Leroy Jenkins Evangelistic Association said the house was virtually empty.[62]

The spokesman, Leroy Allen, has since left the crusade.[63]

Jenkins himself was attending a Greenwood Braves baseball game, and arrived on the scene only after the inside of the house had been destroyed.

An insurance policy from another insurance firm covered Jenkins' Greenwood home and its contents when it was set afire.

Jenkins bought the home, along with a Presbyterian church next to it, for $200,000 the year before and he says he spent $150,000 in repairs to the Victorian structure on Calhoun Avenue which was once known as the Cooner house.

Damage to the mansion by the fire was estimated at $169,000. The Association has received payment from the company for damage to the building.

But in an interview last summer, Jenkins said all other insurance on his Greenwood property had since been canceled by the same company. The evangelist said he did not know why.

At the end of a television show broadcasted by several stations only weeks after the fire, Jenkins himself appeared in well-tailored clothes, telling viewers he lost almost eve-

---

[62] This is simply untrue. The weekend before the fire, two buses carrying supporters from Ohio arrived in Greenwood at the Rev. Jenkins' invitation to visit his mansion on Calhoun Street, and to visit the museum in his childhood home on Stockman Street. For that reason, and also because the Calhoun Street house was becoming cluttered with antiques, the Rev. Leroy Allen and other employees moved some of the beautiful antique pieces of furniture over to the museum from the mansion on Calhoun Street.

[63] At the time this article was written, Leroy Allen had not left the Association, but was serving as pastor at Holy Hill Cathedral in the Rev. Jenkins' absence.

rything he owned in the fire. Despite the insurance coverage, he asked for donations to the Association to help him recover from his loss.

The Greenwood fire is the latest in a string of fires which have struck the LJEA's properties. Feb. 3, 1971, an uninsured Lincoln Continental owned by the Association burned outside the barn on its Delaware, Ohio farm property.

One year later, Feb. 19, 1972, the dormitory for Jenkins' defunct boys ranch burned. Damages, including the cameras and related equipment inside, were set at $250,000. Officials listed the cause of the fire as a faulty oil furnace.[64]

Several Jenkins' employees were subjected to intensive questioning by SLED immediately after the Greenwood blaze. One such employee told the Independent that three SLED agents questioned him before a tape recorder for three hours.

Last May, Jenkins acknowledged that some people believed he was responsible for the fire, but he denied any involvement. He also expressed doubts that any of his employees were involved. "There is nobody who works for me who would do such a thing."

Copyright © Anderson Independent

THE REAL REASON FOR THE $1.2-MILLION-DOLLAR POLICY

The *Anderson Independent* reports that "Leroy Jenkins took out a 1.2 million insurance policy on his Ohio church a week before the building was hit by an unsuccessful dynamite blast." The only inference that can be drawn here is that the Rev. Jenkins

---

[64] If the Delaware City Fire Department officially listed the cause of the fire at the Boys' Ranch as a faulty oil furnace, why did the *Anderson Independent* reporters even mention the incident? To prejudice the reader? One wonders.

is an arsonist who attempted to burn down his church to collect insurance.

The trouble with this theory is that *there was no dynamite blast.*

According to an April 10, 1978, report by the Delaware City Fire Department, firemen responded to a report of a bomb threat that had been called in to the Leroy Jenkins Evangelistic Association offices. The caller stated that a bomb had been planted in the ceiling at Holy Hill Cathedral and was set to go off at a certain time. Finding no bomb, the fire department nevertheless advised police to evacuate the office building, which was connected to the cathedral, until they were informed by two employees that a bomb may have gone off in the church because some ceiling tiles had been blown down and there was some damage to a small area of the ceiling.

Fire inspectors once again investigated and filed a report on the incident:

> *We noticed during our first visit that there was a large amount of [ceiling] tile out, but, due to the open construction above the ceiling and the unfinished work, it had seemed to us that this was some stage of construction or that the wind had blown the tile out. There was also damage to a soffit covering a steel "I" beam which was constructed of drywall and 2x4" wood. This was not noticed on the earlier visit, but due to the stages of construction, it would not have seemed out of place at that time.*
>
> *[Delaware police] Patrolman Matthews pointed out a piece of splintered wood, approximately two and one-half feet long that had burns on it and which had an odd odor and was slightly charred.*
>
> *I inspected the soffit area which the employees indicated had been damaged. This area was about eight feet off the ground, covering the "I" beam, and approximately 6x8 feet in size. The wood was broken and the drywall removed.*

> *Due to the appearance of the damaged area, the debris,*
> *lumber and other construction materials present, it appeared*
> *as though the damage was due to vandalism, and that the*
> *ceiling tile had been blown out by wind.*
>
> *It was also noted that various parts of the wood structure*
> *around the "I" beam had char and burn marks which may*
> *have been caused by welding. It was our opinion at this time*
> *that vandals had caused the damage.*

This report is a far cry from the "unsuccessful dynamite blast" that could have "sent the whole building crashing down," as stated in the *Anderson Independent*. This report would have been easily obtainable by the reporters. Had they seen the report and simply ignored it? At the very least, this is another indication of sloppy reporting.

The Association purchased an insurance policy on the church for one reason only: to obtain a mortgage to pay one of the Association's creditors. Almost anyone who has ever owned a home or a piece of property knows that to obtain a mortgage on that property, it must be insured.

At the time the policy was issued, the Association was deeply in debt to one of its creditors, an agent who purchased television time for the Evangelistic Association. The agent had put the Rev. Jenkins' television program on stations all across the country. Television time is very expensive, and it is easy to fall behind. The agent was a fine person, with a lot of faith in the Rev. Jenkins' ministry, and he had extended credit as far as he could. Now, the reverend wanted to get caught up with the bill.

Holy Hill Cathedral had been built with church funds and donations and never had to have a mortgage on it. Before the bank would issue a first mortgage, the building had to be insured. Fortunately, the agent was willing to accept a weekly payment to discharge the debt, while continuing to put the program on the television stations. For this reason, the mortgage was never taken against the church, and the agent was paid in full in a few years. The church was never insured after that one year.

HOLY HILL CATHEDRAL FILLED WITH VALUABLE CONTENTS

The *Anderson Independent* reports "Holy Hill Cathedral was emptied of most of its contents only days before the weekend blast." The truth is, Holy Hill was *never* emptied of its contents. The beautiful upholstered seats themselves were worth thousands of dollars, having been covered with $35-per-yard material. An ebony grand piano, purchased only a few years before for $20,000, stood on stage. Also on the platform were two Hammond organs, a set of drums, and a complete sound system with sixteen microphone connections. The interior of the church, including the stage, had been lovingly designed by the Rev. Jenkins.

Storage rooms in the adjoining office held church files and records. A staff of several people, including crusade soloist Henrietta Hairston, manned the church office. Their desks and files were in the office, also.

The only items that had been taken to South Carolina at this time were some books and financial records and a computer. An explosion at the church would have been a great loss to the Evangelistic Association and could not have been replaced through insurance coverage.

The *Anderson Independent* reports that the church complex was completed at slightly less than a million dollars. With the valuable furnishings, the loss would have exceeded the $1.2-million-dollar insurance policy, and thousands of dollars would never be recovered. This alone should be proof enough that it would not have been advantageous to stage a fire for the insurance money.

The *Independent* reporters based their assumptions on the vengeful grumbling of a "disgruntled former employee." The Rev. Jenkins had fired this individual, a contractor, because he was not doing the job he was hired to do. The Association later obtained a judgment against the man but was unable to collect it because the man left the area and could not be found. He was probably not the most reliable source for a serious newspaper article.

GREENWOOD MANSION'S IRREPLACEABLE CONTENTS LOST

The Rev. Jenkins' beautifully furnished home in Greenwood could never have been replaced by the insurance money. The five bedrooms were completely furnished and occupied. The Rev. Jenkins lived in the house along with his younger children Candy, Sharon, and Scotty, and a housekeeper.

His married children, Theresa, her husband and her two babies; and Lou, with his wife and little girl, had come to town for a long visit. Their clothes and possessions were a total loss.

The living and dining room was filled with crystal glassware, china, and antique furniture. The appliances—a washer, dryer, freezer, refrigerator, and dishwasher—were new.

After the fire, hundreds came from Greenwood to the fire sale conducted in the yard of the burnt home and saw the pitiful condition of the numerous pieces that were dragged out of the charred, stinking structure.

At first, likely due to the *Anderson Independent* article, the Aetna insurance company refused to pay for the items destroyed in the fire. In 1981, the Rev. Jenkins filed suit against them to recover for his personal belongings and antiques. After a trial before a jury in the Greenwood County Courthouse, the Aetna insurance company was ordered to pay the claim.

The Rev. Jenkins was shocked and puzzled at the *Anderson Independent*'s articles. He did not know at this time that he would be arrested at week's end on a charge of conspiracy to commit arson. The ground had been laid for his betrayal, and the atmosphere so poisoned there could never have been a fair trial anywhere within reach of this scandal sheet.

THE ARREST

LEROY JENKINS JAILED

EVANGELIST FACES 3 CONSPIRACY CHARGES

Anderson Independent, April 18, 1979

Jim Galloway and Rick Ricks

GREENWOOD – Evangelist Leroy Jenkins was arrested Tuesday on three counts of conspiracy, with one count charging him with plotting to burn down the home of a S.C. highway patrolman. Jenkins is being held in the Greenwood County Jail in lieu of $500,000 bond.

Following an investigation that lasted almost a year, during which a federal undercover agent infiltrated Jenkins' organization, the evangelist also was accused of conspiring to burn a Belton home, and charged with conspiring "to commit

*assault and battery of a high and aggravated nature"[65] on an
Anderson Independent reporter.*

*The target of the alleged assault plot, Independent reporter
Rick Ricks, was an author of a series of articles on Jenkins
and his $3 million-a-year ministry published last week by
the Independent.*

*Dressed in white athletic shoes, a gold necklace and the
standard green coveralls issued to county prisoners, Jenkins
exchanged pleasantries with reporters as he entered the
small magistrates courtroom at the Greenwood County Law
Enforcement Center.*

*But the evangelist remained silent after Magistrate
Charles Henderson convened the hearing at 7:15 p.m., three
hours after deputies arrested Jenkins at his newly purchased
home on New Market Street.*

*Jenkins' two grey-suited attorneys flanked him, and four
members of the Leroy Jenkins Evangelistic Association sat
with several reporters attending the hearing.*

*Jenkins' arrest came almost a year after his former
Greenwood home was struck by arson. Three weeks before the
Victorian mansion burned in 1978, Jenkins' church in Ohio
was dynamited - one week after the evangelist took out a $1.2
million insurance policy on the structure.*

*Neither incident, both of which are being investigated by
SLED and federal agents, has been solved.[66]*

---

[65] If *Anderson Independent* editors truly believed Rick Ricks was the
target of a planned assault against him, he should have been taken
off the story. How could he fairly write about a man he had been
told was planning to hurt him? It is a clear conflict of interest by
any journalistic standards.

[66] This is misleading. The suspected arsonist in the Calhoun Street
fire may not have been found, but responsibility for the fire was
never laid at the feet of the Rev. Jenkins. The so-called fire at Holy
Hill Cathedral was ruled by the Delaware, Ohio fire inspector to
have probably been caused by a welding tool used in construction.

According to the warrants issued Tuesday, Jenkins is charged with conspiring to burn the home of highway Patrolman C. R. Keasler, of 228 Greenwood Drive.

Keasler arrested Jenkins' daughter, Candace, in December on a series of minor charges stemming from a speeding ticket. Ms. Jenkins pleaded guilty on all counts.

A federal undercover agent allegedly participated in the plot, along with Frank D. Minor, 23, of Wisconsin, who was arrested and charged with conspiracy to commit arson.

Authorities said Minor and the agent were stopped, loaded down with gasoline, in the driveway of Keasler's house.

The second warrant charges Jenkins with a March 8 conspiracy to commit arson along with Scott Shirley, 23, of Hodges and the federal undercover agent. The purpose of the plot was to destroy the residence of Charles Mullinax in Belton, according to police. Greenwood authorities said Mullinax had no knowledge of the conspiracy.

According to the warrant, Jenkins allegedly furnished the undercover agent with combustible materials "with felonious intent."

Shirley was arrested by Greenwood County deputies at 6 p.m. and was not arraigned Tuesday.

A third warrant charges Jenkins with entering into an agreement, again with Frank Minor and the federal undercover agent, to commit assault on Independent reporter Ricks on April 12.

A call was placed that night to The Independent newsroom, allegedly attempting to lure Ricks to Greenwood by promising information on Jenkins' activities, to be included in the copyrighted series of articles on the evangelist.

Ricks declined the invitation.

Following Jenkins' arraignment, Minor was brought into the courtroom for formal arraignment on the assault charge. His bond of $150,000 for the arson charge was not increased.

In setting the $500,000 bond for Jenkins, Magistrate Henderson said, "I feel this is fair compensation to the state considering the amount the other defendants were required to pay."

County Detective Sam Riley asked Henderson for a bond "sufficient to protect the interests of the state," pointing out that Jenkins has interests outside the state.

The state also asked that Jenkins be prohibited from interfering with or harassing possible witnesses.[67] (see photos on page 275-276)

Jenkins' attorneys, Dave Cole and Dick Arnold, argued that Jenkins should be released on his own recognizance, since the three charges were not capitol offenses, and since his home and the Association is located in Greenwood.

The attorneys pointed out that Jenkins' profession requires that he travel throughout the country to conduct his crusades, and said that Jenkins has committed no serious offenses "in the past several years."

"Due to the seriousness of these offenses, a personal recognizance bond is out of the question," Henderson said. The magistrate pointed out that the arrest came in time for the case to be included in the May 14 general court session in Greenwood.

Arnold and Cole asked Henderson to remain available in case the bond could be raised within the next few hours, but Henderson said he would not consider releasing Jenkins on bond until 9 a.m. Wednesday.

According to an Internal Revenue Service spokesman, Jenkins cannot use funds from his $3-million-year ministry to post bond without losing his tax-exempt status.

Copyright © Anderson Independent

---

[67] This is an ironic statement considering that one of the prosecution's key witnesses would later accuse the solicitor of coaching him in his testimony. See chapter, "A Witness Recants – Too Late."

THE UNTHINKABLE HAPPENS

The Rev. Jenkins' last free hours were spent in his room where he was resting and reflecting after a recent crusade. It was a lovely spring day. Dogwoods and azaleas bloomed profusely. Honeysuckle perfumed the air that wafted in through the open windows.

David, Rev's thirteen-year-old son, was washing the limousine in the driveway, as Eliza, the housekeeper, finished up the last of the dinner dishes.

Suddenly, squealing tires shattered the peace. Fifteen police cruisers pulled into the driveway that curved in front of the mansion, their wheels throwing gravel and dust.

Police tumbled out of the cars, guns drawn, and rushed to the front and back doors.

It could have been a scene from a Hollywood police drama. As Eliza opened the door, the men pushed the terrified woman aside and poured into the house like a pack of commandos.

"Where is Leroy Jenkins? We have a warrant for his arrest," one of them barked as the others lumbered up the stairs and through the house.

The bewildered preacher was handcuffed, hustled into a cruiser, and taken to the police station as his son and housekeeper looked on in disbelief. That afternoon, a nightmare began that would not end for more than five years.

The insidious plot to send Reverend Jenkins to prison was set up and orchestrated by a host of high profile public officials, one of which was the Greenwood Solicitor, William Jones. It was a premeditated plan to get Reverend Jenkins arrested and sentenced to over ten years because he did not want Jenkins to be able to post bond. The authorities knew that in order to prevent Reverend Jenkins from posting bond, the sentencing had to be over ten years by statutory requirement.

In order for this plan to work, there must be witnesses close to Reverend Jenkins to "testify" against him. A plan was devised to arrest two of his employees, Frank Minor and Scott Shirley so they could be coerced into testifying against Jenkins. ATF Agent, Bruce Mirkin was enlisted to setup an ambush and "sham" arrest of himself and Frank Minor for allegedly trying to torch Patrolman Keasler's home.

After successfully arresting Frank Minor and later Scott Shirley, the plan was now in full motion. Once in jail, Greenwood Solicitor, William Jones now had complete freedom and unlimited access to interrogate and wear down both Minor and Shirley through fear and intimidation. Minor said he and Shirley were regularly taken out of their cells each night into rooms where Jones "schooled" them for hours on how to testify against Reverend Jenkins. Jones cast aspersions in their minds about Reverend Jenkins based in part on the inaccurate report of the *Anderson Independent.* Jones convinced them they were doing the right thing and finally, out of exasperation, they both testified against Reverend Jenkins, giving William Jones the "testimony" he had engineered.

Minor, now realized that he and Shirley had been used to help convict an innocent man. Frank Minor later came forward of his own volition to inform Reverend Jenkins' attorneys what really happened. The hideousness of the injustice against Reverend Jenkins is that he was convicted of a crime that NEVER happened through a criminal justice system that did not follow it's own protocols for due process. Reverend Jenkins had not been charged with a felony and he was not allowed to have witnesses testify on his behalf.

TRIAL AND TRIBULATIONS

After persuading the court to reduce the half-million-dollar bond to $150,000, the Rev. Jenkins was free pending trial. He went on with his ministry and the crusades that had been scheduled before the arrest.

Newspapers in South Carolina and Ohio heralded the news of the arrest, but the notoriety did not deter the crowds that came to fill every auditorium where the evangelist appeared. Because of the arrest, the crusades were front-page news. The articles may not always have been favorable. But the end result was that God's name was mentioned over and over in the nation's press. You can't buy that kind of publicity.

The Huntsville, Alabama, crusade, where people filled the arena to the top row, made the front page. The *Columbus Citizen-Journal* of Columbus, Ohio, reported, "The evangelist touched the heads of the faithful, prayed for miracle cures for afflictions ranging from broken bones to cancer."

"She got her miracle," read a photo caption on the front page of the April 30, 1979 *Nashville Tennessean*. The photo captured the joyful expression on a young lady's face as she embraced her friends.

"Stephanie Armstrong, 23, of Columbia, is overcome with emotion after she said her blindness was cured during an evangelistic sermon by Rev. Leroy Jenkins," the caption read.

Believers packed the halls of Nashville's Grand Ole Opry House, shouting their support as the evangelist proclaimed his innocence.

"'If you've read the newspapers, you know I've been arrested in South Carolina. Well, let me tell you right now, I'm not guilty. They have been trying for 23 years to get something on me to stop me because my leadership is so effective, so they planted an agent in my ministry," an article in the *Nashville Tennessean* reported.

"Then Jenkins resumed his mingling with the audience, blessing dozens of persons afflicted with physical handicaps from blindness to paralysis," the article said.

If the arrest did nothing else, it served to get miracles and healing headlined in the newspapers time and again in the spring of 1979.

GOOD-BYE, CHARLIE

Just two days before the trial was to begin, the *Columbus Citizen-Journal* covered a crusade held at the Delaware church:

> Jenkins promised his enthusiastic followers Sunday that he would be acquitted of all the charges against him. But in an interview after the service, he said he could run his multi-million dollar ministry just as effectively within the prison as outside it.
>
> Jenkins earlier had told his followers, "There's not a law or government or the FBI or anybody else that could take away from me what God gave me 21 years ago." The audience responded with shouts of "Amen!"
>
> "When Jesus Christ hanged down from the cross at 33 years of age, people didn't lose their faith and respect for him," Jenkins said. "The government is what killed him,

the same thing they're trying to do to me, the same thing they would try to do with you."

The *Citizen-Journal* article reported the reverend's comments about the Greenwood law enforcement establishment:

> "You give them hillbillies a badge, honey, and a gun and it's dangerous. I'm scared to go out on the street. They don't have as much education as I do. Those little hillbillies will shoot you." The Rev. Jenkins also made reference to the amazing number of detectives and officers gathered in Greenwood for the trial.
>
> "There must be 100 law enforcement people lying around the Holiday Inn getting drunk on the taxpayers' money."
>
> Jenkins said he would rely on a jury to acquit him of the charges.
>
> "There has to be two or three on a jury who will go along with me. If not, I'll just have to say "Good-bye Charlie.""

As the article hinted, there seemed to be an indication that the Rev. Jenkins knew what might befall him. He had told his church months before that God let him see he was going to go to prison, like Paul and Silas. Although he would receive a twelve-year sentence, he would not serve the full term, he said.

Perhaps God was preparing him for what was to come.

A PACK OF OLE HOUND DOGS

Hugh Beasley personified the courtly Southern lawyer in his suspenders and seersucker suits. He had come by the Association offices in Greenwood to offer his services as local defense counsel for the Rev. Jenkins. Holding his fine strawhat in his hands, he spoke passionately of local law enforcement.

"They are just like a pack of ole hound dogs chasing a little bitty rabbit. They will corner him and flush him out, and that will be the end of him. They will show no mercy," Beasley said, his blue eyes flashing behind steel-rimmed spectacles.

"I love that boy," he said of the Rev. Jenkins. "I remember when he used to come around selling boiled peanuts. He was a little go-getter. They just can't stand it that he came back here, so aggressive and successful. They are afraid he's going to upset their apple cart," Beasley said.

"He's going to need a lawyer with a lot of statewide prestige. We are going to have to get the best we can find," he said.

Beasley had served as solicitor in Greenwood County for many years. He resigned to enter the navy in WWII. After years of distinguished service as an officer, he returned to Greenwood and went into practice with his son, John.

Their law offices were directly across the street from the courthouse, and nothing escaped Beasley's attention. A graduate of the prestigious Furman University, he had friends in high places and was widely respected.

On his advice, the Rev. Jenkins retained Kermit King, an esteemed attorney from Columbia, as chief counsel.

SUSPICIONS OF SNOOPING AND JURY TAMPERING

Beasley's navy training had familiarized him with many types of listening devices. He had a strong suspicion that the Association offices were bugged, as well as the Greenwood motel where the defense lawyers were preparing their case.

He first suspected the wiretapping after an incident involving the jury box, which contained the names of potential jurors. Beasley's son, John, was in the courthouse on business when he noticed the jury box standing unlocked and open. The jury box was supposed to be locked at the time of jury selection.

Had someone been going through the names in the box with the intent of rigging a jury sympathetic to the prosecution? Concerned, John Beasley immediately telephoned his father, who went directly to the Association's offices to warn them of possible jury tampering. Just as soon as the senior Beasley had delivered the message, his son, still in the courthouse, saw a clerk receive a telephone call, then walk over to the jury box, and lock it.

The defense team hired an expert in electronic eavesdropping to help them determine whether or not Beasley's private conversations with Association staff members had been compromised by law enforcement officials.

The expert, William Wilde, whose credentials included ten years' experience as a member of the Marine Corps Criminal Investigative Division (CID), testified that his equipment had detected a powerful transmitter emanating from a building near the Association offices. When he and Beasley got into a car with the intent of following the transmission signal to its source, it suddenly stopped.

Later, when the trial got under way, Beasley and King broached the subject of the unlocked jury box and the possible jury tampering, inexplicably incurring the wrath of presiding judge James E. Moore.

"Drop that subject and never bring it up again, or you will never practice law in this court again," the scowling, red-faced judge replied.

Hesitant to antagonize the judge at the very beginning of the trial, chief counsel Kermit King dropped the matter.

The judge also refused to allow the defense attorneys to individually interview members of the jury—a common practice known as voir dire—in an attempt to assemble a fair and impartial jury. Even without the suspected jury tampering, it would have been impossible to find a jury who had not been poisoned by the adverse publicity generated by the *Anderson Independent* and other news media. The only way to allow the reverend even a semblance of a fair trial would be to grant a continuance to allow the pretrial publicity to subside or to grant a change of venue.

Another troubling incident took place that added to the defense lawyers' suspicions of eavesdropping by law enforcement officers. The defense team, who were headquartered in a local hotel room, was preparing to interview someone connected to the case. As a precaution, they called in their surveillance expert to check the room for listening devices. No bugs were found in the room, but Wilde detected a transmission coming from within the hotel complex.

Wilde also observed a vehicle parked across the street from the hotel. The car carried municipal government tags. When the defense team left the room to have lunch at a nearby restaurant, the car followed close behind and parked across the street where he could easily observe the subjects of his surveillance. Three days later, Wilde said he observed the same car parked at a service station across the street from the hotel.

Though they could not prove the government was listening in on their strategy sessions, defense attorneys were certain their attorney-client confidentiality had been breached.

A RUSH TO JUDGMENT

The trial of the Rev. Leroy Jenkins was a mockery of American justice.

The pretrial hearing took place on May 9, 1979. The magistrate determined there was probable cause to bind the case over to the grand jury despite the fact that the state presented hearsay evidence from a single law enforcement officer who had *no firsthand knowledge* of the alleged offenses. This witness, chief detective of the Greenwood County Sheriff's Office, admitted his sole source of information to be ATF Agent Bruce Mirkin, alias Billy Murphy, a man who had proven to be an accomplished liar and schemer who had tried to influence and entrap innocent people into committing crimes *that never took place*. The chief detective also claimed to have had additional conversations with other persons directly associated with the investigation, but he "could not recall their names."

The Rev. Jenkins was indicted on May 17, 1979. The trial was set for two days later. The defense did not know of the existence of the undercover agent or his secret tape recordings until May 13. This is almost unheard of. Normally, the defense is given ample opportunity to study evidence against their client.

At the last minute, a fourth misdemeanor charge—conspiracy to commit assault against newspaper reporter Rick Ricks—was added to the three misdemeanor charges already pending against the evangelist. The solicitor asked the grand jury to return an indictment on this charge *without presenting any evidence whatsoever.*

Faced with three hundred pages of transcripts of taped conversations procured by ATF agent Bruce Mirkin, alias Billy Murphy, King reasonably requested a month's delay. Instead, he was given *three days* to prepare his case.

Three law clerks worked frantically to digest the transcripts that were to be used as evidence against the Rev. Jenkins. There was no way the lawyers could come up with an effective defense in that time.

Although the reverend strongly suspected the tapes had been doctored,[68] the defense had no time to test the recordings for authenticity. Neither did the defense have time to interview and prepare potential witnesses on the Rev. Jenkins' behalf.

The rush to trial also prevented the defense from filing the necessary pretrial motions that would have enabled them to uncover new information that might help their case.

The defense again requested a continuance but was refused outright. Continuances are routinely granted in most jurisdictions. It is not only within the judge's power to grant a continuance, but

---

[68]   This opinion was later seconded by one of the prosecution's key witnesses. See chapter, "A Witness Recants – Too Late."

it is also his duty if the defendant does not have sufficient time for effective preparation. Not to do so is a violation of a defendant's constitutional right to effective counsel and its grounds for appeal.

The defense attorneys found themselves stonewalled at every turn. Their client was sinking in the mire of Greenwood-style justice, and they did not have a rope to throw him.

The Rev. Jenkins' Ohio attorney, Henry Eckhart, summed up the feelings of many trial observers when he later told the state newspaper in Columbia that the reverend "went down to South Carolina and got railroaded."

EXPLETIVES NOT DELETED

The trial convened on the morning of May 17, 1979, despite defense counsel's continuing protestations that they were not ready.

Bruce Mirkin, alias Billy Murphy, the ATF undercover agent who had been sent to spy on the Rev. Jenkins, took the stand. The two codefendants, Scott Shirley, who had been out on bond, and Frank Minor, who had been kept in jail ever since the arrest the month before, also testified.

The prosecution's case hinged primarily on the testimony of Mirkin, whose "investigation" was based on lies and deceit.

Portions of the many hours of tapes secretly recorded by Mirkin during what the Rev. Jenkins believed were private conversations in his home were played in court for everyone to hear. Taken out of context, the tapes did not cast a favorable light on the reverend. This was not because he had conspired with anyone to commit arson or assault; he had not.

It is true that he talked about getting even with the people he felt had hurt him. Anyone who knows the Rev. Jenkins knows he has a temper. But they also knew he would never do anything to hurt anybody.

Patrolman Keasler had arrested the Rev. Jenkins' teenaged daughter, roughing her up and bruising her in the process. What father would not have been angry? Reporter Ricks had coauthored a series of articles that contained a number of rumors, misstatements, and outright lies about the reverend's life and work. Who would not have been angry?

Is there anyone who, at some point his life, has not savored the idea of revenge against those who have hurt him? "I'd like to wring his neck" or "If I get my hands on him, I'll kill him" are common expressions of anger.

Talking and doing are two different things. In order for Leroy Jenkins to be guilty of conspiracy, he had to have the intent to follow through, which he did not.

What appeared to turn the jury against the evangelist the most was the fact that, while hanging around with his supposed friend Murphy, his conversation was liberally salted with common expletives, which shocked those who thought a preacher ought to be above such things.

"I am so embarrassed," the Rev. Jenkins confided at one point during the playing of the tapes. "I could just crawl under this table."

As embarrassing as the tapes might have been, bad language is not a crime. If it were, the prisons would be overflowing. The prosecution also pointed out that the reverend had been seen in certain night spots around town. This too, while not illegal, was certain to prejudice a jury in a small, conservative Southern community.

The defense called only one witness, the defendant, who was subjected to an absurd, abusive, and, at times, almost incoherent cross-examination by Eighth Judicial Circuit Solicitor William T. Jones.

Jones' behavior in the courtroom was startling. Jumping up and down, waving his hands, the prosecutor bullied the jury and the defendant throughout the trial. He attacked the Rev. Jenkins' ministry, accusing him of "sucking" money from people. The accusations were never proved, and they had nothing to do with the charges at hand. But such highly inflammatory remarks surely had their desired effect.

Jones questioned the evangelist about the fire that destroyed his Greenwood home and the alleged "dynamiting" of his church in Delaware, Ohio, implying by reference that he had been responsible for these two incidents. That no such thing had been proved[69] did not seem to matter. Jones repeatedly questioned the defendant about these events even though the judge had ruled beforehand that they were not to be introduced into the trial.

In commenting on the reverend's character, Jones remarked in his closing argument that the defendant's private life and his religion were pertinent to the charges at hand.

"Well, what does make any difference to try to sight up (sic) a man as to whether or not he has the capacity, the willingness to commit a crime?" Jones asked.

"Where would you get it from? Those things are valid things to take into consideration as to having, his having malice in his heart, wickedness, as to his not caring about the rights of others. A man's home is his castle, Mr. Foreman,[70] and he's going to parade around here as a minister and tell you he's done changed his mind about this man Keasler out yonder, when he done found out that his daughter kicked him and messed all around with him when he's just trying to arrest her for speeding, and he done changed his mind?"

Jones' almost-incoherent ramblings were breathtaking. It is an elementary rule of evidence that a defendant's bad reputation or prior "bad acts" cannot be brought into evidence unless the defendant himself makes it an issue.

---

[69]   The solicitor either did not know or did not reveal that there had been no dynamiting of the Delaware church.

[70]   An ironic statement, since the prosecutor obviously did not consider the Rev. Jenkins' home to be his castle.

The solicitor even went so far afield as to make personal attacks on the evangelist's appearance.

At one point, Jones took off his shoe and banged it repeatedly on the bar that separates the jury from the rest of the courtroom. His behavior brought back images of Soviet dictator Nikita Khrushchev pounding his shoe on the table at the United Nations, shouting, "We are going to bury you." It was disturbing to watch someone who seemed so out of control.

"If he's not guilty, I'll eat my shoe," Jones said banging away. It was an awesome display of temper and personal animosity.

INTIMIDATION OF POTENTIAL WITNESSES

Staff members arrived from Ohio to lend their support and to testify if called upon.

Taffy Douglas, head of the Faith Enterprises division of the Leroy Jenkins Evangelistic Association, which secures radio and television time, came to help. Ms. Douglas had been a radio station owner and had her own television program in Dayton, Ohio. A black woman in a largely white market, she had risen to the top of her field. She is a highly respected broadcast professional, not easily intimidated.

From the moment of her arrival, Ms. Douglas noticed men following her. She did not know who they were, but she and another woman of color traveling with her said they felt so intimidated they had to leave town.

Another friend, Joe Mason, who is also African American, had been present many times when Mirkin, alias Murphy, had secretly taped conversations with the Rev. Jenkins. Mason could have refuted much of the agent's testimony. But he said he believed he would be harmed if he testified, and so he did not come forward.

While many, including the author, were ready and willing to serve as character witnesses, with so little time to prepare, no one was called to testify that Rev was not the one-dimensional person he was portrayed to be in court. No one told of his sense of humor, his kindness, his generosity, or any of his many good qualities.

THE DEFENSE

Chief defense counsel Kermit King, accustomed to the more genteel courtrooms in Columbia, South Carolina's capital, seemed to have been caught off guard by the coarse antics and language of William Jones.

As a defense, King argued two principles of law: conspiracy and entrapment. A conspiracy, King told the jury, requires criminal intent. In other words, if some friends are sitting around talking about how they need money and one says, "Let's go rob a bank," and another agrees, they would not be guilty of a conspiracy unless they really intended to rob a bank. Even if the reverend had made careless comments in the privacy of his home about how he would like to beat up a reporter who had been writing negative stories about him, for example, there was no proof he actually intended to do so.

As far as Rick Ricks was concerned, the Rev. Jenkins had indeed been angry at the *Anderson Independent* reporter. He was so angry, in fact, that he told one of his employees that he had called Ricks up on the telephone and told him he was going to give him a black eye. If he had intended to have someone assault Ricks, it would have been extremely stupid of him to show his hand by calling Ricks beforehand.

As someone smart enough to dig his way out of poverty to become a highly successful evangelist of international repute, it is doubtful the Rev. Jenkins would risk all he had accomplished over a grudge against a small-town reporter. Besides, as everyone knew, the reverend liked to fight his own battles.

The evangelist had been verbalizing his anger toward the reporter for months. That not a single hair on the reporter's head was ever touched was proof enough that the Rev. Jenkins lacked criminal intent.

Regarding the entrapment issue, King argued that there would never have been talk of assault or arson without the urging of the federal agent. This argument is supported by one of the prosecution's own witnesses who later told the evangelist's lawyers that there was never any talk about fires or assault unless Mirkin was present (see chapter "Trial and Tribulations").

Even *Mirkin* admitted that he had initiated the conversations with the Rev. Jenkins in which he prodded the evangelist to take action against Patrolman Keasler and others.

Jones' question to the jury that "how in the world can [someone] be persuaded to do [something] if he didn't intend to do it?" missed the point.

Perhaps the solicitor didn't understand the legal definition of *entrapment*: an act by police or other government officer of inducing a person to commit a crime he had not contemplated nor would have committed *if not for the inducement*.

It is more likely that the prosecutor knew the definition but wanted to muddy the waters.

King pointed out that it would be highly unlikely for the reverend to conspire with a relative stranger, especially one who had tried to take advantage of his daughter as Mirkin had done, and not with someone much closer to him. Why would Rev feel he could trust Mirkin?

Mirkin had also accused the Rev. Jenkins of associating with "mobsters." The so-called mobsters were the Chicago security firm hired by the evangelist to protect him from the crowds following his crusades. If these men had indeed been "mobsters," King argued, why wouldn't the reverend have hired *them* to carry out his "conspiracy"?

There were inconsistencies throughout Mirkin's testimony. The defense counsel pointed out that the ATF agent claimed to have recorded some conversations he had with the reverend and not others. That's a huge red flag. Why didn't he? Did other tapes exist? Could the conversations Mirkin did not record have exonerated the Rev. Jenkins? It is against the law to withhold exculpatory evidence, which, in this case, would be evidence favorable to the reverend and the prosecution hid from the defense. The reverend told his attorneys that many of the tapes contained only parts of his conversations with Mirkin.

Mirkin had excuses for the times he did not wear a recording device. One time, he said it was hot, and he had to take off his shirt, so he could not wear a wire. At one point in his closing argument, King said, "You can ask Mirkin what time it is, and he'll tell you how to make a clock."

Referring to Patrolman Keasler's arrest of the reverend's daughter, King added, "Isn't it remarkable that Mirkin just happen to arrive in town at a time when Jenkins was upset over the arrest of his daughter?"

At one point, Mirkin was caught in a lie he told the jury. Though one segment of the tapes revealed that the agent had urged the Rev. Jenkins to try marijuana, Mirkin denied he had ever tried to get the reverend to commit an illegal act. But wait—wasn't the general idea to goad the reverend into an illegal act?

In another segment, King pointed out a recorded comment the Rev. Jenkins made to Mirkin in which he said, "You know, you told me one time that you could kill somebody; that bothered me." The reverend also told Mirkin he did not want him to burn down any houses or assault anybody.

It just didn't add up, the chief defense counsel reasoned. Mirkin kept talking about how he wanted to protect the people who were allegedly targeted by the evangelist. But if he really believed the reverend wanted to have homes burned and people beaten up, why did the agent expose those people to such peril?

They were not warned they were targets of the so-called conspiracy until close to the time of the faked arrest. The truth was that Murphy knew the Rev had no intention of harming those people.

Warning of the danger to society of "overzealous policemen," King pointed out that Mirkin had originally been sent by the ATF to investigate the fire at the reverend's home. Having failed to uncover anything incriminating against the reverend and no doubt feeling pressure to justify the waste of taxpayers' money, Mirkin had to come up with something. After many months of goading and scheming, all he would come up with were four feeble misdemeanor conspiracy charges filed in state court.

Later, one of the prosecution's key witnesses would sign an affidavit saying he had lied on the stand and that the Rev. Jenkins had not been a party to any plan to commit arson. In fact, the witness said, the reverend had repudiated—or renounced—the ATF agent's plot (see chapter "Trial and Tribulations"). Even if someone is involved in a conspiracy, if he repudiates the conspiracy, he is not guilty of the conspiracy according to the law.

THE VERDICT

The outcome was guaranteed even before the trial began. In the end, the jury rejected the defense's plea of entrapment. A week after it began, the trial ended.

The reverend had been given the *maximum* sentence allowed— five years each on the four misdemeanor counts. Ultimately, the twenty-year sentence was reduced to twelve. Twelve years in prison is a long time, especially when you consider that the average sentence for homicide in the United States is twelve years and five months.[71]

When the judge announced the verdict, a phalanx of officers who had formed a human barrier between the reverend and his friends and family members grabbed the minister and hustled

---

[71]   Bureau of Justice Statistics, Prison Sentences and Time Served for Violence, 1995.

him back to jail. He was not permitted to spend even a moment with his seven children, who were sobbing in the first row of seats.

He would not see his ten-year-old son Scotty or his other minor-age children again for years. Later, the reverend reflected on his arrest and conviction:

He [ATF agent Bruce Mirkin alias Billy Murphy] was sent here to do what he did, and he didn't stop until he'd gotten the job done.

In posing as a friend, employee and later as an arsonist for hire, Mirkin hounded and tormented me. I thought he might actually kill somebody, and I didn't want that to happen.

He was trying to entrap me, and I was talking to him, trying to find out who sent him, and what he was trying to do to me.

The Rev. Jenkins had been tricked by a practiced deceiver, targeted by a hostile and determined prosecutor, and sentenced by a judge who obstructed the defense every step of the way.

It had taken at least six federal agents, as well as countless state and local law enforcement officials, more than seven months to make a case against the Rev. Jenkins. Could the hundreds of man hours devoted to this case have been better spent solving crimes of murder, rape, robbery, and other felonies? There must have been many such unsolved crimes in South Carolina. The Rev. Jenkins harmed no one.

At first, it seemed the forces of evil had prevailed. But the evangelist's lessons learned in the rough-and-tumble scramble from poverty to prosperity, combined with the power of a mighty God, would see him through the dark days to come.

APPEALING TO A HIGHER COURT

Dr. Gilbert Holloway and his wife, June, both respected and gifted evangelists from Deming, New Mexico, came to Greenwood following the trial to help with the management of the Evangelistic Association. They spent two days in Greenwood wandering around, meeting and talking to the townspeople in an attempt to understand what happened.

The Holloways had known the Rev. Jenkins since attending one of his crusades in Florida in 1963 and considered him a man of boldness, daring, and courage. They were shocked and saddened to see a man so highly gifted in the spirit and with such a successful ministry wind up in a South Carolina prison, so they appealed to the State Supreme Court to grant a new trial.

"Leroy spent money in a constructive way in and about Greenwood, and, of course, the citizens were happy to take his money, but they criticized him behind his back for his aggressiveness, flamboyance, and very positive attitude.

"Like most gifted persons, he is temperamental, and has quite a temper on occasion," Dr. Holloway continued. "But anyone who knows the Rev. Jenkins knows he could never hurt anyone."

Dr. Holloway was especially critical of Greenwood's brand of justice.

"Everything went wrong at the trial," he said. "The judge was a crony, a former law clerk in the office of the prosecutor. The prosecutor was an able trial lawyer who showed extreme animosity toward Brother Jenkins. He was extremely aggressive and competent, bullying the judge, the jury, and all present."

"A lawyer in town told me the jury box had been tampered with, and there is a real question if the jury was hand picked with friends, relatives, employees, or persons obligated in some way to the prosecutor," Dr. Holloway said. "I believe the trial was grossly unfair and improper. First of all, the judge should have disqualified himself, or been disqualified by law. He was too close to the prosecutor.

"Second, the defense was not given proper time in which to prepare. This in itself is reason for a mistrial, and I hope the South Carolina Supreme Court will throw out the whole business when it comes up on appeal in due course of time.[72] It is gross injustice to a good and decent man. It stinks to high heaven, and it is a shame

---

[72] The South Carolina Supreme Court did not order a new trial.

and disgrace upon the people of South Carolina, and indirectly upon all Americans and their sense of justice and righteousness."

Another longtime supporter of the ministry, June Dunlevy, appealed to the state Supreme Court, sharing an experience in Greenwood that illustrated the feeling of ill will some people had for the Rev. Jenkins and that a plot to entrap him had been in the making for a long time.

In her letter to the high court, she told of stopping to buy gasoline following a crusade she had attended in Greenwood. She struck up a conversation with the attendant.

"We are from Boone, North Carolina," she told him, "and are on our way home. I can tell you that nothing has ever happened to me like happened here yesterday. We have been attending the two-day Leroy Jenkins crusade at the civic center. A little Baptist lady from Monroe, North Carolina, received her sight after being blind for five years."

Mrs. Dunlevy said the attendant replied, "Is that right? We stay awfully busy here, and I have never been to one of his crusades, but I'm going to watch him on television some time."

Mrs. Dunlevy said she hoped he would. Then she said the attendant remarked, "Rev. Jenkins has been down here for about a year. He has stirred up a lot of things down here, and I don't doubt that a lot of it is true, *but they are out to get him.*"

Deeply troubled, Mrs. Dunlevy said she realized the importance of the attendant's words when Rev was arrested.

Thousands of other supporters appealed to the South Carolina justice system, calling for the reverend's release or, at the very least, a new trial. Their pleas fell on deaf ears.

A WITNESS RECANTS — TOO LATE

A month following the trial and conviction, one of the witnesses who testified against the Rev. Jenkins came to the reverend's attorneys and made a shocking confession. He told them he could no longer live with the lies he had been coached to tell in court.

Frank Minor signed a sworn affidavit stating he had been instructed in what to say in court by Eighth Judicial Circuit Solicitor William T. Jones,[73] who led him to believe he would "get off easy" if he cooperated.

In his statement, Minor said he wanted to tell the truth and clear his conscience. Unfortunately, it was too late to help the Rev. Jenkins.

"It's been on my conscience," Minor said, "and I think the truth should come out. I don't think a man should get what is happening to [the Rev. Jenkins] for something he hasn't done, something he was dragged into."

---

[73] Not to be confused with his son, current Eighth Judicial Circuit Solicitor William "Townes" Jones, IV.

"I AM NOT BURNING NOTHING DOWN"

Minor was working as a house painter at the Rev. Jenkins' home on New Market Street at the time of his arrest. He said he had been pulled into the conspiracy by ATF Agent Bruce Mirkin, known to him as Billy Murphy.

"Before Murphy came down, there was never any discussion about burning anybody's house. That's all he would say, 'I'm a torch by trade.' Nobody would ever pay that much attention to it. I would say, 'No, I'm not burning anything,' and nobody else wouldn't even talk about it. I don't think it was ever taken seriously at all."

In his sworn statement, Minor said there were blank spaces in the tape recordings made by the ATF agent that were used as evidence against the Rev. Jenkins.

"There were missing portions in the tapes," Minor said. "There were different things that I said and that Mr. Jenkins said that weren't on the tapes.

"I remember when we were sitting at the back door getting ready to leave [allegedly to burn down Patrolman Keasler's house]. Mr. Jenkins said, 'If you guys go out and get into trouble you are on your own.' That wasn't on the tape.[74]

"When Murphy got up to start it, it was the first I ever heard of any fire. I said, 'Uh, uh, I am not burning nothing down.' And that wasn't on the tapes."

---

[74]   A person is not legally accountable for the criminal conduct of another if, before the commission of the offense, he terminates his efforts to promote such commission and gives a warning to law enforcement officials or makes a proper effort to prevent the criminal activity. Withdrawal from a conspiracy requires either making a clean breast to authorities or communicating the abandonment of the conspiracy in a manner reasonably calculated to reach co-conspirators. Black's Law Dictionary, West Publishing Co., 1991.

Minor said when he challenged law enforcement officers about the missing portions of the tapes, he was told it was because his voice was "too low to be picked up"[75] (by the recorder) and that there was a "bad spot" on the tapes.

He said he also was told that he was "imagining things."

"I blew up the night that I heard [the tapes]. I said, 'I'm not helping you. You are not telling the whole truth.' And they said, 'Frank maybe you think so hard and that's why you think it should be on there, but it's not.'

"And I said 'Hell no. I know it should be on there.'"

"I AIN'T DOIN' IT"

Minor described what happened when he and the ATF agent pulled up to Keasler's house.

"That's another part that's missing on the tapes. I said, 'I'm not going to do it. Let's leave.' I said, 'I'll find [Keasler] in a couple of weeks and punch him in the nose.' And Mirkin said, 'No, we are here, and we are going to do it.' And he whipped down in the driveway.

"I was a passenger just riding. Then when we got there, Mr. Mirkin said, 'Come on, let's get to it.' And I said, 'No.' I said, 'Uh, uh, I ain't doing it.' And I set in the car, and he got out and started up toward the house and he got up in the carport of Mr. Keasler's house, and then SLED agents and cops came from all over the place.

"I never got out of the car or even attempted to get out of the car. I sat there with my hands crossed and just sat there in the car."

---

[75] This is a strange comment, considering the fact that the ATF is certain to have the most sophisticated equipment taxpayer's money can buy.

When reminded by the Rev. Jenkins' attorneys that Bruce Mirkin later testified in court that Minor had gotten out of the car also, Minor said he became angry upon hearing that.

"I got mad then sitting in the courtroom. I got mad and started to blow up, and they told me to leave the courtroom, go get some water, and go to the bathroom or something."

"YOU DIDN'T KNOW WHAT TIME THEY WERE COMING"

Minor said that an agent from the South Carolina Law Enforcement Division (SLED) and the ATF agent Bruce Mirkin, alias Billy Murphy, talked to him in jail and told him what he had to do.

"They told me that Murphy was a federal agent and that I was just dead caught and might as well confess, that if I would tell them the truth and go to court and say that I was working for Mr. Jenkins my chances were 99 percent sure probation. They just wanted me to testify that Mr. Jenkins was guilty," Minor said.

"[The solicitor and the detectives] would say, 'If you go along with us and if you help us we are 99 percent sure you will get probation.[76] But if you don't help us, you could get a whole bunch of time.'"

Scott Shirley, who had agreed to testify against the Rev. Jenkins, was released on $35,000 bond.

However, Frank Minor was held in jail until the trial. Minor's bond was originally set at $150,000—an excessive amount considering the charges—and his family was not able to raise the necessary funds.

---

[76] Before testifying, Minor said Jones approached him and said, "I haven't promised you a God d____d thing now, have I?"

TORMENTING A MOTHER

Officials later told Minor his bond was reduced to $35,000. But on two separate occasions when his mother traveled to Greenwood from out of state, after struggling to come up with the money, she was told there had been a "mistake" and that her son's bond was still set at $150,000.

"They just locked me up in the cell and kept playing with my bond, putting it up and down and not letting me out," Minor said. "They'd come back there and feed me, you know, and they would go buy me hamburgers, and they'd let my girlfriend bring me food every night and sneak me out and take me up front to the detective's office, and stuff like that.

"They talked to me off and on all day long—yes, sir," Minor recalled in his statement, "During the day and during the night. They'd come and get me all different times of the day. You wouldn't know what time they were coming. They would tell me things like, 'You don't want to get out of jail because if you get out of jail, Mr. Jenkins is going to have you killed.'"

Minor's lawyer, Joe Pracht, offered to take his case for free on one condition.

"He said that he didn't want no money from me; all he wanted to do was see justice taken and Mr. Jenkins to get what he had coming. He said that he hoped that they would hang the son of a b____ and stuff like that.

"He told me there was no way in the world he would take the case if I did not plead guilty, but if I pleaded guilty, he would be glad to take the case and was 99 percent sure I would get probation."

"YOU CAN GET A WHOLE BUNCH OF TIME"

In his sworn affidavit, Minor told how the detectives and Jones, the solicitor, coached him on what he was to say on the witness stand, despite the fact that Minor told them repeatedly that the federal agent was the one who promoted the plans to commit assault and arson.

"He was the one that tried to get him to do it," Minor said.

"When Willie T. Jones [Jones was frequently referred to as Willie T. behind his back] talked to us trying to get us ready for court, if we would say, 'No, that's not the way it happened,' he would blow up like a wild man. He would start screaming and hollering and going, 'We don't have to help you godd____it, and if you don't want our f____ing help, f____ you, we don't need you.'[77]

"And it would just make me and Scott so scared and worried. He'd be telling us, 'Well, you can get a whole bunch of time or you can get a little bit of time.'"

"About three days before I went to court, I had a meeting with [Jones] one night. He told me he thought Mr. Jenkins was a devil and son of a b____ and a motherf____ and stuff like that, and it was plain to see all he wanted to do was hang Mr. Jenkins. What his motives were or what his hatred was, I don't know."

---

[77]   Jones' profanity is a bit ironic since he found it so objectionable in court when replaying tapes of private conversations between the Rev. Jenkins and the ATF agent. It seems unbecoming of an officer of the court.

"THERE WOULD BE THINGS I'D KNOW WASN'T EXACTLY RIGHT"

Minor said police officials joked about the fact that the reverend's attorney had been given three hundred pages of transcripts and, with only three days to prepare a defense, would never be ready in time for the trial.

"They would be all of them talking about how much they hated [the Rev. Jenkins] and be laughing about him and stuff in the back. They would have us in the back room calling him all of these names and stuff, and these questions would come up, and they'd start saying you know, 'Hey, I want your testimony to be perfect when you get up there,' and you know [Jones] would read over these papers to refresh your memory to make sure you say everything like this.

"And then we would read over the papers, and there would be things I'd know wasn't exactly right, and when we would question them about it or say, 'You know, I don't think Leroy did that,' they would just blow up. And they would say, 'Well, we don't have to help you,' and just start hollering and screaming."

When asked to give a statement about his involvement in the alleged conspiracy, Minor said he asked that his attorney be present but was told they couldn't get in touch with the attorney. He said he only spoke to his attorney twice and then only briefly before the trial.

Minor said officials did not use a tape recorder when taking his statement[78] and that he was coached in what to say in both the statement and on the witness stand. He said when the statement was typed up and he was asked to sign it, he didn't want to read it.

---

[78]   This seems very odd, since tape recordings seemed so crucial to the prosecution in the case against the Rev. Jenkins. Could it have been that they were afraid the public might learn of their intimidation of the witness? Perhaps all such interviews should be tape recorded to protect both the police *and* the suspect or witness.

"I was so disgusted with myself for giving it… They said, 'You want to read it?' And I said, 'Hell no.' I just signed it."

At one point, Minor said he was taken into the courtroom while the ATF agent was on the witness stand.

"They wanted us to watch him and get an example from him, you know, how to get up there and take care of ourselves and be strong."

While giving the affidavit to the reverend's attorneys, Minor was reminded by the reverend's lawyers that he had sworn on the witness stand that he had not been promised anything in exchange for his testimony.

"I was promised 99 percent probation," Minor said.

When asked why he had not told the truth, he said, "I just wanted to help myself."

THE FIX WAS IN

Minor said that during the first couple of days of the trial, the solicitor already knew how much time the Rev. Jenkins would get.

"Everybody would go home [after a day in court], supposed to be back the next day. Mr. Jones would have them keep us over, and there would be a meeting. Maybe fifteen of us would all go in a room and sit in the courtroom or somewhere, when everybody would be gone, and talk about the case.

"They were talking about how much time he was going to get. I heard twelve years pop up. It was Willie T. Jones. He said, 'I'd say he was going to get twelve years. We have got to give him over ten years because he will get out on bond if we don't.'[79]

---

[79]   According to South Carolina law, only the state Supreme Court can set an appeal bond for a person sentenced to more than 10 years. It was highly unlikely the high court would allow the reverend to go free on bond while he was appealing his case. At the time this book was written in 1998, the last time granted such an appeal was in 1954.

"When they took us back [to the jail], I told some people how much time Mr. Jenkins was going to get, and then that's exactly what he was sentenced to, twelve years."

Minor was sentenced to ninety days in jail the day after the Rev. Jenkins, minus time served, and two years' probation.

"I had Joe Pracht [Minor's lawyer] speak on my behalf," Minor said "He told the judge a lie. He told the judge that I had never owned a car in my life or anything and that I was just dragged into this thing as a poor innocent little child," the twenty-three-year old said. He added, "I have a van right now. I have a '78 Ford Pickup that I have at my mother's, and I have a motorcycle."

Minor was asked if there was any question in his mind that the idea of burning anybody's house and assaulting the *Anderson Independent* reporter was first brought up by the federal agent Bruce Mirkin.

"I'm positive it was first brought up by Mirkin," he said.

PART 2:
FROM PRISON TO PULPIT—
THE LONG ROAD BACK

When the Son of man shall come in his glory,
and all the holy angels with him,
then shall he sit upon the throne of his glory:
And before him shall be gathered all nations:
and he shall separate them one from another,
as a shepherd divideth *his* sheep from the goats:
And he shall set the sheep on his right hand, but the goats on the left.
Then shall the King say unto them on his right hand,
Come, ye blessed of my Father,
inherit the kingdom prepared for you from the foundation of the world:
For I was an hungred, and ye gave me meat: I was thirsty,
and ye gave me drink: I was a stranger, and ye took me in:
Naked, and ye clothed me: I was sick, and ye visited me:
I was in prison, and ye came unto me.
Then shall the righteous answer him, saying, Lord,
when saw we thee an hungred, and fed *thee*?
or thirsty, and gave *thee* drink?
When saw we thee a stranger, and took *thee* in?
or naked, and clothed *thee*?
Or when saw we thee sick, or in prison, and came unto thee?
And the King shall answer and say unto them, Verily I say unto you,
Inasmuch as ye have done *it* unto one of the least of these my brethren,
ye have done *it* unto me.
—Matthew 25:31–40 (KJV)

FROM THE INSIDE LOOKING OUT

Rushed from the courtroom following his sentencing in Greenwood, the Rev. Jenkins was hustled into a waiting patrol car. A detective sat on either side of the stunned and shaken evangelist as the patrol car, followed by a convoy of police cruisers, set out on the late-night trip to prison in Columbia, South Carolina's capital, where he would await assignment to a permanent facility.

Heavy rain drummed on the roof of the car as the reverend fought to control his emotions. He had not even been allowed to say good-bye to his young sons Scotty and David, who were still living at home, nor other members of his family and friends.

"Rev," said one of the detectives, "my mother loves your ministry. Her favorite song is 'Amazing Grace.' Would you sing that for her tonight?"

Choked with feeling, the prisoner softly sang that favorite gospel tune to the beat of the windshield wipers. Unknown to him, the patrol car radio beamed the song across the airwaves, and it was heard by every patrol car in the listening area.

"Through many dangers, toil and snares, I have already come. 'Tis grace hath brought me safe thus far, and grace will lead me home."

Many who heard that plaintive melody could not fail to be stirred by the song. They knew what awful trials lay ahead.

HOME SWEET HELL

The Kirkland Reception and Evaluation Center in Columbia was a filthy, cockroach-infested facility used to warehouse prisoners until they were permanently assigned to an institution. Many of the cells were in the basement near a pile of rotting garbage.

Here the Rev. Jenkins was strip-searched, showered, and issued prison clothing. The physical invasion was horrifying, humiliating, and painful—both to the body as well as the mind.

Buses filled with Ohio church members parked across the street from the R&E Center in the hope of catching a glimpse of their pastor through one of the grimy, smudged windows. They waved and blew kisses to the window they had been told was his and to the shadowy figure behind it. It was inconceivable to them that their pastor could be behind those bars.

Eventually, the buses drove off, and the reverend left the R&E Center for a new life at Kirkland Correctional Institution, a maximum-security facility where the worst offenders—felons convicted of rape, murder, and other heinous crimes—served out their time. (see photo on page 265)

Despite the fact that the prison was relatively new in 1979, on a scale of toughness, Kirkland was second only to Columbia's notorious Central Correctional Institute.

The Rev. Jenkins was assigned to a pod of four cells, each housing four prisoners. Right away, things got tough for the evangelist. His notoriety made him a "mark." Other inmates often tried to extort money from him, either through feigning friendship or through intimidation.

True friends were at a premium. While walking in the prison yard during exercise time, Rev became acquainted with another convict, a doctor. The doctor had already served the major portion of his sentence and was due to be released in a year. But he would never be released. One day he was found hanged in his cell. No one knew what anguish had driven him to this desperate act or even if he died by his own hand.

Visits from the outside were severely restricted. In order to see his family or his lawyer, the Rev. Jenkins had to pass through an area where inmates were strip-searched before entering or leaving the visiting room. Though he looked forward to these visits from his family, the humiliating and demoralizing searches were nearly impossible to bear.

One day while June Buckingham, the reverend's office manager, sat with him in the visitors' area, a brawny man in a muscle shirt ambled over.

"Don't worry, lady. Rev, he's our man. We'll watch over him. Won't nobody bother Rev when we're around, will they, Rev?" he said, his voice dripping with sarcasm.

Such assurances offered little comfort. It was difficult to distinguish friend from foe. The evangelist had seen a man's leg grasped through the bars of his cell and snapped like a twig. Kirkland was a cruel place. Evil abounded within its walls.

After an unspeakable attack by other inmates, the Rev. Jenkins became traumatized. He could not eat and quickly lost sixty-five pounds. His spirit became tormented by the wickedness that surrounded him. Alarmed, his family and staff, who were frantically searching for a way to have the twelve-year sentence appealed, decided something had to be done to lift his spirits and encourage him to eat. Otherwise, he might starve.

Mrs. Buckingham made an appointment with William D. Leeke, superintendent of the South Carolina Department of Corrections. His imposing desk and luxuriously appointed office were quite a contrast to the barren visiting area at Kirkland. Leeke regarded his visitor with cold, dark eyes as she pled the reverend's case.

"Mr. Leeke, it is like putting Billy Graham behind bars. This man is spiritually sensitive. Not only does he suffer physical deprivation, but his spirit is also tormented by the evil that surrounds him."

Leeke appeared to be unmoved.

"Mrs. Buckingham, we didn't sentence this man. We are simply his custodians while he serves his sentence," he said evenly.

It was evident that Leeke was to be of no help at all.

THE GOOD SAMARITAN

Letters and phone calls flooded the prison system, inquiring about the Rev. Jenkins' welfare and begging for his release. Prison officials were aware of the outpouring, but it didn't ease his treatment. It did, however, put officials on notice that the world was watching.

The newspapers were quick to print any solid news, and even some rumors, about his treatment. Officials knew that if the Rev. Jenkins was harmed, it could give the entire system a black eye.

Still desperately seeking someone within the prison system who could improve the reverend's plight, Mrs. Buckingham called on Jesse Strickland, the deputy commissioner of the Department of Corrections.

This meeting was a stark contrast to the meeting with Commissioner Leeke. Strickland was a strikingly handsome man with thick, wavy hair, smiling eyes, and a courtly Southern manner.

"Come in, Mrs. Buckingham," he said, indicating his spacious office overlooking the prison complex. "Have a seat and tell me about the Rev. Jenkins."

Near tears, she recounted the story of a man, greatly gifted by God, who had been goaded and tricked by an ATF agent posing as a friend into making careless statements in the privacy of his own home. She told how these statements were secretly recorded by a tape recorder strapped to the agent's body and were later taken out of context and used against the reverend in a sham of a trial.

Jesse Strickland was a giant of a man, more than six feet tall, and hard as nails. He had been warden at the infamous Central

Correctional Institution, where he was known to wade into riots there with nothing but his powerful personality and the respect of the men in his custody to protect him.

Strickland was a legend. The men in the prison system respected him. He was fair, but fearless; just, but merciful.

"Mrs. Buckingham, I will see what I can do," he said when told of the reverend's plight. "I will go see him."

And there was more.

"First of all, I will grant your request that you be allowed to see him every day to pick up the mail that is flooding in here for him and bring him food from home for his lunch so that he will stop losing weight," he said. (see photo on page 266)

Then Strickland revised the visitation list to include the Rev. Jenkins' adult children and several associates in the ministry. Additionally, he was allowed to have two visitors every day. It was more than anyone could have hoped for.

True to his word, Strickland went to see the Rev. Jenkins at once.

"Rev. Jenkins," he said, "you've got a lot of people out there who love you. I'm not going to let you do anything to yourself. You've got to eat and stay well, and one of these days you will be free," he said.

"It seems like a long road ahead, but there is light at the end of the tunnel, and I want you to remember that," he said.

Then the assistant commissioner wrote down his private home phone number.

"I will be your friend," he said. "Call me anytime whenever things get too much for you."

Years later, when Jesse Strickland visited the Holy Hill Cathedral in Ohio, the Rev. Jenkins introduced him to the congregation.

"This man made it possible for me to survive in the prison," he said of Strickland. "He had to do some talking and some fighting, but he did what he could for me. His hands were tied because of who I was and the surveillance I was under from higher-up, but he did what he could for me.

"He wasn't afraid to be seen with me, and he came and visited me many times. His son came up every Sunday to see me and bring me things I needed. His wife and his family, also.

"Everybody knew who these people were, but they befriended me and didn't care who knew it," the reverend said.

Strickland received an ovation from a grateful congregation.

A PROPHECY

Kirkland permitted church services every Sunday, each denomination having its turn. The Rev. Jenkins was asked to speak one Sunday and invited several guests from outside.

On that day, he preached the dignity of every man, pointing out that all were fallible and none free from sin. He told how God could forgive and cast the memory of the sin as far as the east is from the west.

"Man looks on the outward appearance, but God looks on the heart," he said.

When he gave the altar call, many men came out of their seats and moved to the front of the makeshift church to publicly commit their lives to Jesus Christ.

There was a new freedom of the spirit in the men that day. It was evident in the way they squared their shoulders as they strolled out of church and in their eyes as they exchanged greetings.

The Rev. Jenkins also made a peculiar prophecy that day.

"Everywhere I go there are signs that say don't go beyond this point. So one day, I said to myself, I am going to try the back way. I walked out there, and sure enough, there was no sign there, but there was a gate, another gate and a guard house," he said.

"When I leave here, I'm going out that back gate."

No one could know it at the time, but the prophecy came to pass exactly as the Rev. Jenkins described it. Later, he spoke of the incident to his Ohio congregation: "See, if you speak something and you are a prophet of God, it will come to pass. God was there, even inside that prison. The important thing is that he doesn't leave you when you walk in those gates."

PARTY TIME

Visitors are the only bright spot in a prisoner's life, so inmates tried to make the visiting area at Kirkland as cheerful as possible. The room was large and well lighted, with windows on three sides. A soft drink and a sandwich machine provided refreshments for inmates and their families. Visitors sat at square tables in brightly colored, molded chairs. Each table had a tin can for cigarette butts. These were also used for spittoons.

Determined to dispel the gloom of the institutional setting, the prison's Jaycee chapter decorated the visiting room walls with floor-to-ceiling paintings of *Sesame Street* characters to entertain the children who came to visit their fathers. The Rev. Jenkins helped with this project and received a commendation for his efforts.

One evening the prison hosted a covered-dish dinner for inmates with good disciplinary records. Guests—approved beforehand by prison officials—brought refreshments. Everyone wore their best clothes.

At first, the inmates and their families kept to themselves. Then a few walked from table to table, quietly introducing their families and friends to the other inmates and their guests.

A troupe of cross-dressing inmates had done what they could to decorate the visitor's area for the party and tried to enliven things by prancing around in outrageous costumes. They managed to break through the gloom and stiffness of the event as they strutted about in net shirts and tight satin pants tucked into knee boots. Their cheerful conversation and clownish behavior lifted everyone's spirits as they flitted from table to table. The dismal room became as lively as a Paris bistro. Finally, the inmates loosened up enough to enjoy themselves. For weeks afterward, they recounted every moment of this happy event. It helped to relieve the mind-numbing sameness of their lives.

APPEALING TO REASON

F. LEE BAILEY CONSIDERING HANDLING JENKINS' APPEAL

The State of Columbia, South Carolina, May 31, 1979

(COLUMBIA) Renowned defense lawyer F. Lee Bailey was in Columbia Wednesday to discuss the possibility of handling the appeal of evangelist Leroy Jenkins' conspiracy conviction.

The Boston attorney, whose famous clients have included Patricia Hearst and Jack Ruby, flew into the South Carolina capital on his private airplane to meet with Jenkins and the minister's lawyers.

Bailey said he would decide in a week or two whether to handle the appeal. "A lot is left to learn about the case," he added. "It has many extraordinary aspects."

Meanwhile, Jenkins' attorney, William Gambrell, said Jenkins has "less than a 50-50 shot" at being released on bond during his appeal. He said the lawyers expect to appear before the State Supreme Court June 11 or 12 with the request.

Gambrell said research into the question of appeal bond indicates no one since 1954 had been freed from custody while appealing to the Supreme Court. "That's an awful tough track record to go up against."

The lawyer said Jenkins is pointing out the swiftness of the trial (he was arrested April 17 and tried from May 17-22) in justifying the request.

"This fellow, not considering whether he's good, bad, horrible or angelic, has not had a second to attend to his personal matters, such as who is going to take care of his children," he noted.

Copyright © The State

FAMED ATTORNEY OFFERS HOPE

Newspapers throughout South Carolina and Ohio also ran banner headlines about the appeal. The combination of the two well-known personalities seemed to fascinate the public, and the Leroy Jenkins' saga remained on the front page.

F. Lee Bailey flew his own private Learjet to Kirkland prison to have a conference with the notorious prisoner. Distinguished-looking in a gray pin-stripe suit, the silver-haired celebrity received star treatment from the guards and the warden.

The Rev. Jenkins was brought into the conference room, the strain of the last few weeks showing on his haggard face.

"Reverend," Bailey, said "I am happy to meet you, but not under these circumstances. Why don't you tell me what has happened to you, and we will see what I can do about it."

Bailey's courtesy and concern were in such stark contrast to his treatment by the South Carolina prison system, it brought tears to the evangelist's eyes. He could stand adversity, but sympathy caught him off guard. Perhaps Bailey could do him some good, after all.

Bailey seemed fascinated with the incredible story of the arrest and trial and the way the Rev. Jenkins had been isolated from friends and family in a maximum-security prison.

Assuring the reverend he would obtain the trial transcripts and file a habeas corpus motion to win the evangelist's freedom pending his appeal, he agreed to take the case.

Bailey could not have been more encouraging. He was a person of great stature in the legal field, and he seemed confident he could help. It was a great relief.

HOPES DASHED

Unfortunately, Bailey had never tangled with the South Carolina justice system. On June 12, 1979, the state Supreme Court denied Bailey's request that the Rev. Jenkins be released on bond pending appeal. Just as Greenwood Solicitor William T. Jones had predicted, the length of the Rev. Jenkins' sentence had made his release highly unlikely.[80]

The Supreme Court did not give any reasons for its actions but made its decision after hearing arguments from representatives of the attorney general's office, who claimed prosecution witnesses had received "anonymous threats before, during and after" the trial. The prosecutors declined to name those individuals.[81]

Prosecutors used the same reasoning to battle the defense attorneys' petition asking the US District Court in Columbia to release the evangelist on bond. Prosecutors told the federal

---

[80] South Carolina law dictates that only the Supreme Court can grant an appeal bond for a sentence of over 10 years. The reverend's attorneys argued that since his 12-year sentence was not for a single offense, but for four counts of conspiracy at three years each, their client should be entitled to bond. The court rejected this argument.

[81] *Anderson Independent*, June 13, 1979.

court the Rev. Jenkins was "dangerous" and "might seek reprisals" against witnesses in his trial.[82]

The petition to the federal court also was denied.

Kenneth Fishman, an associate of F. Lee Bailey, called the Supreme Court's decision "arbitrary" since they gave no reason for denying the bond.[83] While acknowledging that it was within the court's discretion to deny bail, that denial should be based on sound reasoning, he said.

It was now up to the Supreme Court to decide whether or not they would consider the appeal of his conviction.

None of this came as any surprise to the Rev. Jenkins. Weeks earlier, while Mrs. Buckingham and the reverend's son Dennis were visiting him at Kirkland, he made a strange remark. He said that God told him the efforts to appeal his sentence were in vain. Taking a napkin, he drew a map showing that he was to be moved seven different times from one prison to another. The last prison would be close to a road, and after that he would be set free.

PLEASE RELEASE HIM, LET HIM GO

While F. Lee Bailey and the defense team appealed the verdict in the courts, the public appealed to South Carolina's governor for the reverend's release.

---

[82] The State, Columbia, S.C., Oct. 4, 1979. This was a case of "smoke and mirrors" on the part of the prosecution. No one connected to this case was harmed in any way before, during or after the trial.

[83] The Index-Journal, Greenwood, S.C., Oct. 4, 1979.

LETTERS PLEAD FOR JENKINS' RELEASE

Anderson Independent, July 17, 1979

Clisby Williams and Randy Loftis

(COLUMBIA) Pleading for the release of convicted evangelist Leroy Jenkins, the hand-written and often grammatically incorrect letters[84] arrive daily at Gov. Dick Riley's office.

Jenkins, hoping to be released on bond until the appeal of his conviction on four conspiracy charges is settled, is marshaling supporters as he runs his ministry from Kirkland Correctional Institution in Columbia.

"I miss him so much on Sunday on the television," one man wrote in a typical letter to Riley. He's needed to heal the sick also to deliver the dope addicts."

"The Bible tells us, 'Touch not mine anointed, and do my prophets no harm," a man wrote. "Every day Rev. Jenkins is kept in the Kirkland Correctional Institution you are harming God's prophet. Why? Because you have the power to free him.

"Therefore, you are standing in the way of sinners being saved, drug addicts being freed, and the sick being healed. On judgment day, how will you explain to God your reason for hindering His works by keeping Rev. Jenkins in prison?"

What many of Jenkins' supporters - well over 100 have written Riley - apparently don't realize is that the South

---

[84] Was this comment essential to the story?

Carolina governor cannot pardon or release a prisoner, said Marion Brown, Riley's press secretary.[85]

Riley's only authority over sentencing is that he can commute a death sentence to life imprisonment, Brown said.

A group of Jenkins' family and supporters met with Riley's legal aide shortly after Jenkins was sentenced in late May on charges of conspiring to assault a highway patrolman and to burn a Belton man's home; and conspiring to assault a newspaper reporter.

"We made it clear the governor just does not have the authority to intervene," Brown added. The letter-writers will be given the same answer, he said.

The letters, from all over South Carolina and a number of other states, apparently were prompted by fund-raising letters mailed by Leroy Jenkins Defense Fund.

"If you believe in the ministry, and that I should be out tending to lost souls, write Gov. Richard Riley and tell him you are my friend and that you want me freed," Jenkins wrote on July 10. "Then write to me, telling me of your prayer requests. I pray over these requests each day here in the prison, and I believe God for the answer.

"PLEASE DO NOT FORGET ME OR LET ME DOWN! I need your help, your prayers and your love."

Another letter, seeking money to keep Jenkins' remaining television and radio programs on the air arrived at the Governor's office last Friday.

A black and white drawing on the front of the letter depicts Jenkins clutching prison bars while a crucifix tilts across the background. To one side are the words: "Jesus Yesterday... Jenkins Today???"

---

[85]   While the governor's office may have been unable to help the Rev. Jenkins, the letters from supporters drew public attention to his plight, a fact that let prison officials know the evangelist had not been forgotten by his friends, and that his treatment would be closely watched.

"This is a very hard burden that I am having to bear," Jenkins writes inside. "God only knows what I go through daily. I have been very patient while I am waiting in this awful place. Without your prayers and support, I would not be able to make it."

The response to the fund-raising campaigns has been "very gratifying," June Buckingham, secretary of the Leroy Jenkins Evangelistic Association Inc. said Monday. She declined to say how much had been raised for Jenkins' defense.

To avoid any violation of federal regulations governing the LJEA's tax exempt status, contributions to LJEA are kept separate from those to the defense fund, she added.

And an offer of help has come from another source; the National Ministers Association with headquarters in Tujunga, Ca.

The Rev. Dr. R.E. Davis, Association director, said the organization's presiding council has volunteered to accept custody of Jenkins if that would help win him an early release.

If he is successful in being allowed bond by a federal judge, the organization members would sign his bond, Davis said. The Association would provide a cash bond "if financially possible," he added.

Davis, who said his organization has 400,000 minister members nationwide, said the NMA was informed of the Jenkins case by a Greenwood minister. After investigating the case, the council decided to support Jenkins' release from prison, he said.

"We're not trying to judge his complete innocence or guilt," Davis said. "We're trying to judge the fairness of his trial."

NMA council members believe Jenkins was "overconvicted" or given too harsh a sentence, Davis said.

The NMA was formed seven years ago to promote public trust in the ministry, and to combat what members consider to be government attacks on Christianity and freedom of religion, he said.

Jenkins continues to direct his organization from prison, and his mother has "done a beautiful job" in carrying on his crusades, Mrs. Buckingham said.

The nationally known faith healer, whose organization brought in $3 million in donations in 1977, declined an interview request Monday, on the advice of his attorneys.

By the next crusade, scheduled for Sept. 9 in Baltimore, Jenkins' supporters hope he'll be out of prison.

A petition filed in federal court in Columbia asks that Jenkins be released on bond - a request denied by the S.C. Supreme Court - until his appeal is decided.

The prosecution is expected to oppose Jenkins' release, as it did before the state court, said Ken Fishman, an associate of trial lawyer F. Lee Bailey, who is representing Jenkins.

No date has been set for the petition to be heard in court.

The people on Jenkins' mailing list received two appeals in one envelope last week, one from the LJEA and one from Jenkins' defense fund. Both letters bear the same return address - Box F, Greenwood.

In the defense fund letter Jenkins writes that he has gotten no support from other evangelists - Billy Graham, Oral Roberts, and most notably, his long-time associate, the Rev. Richard Diamond.

"You know that I have supported all these men with my prayers, and this neglect really hurts," Jenkins says.

"But their time will come. I only hope that YOU will stand by me in this time of REAL TRIBULATION!"

Jenkins begins the LJEA letter by saying he is dictating it from his prison cell. He says he was arrested and tried "within the space of a week's time." It was actually one month.[86]

---

[86] The trial date was set for three days after the reverend's indictment. This was all the time given the defense to review 300 pages of transcripts from the tapes, and to prepare a defense.

The evangelist continues to insist that no crime was committed and no one was hurt. He blames his conviction on a conspiracy by government agents.

"I am a prophet of God, and each prophecy that I have made has come to pass," he writes. "God has spoken to me and inspired me to write this letter to ask for your prayers and support and to have you sit down and spell out three of the most important things you want God to do for you and to get them in the mail to me right away. GOD HAS TOLD ME TO TELL YOU TO ANSWER THIS LETTER, NO MATTER HOW YOU FEEL."

Jenkins closes by asking 1,000 people to send his Association $100 each, and by assuring his followers that "BEHIND EACH CLOUD THERE IS A SILVER LINING. I am sure mine is around the corner, and so is yours." On the back of the letter is a place for a prayer request and a form where a contributor can say, "I want to stand with you and be a part of your silver lining. Here is my donation in love of $____"[87]

Copyright © Anderson Independent

---

[87]   It is common practice for preachers, animal rights organizations, veteran's groups and just about everyone else to ask for donations in mail-outs. If an organization does not ask for money, it will not receive it.

BREAKOUT: A BRIEF TASTE OF FREEDOM

The distance from the prison ward to the high chain-link fence surrounding Kirkland Correctional Institution was only several hundred yards. But it might as well have been a thousand as far as the Rev. Jenkins was concerned.

This night, in a planned escape attempt, he would run across the yard, exposing himself to rifle-toting guards in the towers. Would they see him? Shoot him? He couldn't be sure.

Dressed in black from head to toe, including black gloves to cover his hands, the reverend stayed in the cover of the buildings as long as he could. Finally, he took a deep breath and made his dash for freedom.

Escape from Kirkland was said to be impossible. To get in, visitors had to pass through a number of checkpoints and a long underground tunnel. Heavy barred gates hung from the ceiling, ready to drop at a moment's notice.

The only other way into or out of the prison was through a back gate, which was used for deliveries. Trucks carrying food or supplies drove directly through this gate after guards, using mirrors attached to long poles, inspected the chassis.

This back gate was the reverend's planned escape route. Now, he ran toward it, praying the full moon did not illuminate his movements.

The escape wasn't the Rev. Jenkins' idea. He had been approached by a guard who offered, for a fee, to let him out the back gate.

At first, he didn't take the offer seriously. But the reverend's innate sense of justice was offended by the corruption among prison guards who, among other things, were rumored to bring drugs into the institution.

"They think their little tin badges make them something," the evangelist once said during a church service at Kirkland. "They go around with their noses so far in the air if it rained it would drown them. A lot of them are worse than the people they are guarding," he said.

After the guard Robert Charles Schively approached him several times with the offer, he reported it to Jesse Strickland.

Commissioner Leeke was out of town, and Strickland had control of operations in his absence. He decided to pursue the matter. He and Warden J. L. Harvey recorded a telephone conversation between the Rev. Jenkins and the guard in which Schively repeated his offer to let the evangelist out of the prison's back gate in return for $6,000. With this tape as backup evidence, Strickland put his plan into action.

For a rock-solid case, it was imperative the guard be caught red-handed. The Rev. Jenkins would have to slip unnoticed out of his ward and walk across several hundred yards of open ground before reaching the gates. Once there, he would slip through the gates, walk up to the guardhouse, and hand Schively the money.

The plan had risks. In order to avoid alerting Schively, the scheme remained secret from all but a chosen few. The officers watching the prison's perimeter wouldn't know the escape was staged, and there was a very real possibility they would try to shoot the would-be escapee. Reverend's secretary and his son

Dennis were at the prison the night of the planned escape. June Buckingham had secured the $6,000 in marked bills underneath her clothing and smuggled the money into the prison. June and Dennis waited in a windowless room as the operation unfolded outside. They strained their ears, listening for the sound of gunfire and praying for silence.

Hugh Beasley, the evangelist's Greenwood attorney, was so concerned that something might go wrong, perhaps a double-cross in which the reverend would be shot in a supposed escape attempt, that he insisted on notifying the South Carolina Law Enforcement Division's chief Pete Strom, a trusted associate. Strom alerted his men to the plan, and they were planning to be on the scene when the Rev. Jenkins made his way through the gate.

If he successfully passed the money to the guard and made it through the gates, the Rev. Jenkins was supposed to fall to the ground. Strickland would be waiting in a van, ready to take charge of the operation.

If all went well, Strickland promised the reverend he would be transferred to an open institution, with no fences, no armed guards, and unlimited visiting privileges. It seemed like a worthwhile risk to take.

The Rev. Jenkins waited in the conference room until it was dark enough outside to give him some cover. Finally, Strickland gave the word, and the escape attempt began.

First, the reverend had to distract the officer guarding his ward. He gave the man a copy of his autobiography, *How I Met the Master*, and then asked the officer if he could use the telephone located outside the ward. The guard became absorbed in the book, forgetting he had an absent inmate. This lapse would be soon discovered when the guards conducted their routine prisoner count.

Knowing his time was running out, the Rev. Jenkins left the safety of the shadows and ran across the yard.

"Open the gate," he called out, but the guard's response stunned him.

"Go back; man, go back," he said, appearing in the door of the guardhouse with a rifle in his hands. "Go back. It's too risky. You'll get us both in trouble."

"It's too late to go back," the prisoner said. "I got your money right here. Open the gate."

"Drop the money," the guard shouted. "Leave it right there."

The Rev. Jenkins' instructions were to hand the money directly to the guard, so he kept walking, his heart in his mouth. Would the guard double-cross him, take the money, and shoot him as an escapee, as Hugh Beasley had feared?

"Open the gate. Open the gate," the reverend shouted as he handed the money to the guard. The guard grabbed the bag, threw it behind him onto the desk, and opened the gate just enough to let the Rev. Jenkins squeeze through.

By now, the guard dogs who patrolled the area snarled and leapt up onto the chain-link fence, the only thing separating them from the escapee.

"Open the next one," shouted the Rev. Jenkins, tugging at the gate that would let him through to the outside.

Slowly the second gate opened, and the Rev. Jenkins stepped outside the prison grounds.

He was too preoccupied to appreciate these few seconds of freedom. Squinting into the darkness, he looked for the van in which Strickland was supposed to be hiding. He could see it parked far away on one of the hills overlooking Kirkland. That was not part of the plan. Had he been betrayed?

Just then, men dressed in fatigues appeared from every direction.

"Hit the ground," they yelled as they ran past him to the gate to stop it from closing. SLED agents had taken over the operation and were taking the corrupt guard into custody.

Strickland, dressed in black, raced down the hill where the van was parked and threw himself on top of the Rev. Jenkins, knocking him to the ground to shield him from any gunfire that might erupt.

All of this activity did not go unnoticed by the prisoners. Suddenly, June and Dennis heard excited voices somewhere outside the room where they were isolated say, "Hey, man, did you hear? Rev. made it outside. He's gone, man—he made it out!" As always, the prison grapevine was the first with the story.

After it was over, everyone involved in the operation met at Goodman Correctional Institution, the open facility where Strickland had promised to transfer the reverend. Adrenalin still flowed, and the agents in their camouflage and Strickland in his black perched on desks, telling and retelling the events of the night. The guard had been caught red-handed, and the Rev. Jenkins was safe.

"June," he said, "come back tomorrow with all my children and grandchildren. Bring steaks, and we will have a cookout on the grounds, here."

Everyone went home rejoicing at the Rev. Jenkins' comparative freedom. He would be able to see his entire family now, and time would go much more quickly in this atmosphere.

The newspapers were told of the escape, but the reading public would never know of the nerve-shattering night spent at Kirkland or the dangers their pastor faced.

JENKINS ESCAPES FROM PRISON—SORT OF

Greenville News, July 31, 1979

Duncan Mansfield

(COLUMBIA) - Incarcerated evangelist Leroy Jenkins participated in a fake escape from Kirkland Correctional Institution Sunday night.

Prison guard Robert Charles Schively, 23, was charged with assisting a prisoner to escape in connection with the incident, state Department of Corrections spokesman Sam McCuen said Monday.

According to McCuen, Jenkins told J.W. Strickland, assistant deputy commissioner for operations and security, during a "routine interview" last Tuesday that he had been approached several times recently "to feel him out about arranging an escape if some money could be passed."

McCuen would not say who made the offers to Jenkins, who has been held at Kirkland since May 22, serving a 12-year sentence for conspiracy to assault two men and burn two houses.

Strickland responded by asking Jenkins to help officials correct "the hole in our operations involving a correctional officer," according to McCuen.

Jenkins consented.

"We arranged for Mr. Jenkins to have his personal money, or money from his operation, sent down to him," McCuen said.

When the $6,000 needed for the alleged payoff arrived from the evangelist's Greenwood based organization, the Leroy Jenkins Evangelistic Association, law enforcement officers documented the serial numbers of each bill, McCuen said.

About 9 p.m. Sunday, prison officials and State Law Enforcement Division agents staked out the double gates guarded by Schively.

"He, (Jenkins) approached the first gate and the officer pushed the button and let him in," McCuen said.

"They met briefly. He went to the second gate and the officer pushed that button. And that put him outside."

According to McCuen, Jenkins "took about two steps and the trap was sprung. We arrested the officer on the spot and confiscated the $6,000.

"It happened in about two seconds," McCuen said.

Specifically, the warrant against Schively charged him for "being an employee of the Department of Corrections and aiding and abetting an inmate's escape," McCuen said.

If found guilty, Schively faces a maximum penalty of 20 years imprisonment.

Schively was expected to be held at the Richland County Detention Center last Monday following questioning, according to law enforcement officials.

Jenkins has subsequently been transferred to another unnamed facility, McCuen said.

The case is still under investigation, he said.

The decision to move Jenkins to another institution "is a routine procedure any time you have an inmate involved in something you are investigating," McCuen said.

Asked if corrections officers believed other inmates or guards participated in the alleged escape payoff, McCuen responded, "That's something we're looking into."

McCuen joked there was "no going rate," for the price of escape from Kirkland, but added $6,000 "is a pretty hefty figure."

He added that payoffs of this kind were uncommon at Kirkland, and of the few which have occurred, "none of them have been this big."

June Buckingham, who has administered Jenkins' Greenwood organization since his conviction, declined to comment on the incident Monday.

Jenkins' case is currently being appealed to the state Supreme Court. His attorneys, which include famed Boston counselor, F. Lee Bailey, have said it will probably be several months before the appeal is heard.

DOUBLE-CROSS

The day after the "escape," the Jenkins family gathered at picnic tables on the wooded grounds surrounding Goodman Correctional Institution, a minimum-security prison to which the Rev. Jenkins had been moved. Steaks sizzled over a charcoal fire in the brazier. There was a faint breeze with the touch of fall in its bite.

Suddenly, the cheerful, casual chatter ceased as the Rev. Jenkins dropped to a bench, his face in his hands, tears pouring from his eyes.

"What's the matter, Dad?" his children said as they rushed to his side. "You ought to be happy now. Things are going to be better for you here."

"Pack up the things and leave right now," he said. "They are not going to let me stay here. I am going to be moved."

Through the years, God had spoken to the evangelist in many ways. Before he had even been approached by the guard who offered to help him escape, he told the congregation at a Kirkland church service that he would leave the prison by the back gate. That prophecy had come to pass. Now, his sense of foreboding was almost unbearable.

Reluctantly, the children repacked the picnic baskets, doused the fire, and said their good-byes. Just then, a public-address system cackled to life.

"Leroy Jenkins, report to the office," a voice announced.

"There it is," the reverend said. He squared his shoulders and marched over to Jesse Strickland's office. There, he received the bad news.

At first, Strickland could not bear to tell the Rev. Jenkins what had transpired once Mr. Leeke had returned to town and had been informed of the events of the previous night. He struggled for the words.

The reverend finally spoke up.

"Jesse, I know what you are going to tell me, and I know you just can't stand to do it. Just give me the bad news, and get it over with," he said.

"Rev," said Strickland, "Mr. Leeke leaves me in charge when he is gone, and he has never before interfered with my decisions. But this time it is different. He just won't go along with me on this one. I am sorry, son, you are going back to R&E for assignment to another institution."

"For your own safety," he added. "We won't send you back to Kirkland."

The shock this betrayal brought and the horror of his transfer back to miserable quarters in the Reception and Evaluation Center would have been unbearable if God had not warned the reverend in advance.

And so, the Rev. Jenkins returned once again to the dreaded R&E Center to wait until things cooled off so that he could be assigned to another institution.

Strickland weighed in on the reverend's behalf, insisting that this time his friend should not be caged in the filthy basement but have use of the duty room, where the officers were accustomed to lounging and watching TV.

There he slept on a fold-out sofa. Under constant surveillance, he managed a few moments of privacy with a blanket hung over the iron bars.

Still, things were tough. Schively's father had been a guard at the institution in earlier times, and the Schively family had many friends among the officers. The reverend's visits were restricted, and the guards treated him rudely.

Just when things seemed as though they could not get worse, they did. The knife wound the Rev. Jenkins received when he was brutally attacked at Kirkland still troubled him. He knew he needed treatment for the injury to his muscles. At the time, the reverend had hesitated to report the incident because he was new at the facility, and retribution could be severe, especially when there was no one to watch his back.

Now that he was at R&E, he reported the injury and was sent to State Park Medical Center for treatment. There, he was kept in a locked room, with just one small, square window into the hall. He received no visitors. Family and staff had no idea what was happening to him or how he was being treated.

During the entire month of August in 1979, he was kept in limbo, either in State Park Medical Center or in the R&E

Center, treated miserably and in deep depression over his betrayal by prison officials.

FOLLOWERS OF JENKINS SAY STATE BROKE PROMISE

Anderson Independent, October 13, 1979

Clisby Williams

(COLUMBIA) Followers of imprisoned evangelist Leroy Jenkins are protesting that state prison officials reneged on an agreement to transfer the Greenwood faith healer to a minimum-security prison after he cooperated in a prison guard's arrest.

In the past two weeks the S.C. Department of Corrections has received about 15 calls a day and about 200 letters asking that Jenkins be moved to a minimum-security prison "like you promised," department spokesman Sam McCuen said Friday.

After Jenkins faked an escape attempt to help catch a guard who offered to let him out of prison for $6,000, Jenkins was told he'd be moved to a minimum security prison, Jesse Strickland, department director of regional operations, confirmed.

That decision later was overruled by corrections department head William Leeke. Leeke ruled that under department policy, Jenkins must serve one year before being transferred, McCuen said.

Although Strickland said it's "not absolutely unheard of" to waive the policy in the case of a prisoner who's cooperated with authorities in some way. McCuen said Leeke believed "it's in the best interest of the agency not to make an exception."

But Jenkins' associates think Leeke "should stand behind the promise," said June Buckingham, spokeswoman for the Leroy Jenkins Evangelistic Association.

Jenkins, a flamboyant evangelist and faith healer who moved from Ohio to his native Greenwood in 1977, has

been imprisoned since his May 22 conviction on four con-
spiracy charges.

He was sentenced to serve 12 years for conspiracy to burn
the home of a highway patrolman and to assault the patrol-
man; conspiracy to burn the home of a Belton man; and con-
spiracy to assault an Anderson Independent reporter.

The case has been appealed, and Jenkins hopes to be released
on bond until the appeal is settled. So far, however, he has
been denied bond by circuit court, the S.C. Supreme Court
and U.S. District Court.

In July, Jenkins was back in the headlines again after
his faked "escape" in which a guard let him out of Kirkland
Correctional Institution. Jenkins, watched by state law offic-
ers, walked only a few steps past the prison gates before the
guard was arrested.

The guard, Robert C. Schively, later pleaded guilty to aid-
ing and abetting an escape and was sentenced to three years in
prison, to be suspended on service of 15 months.

Since the faked escape, Jenkins has been in protective
custody - solitary confinement - twice. The first time was at
his own request. The second was last weekend, after prison
officials learned that another inmate had said he'd been paid
$500 to kill Jenkins.

An investigation showed the "threat" was a hoax,
McCuen said.

The seeds of the present controversy were planted when
Jenkins and prison officials were working out the details of
how the guard would be arrested.

For Jenkins' own safety, Strickland said, Jenkins had to be
moved from Kirkland after the guard was arrested.

Strickland said he and Kirkland Warden J.L. Harvey
told Jenkins it would probably be best to put him "in an
open institution."

"We felt it would be best if he went to a smaller, open
institution for his own safety," Strickland said.

A transfer to minimum security was not a condition of Jenkins' cooperation, Strickland added.

So, on the night when the guard was arrested, Jenkins was transferred to the 120-inmate Goodman Correctional Institution in Columbia, a minimum-security facility mainly for elderly and handicapped prisoners, Strickland said.

The next day, Leeke, who had been on vacation, returned and decided against that arrangement.

Strickland said he didn't "quiz" his superior on the decision. Leeke "felt it was in the best interest of Mr. Jenkins and the agency to have him in a more controlled environment," Strickland said. "That's his prerogative."

Copyright © Anderson Independent

AN ANGEL IN THE DARK

Swish. A sound.

Startled, the Rev. Jenkins' eyes flew open in the darkness. *Swish.* There it was again, a soft sound like that of corduroy-clad legs brushing together. *Swish, swish.* The reverend slowed his breathing, straining to hear. Was the sound coming from the left? Or the right? Was it close? Was it coming for him?

He already knew what the swishing sound was. It was the sound of a body slithering across the polished tile floor. A jailhouse sound—a portent of evil.

In prison, men use the cover of night to crawl between cots to make deals or to settle scores.

The Rev. Jenkins' muscles tensed, ready to fight if he had to, wondering who tonight's target was, and hoping it was not he. The swishing sound ceased, and the reverend slowly allowed his breathing to deepen. Sleep was now impossible, so he waited for the light to come, letting his mind drift over the events of the last few weeks.

Following the faked escape attempt and the arrest of the prison guard, the reverend was transferred to the medium-security Manning Correctional Institution in September 1979. It was an improvement over Kirkland, but the lack of privacy made it a torment. Here, a man would give a piece of his soul, if he had any left, for one minute of solitude.

Jesse Strickland had kept his promise to see that the Rev. Jenkins' daily visitation schedule was still in effect and that he received his home-cooked lunch and fresh clothing.

He was able to keep up with the work of the ministry, dictating letters to his supporters and supervising, even at a distance, what needed to be done to keep the office going. These were small victories, but small victories are rare on the inside. Defeats are legion.

He listened again for the sound. Nothing. Finally, he dozed.

In the morning, he awoke to see medics carrying off a blood-soaked body. Someone had stabbed an inmate in his sleep. The prison grapevine soon reported him dead. He was never seen again.

"That's not going to happen to me," the evangelist promised himself. He was more determined than ever to survive no matter who tried to break him.

And try they did.

Dr. Gilbert Holloway, the Deming, New Mexico, evangelist who had come to South Carolina to help run the ministry in the Rev. Jenkins' absence, wrote of his concerns:

> [Mrs. Holloway] and I visited Leroy in jail at the Manning Correctional Institute on the periphery of Columbia, S.C. We spent nearly three hours with him. He is very thin, having lost about 40 pounds in weight, and is very nervous and often upset. Twice he has been attacked by other inmates, once seriously by seven men. His right leg, arm and hand are still sore from this felonious assault.
>
> I do not know if this assault had homosexual overtones, as I had not the heart to ask him about it, but there is constant danger of such violence in prison.

Leroy Jenkins is suffering, hurting, near to nervous exhaustion, even to serious illness, and what is being done about it?

It is alright for the prosecutor and judge, the warden and commissioner of corrections, and all the authorities to go home to their wives and comforts each evening, but what about this man of God in jail for misdemeanors that are not even themselves established in a fair trial, in a decent court of law?

The Rev. Holloway's concerns were not exaggerated. The Rev. Jenkins was constantly under threat of harm from inmates who wanted to extort money from him. The guards were no help. Just to keep the peace, they often turned a blind eye to the goings-on behind their backs.

Refusing to give in to the extortion, the evangelist squared his shoulders and marched through the corridors and underground tunnels at Manning, letting everyone know just where he stood with the Lord and stubbornly doing what he could to improve things around him.

"THEY TOLD ME I WOULD LOOK LIKE AN OLD MAN"

The Rev. Jenkins later shared his experiences at Manning, describing how he managed to keep the prison system from breaking his spirit.

"[Prison officials] told me that when they got through with me I would not be so 'prestigious and flamboyant.' They told me I would look like an old man when they got done with me. They tried everything," he told his Ohio congregation.

"They put me in the kitchen mopping floors, and I would mop and sing. Everything they would make me do, I'd sing as I did it. I said, 'I like mopping floors. My mother used to make me scrub floors, and I'm used to it.'

"They made me cook and I said, 'I used to cook meals for my sisters and brothers, and this makes me feel right at home.'

"So they took me out of the kitchen and put me in the barbershop. I told them I was a professional barber. The Lord taught me how to cut hair. I styled it for the men and made them look like they were going to Hollywood.

"I painted the barbershop and put cartoon characters on the walls. I had June bring some drapes, and they are still there. The warden came in and asked where the drapes came from. I said, 'Aren't they nice?'

"He said, 'Yes, but where did they come from?' I said, 'Boy, they really make this place look good.' I never did tell him where they came from.

"So I kicked back in the barbershop with my TV and my hot plate and all, and did everything I wanted to do, and it was private.

"Then I was manager of the canteen. I could get anything I wanted. I moved from there to the school. Here I was, hadn't finished the fifth grade, and I was a teacher's assistant!"

Fighting the dreary sameness of the prison uniforms, the reverend added his own personal touches to his garb. In addition to the requisite blue jeans, he wore a fresh, white shirt each day and colorful sweaters, each with the initials REV over his heart. That is how he wanted to be known, and the inmates obliged him, calling him "Rev."

"YOU'LL NEVER GET TO PREACH IN THIS INSTITUTION"

The Rev. Jenkins never ceased to try to preach, wherever he was. When he first came to Manning, Warden Kenneth McKellar said, "You can be sure of one thing—you'll never get to preach in this institution." The following month, prisoners received an invitation:

Dear Fellow Inmate,

The warden has given his permission to have a show at
Manning on Thursday, Sept. 20th at 7 o'clock, featuring
my Crusade Band and Singers.

 This 11-piece concert band is the one that plays before
thousands in auditoriums in the South, where my crusades
are held, such as the Atlanta Civic Center, the Fox Theater
in Atlanta, the Charlotte Coliseum, the Savannah Civic
Center, Asheville Civic Center, the Township Auditorium
in Columbia, and Memorial Auditorium in Greenville, S.C.

 In addition to the band, which features trumpets,
saxophones, and other brass instruments and which is
conducted by John Cooper from Greenwood, my Crusade
Team Band will be playing also. This band is famous for
its jazz-gospel sound. This team has blessed thousands
from Madison Square Garden to Cobo Arena in Detroit,
and the International Amphitheater in Chicago.

 Also appearing on the program will be my sons, Danny
and Dennis, and my daughter, Candy, singing several of
the songs they have recorded.

 I hope you will come to the concert, and I am sure you
will enjoy these fine entertainers.

Sincerely,
Reverend Leroy Jenkins

 On the night of the "show," the room was filled to capacity.
Resplendent in his black tuxedo, diamond ring, and watch
brought in to him for the occasion, the evangelist introduced the
musical portion of the program.

 First, the Nashville Cloggers took the stage, costumed in
frilly red-and-white checkered dresses, bouncing merrily as they
pounded out the steps of the old-time dances. The men loved it,
of course. How long had it been since a pretty girl smiled at them?

Singer Jamie Marvelle from Nashville, dramatic in a black Stetson and Van Dyke beard, entertained, while the Crusade Team Band, in their black tuxedos, with horns gleaming, played as though they were giving a command performance for the Queen of England.

One of the officers in charge of night operations at Manning introduced the reverend, speaking with feeling of the great respect and love he had come to have for this very special prisoner.

"This man is your friend," he said. "Listen to him, for he has your best interests at heart."

The Rev. Jenkins' sermon fell on receptive ears. He spoke of the Lord and His forgiveness, sharing his favorite Bible passages, and how he applied the Scriptures to his own lessons in life. His often-humorous reflections brought laughter into the dimness of the prison. God's people, he believed, should make a joyful noise unto the Lord. Then he called upon the men to make a commitment.

"Men, we are here, and that can't be helped," he said. "But I promise you that if you give your heart to the Lord, he will make things work for you.

"Try to do your best and think of the other fellow. Love is the greatest gift that God gave us."

When the Rev. Jenkins asked those who would give their hearts to the Lord to stand, everyone in the room arose and raised their arms in dedication.

"God," prayed the evangelist, "you see these hands raised to you. Now, I'm asking that these men be granted mercy, that their days here will be easier, and that many of them will go home much sooner than they are supposed to."

Warden McKellar, who was watching the service from the back of the room, appeared contemplative. Not only had the preacher held a crusade, but he also had the attention and cooperation of the entire prison population. It was said to be the most unusual thing ever seen at that institution.

Afterward, officials noted that things were much better at Manning. Disorderly incidents had decreased markedly, and many of the men were paroled earlier than expected.

Following the crusade, inmates began to hold prayer meetings in a supply closet, where they could worship in private. They sang, prayed, and spoke in tongues as the Holy Spirit filled them.

One day, an inmate in a wheelchair challenged the prayer group.

"If you say that God can heal, ask Him to heal me," he said, glaring at the men. He had been shot in the spine and was a helpless paraplegic.

The group prayed for him and then did not see the man again for several months. One day he walked up to the Rev. Jenkins.

"Do you remember me? I was the fellow in the wheelchair that you prayed for. I used to hate you guys, but you prayed for me, and even though the doctors had given me up, God healed me."

Not everyone was happy about the closet prayer meetings. One day, an officer yanked open the door and raged at the men.

"Shut up that g____ racket!" he ordered.

Outraged, the Rev. Jenkins rose up and confronted the guard, who had a reputation for mistreating the inmates.

"We have permission to have this meeting, and I hope you die," he said, his famous temper getting the better of him.

Shortly after the incident, the guard dropped dead of a heart attack while walking through the prison tunnel. His widow sued the state claiming that her husband had been subjected to unusual danger because he had to care for Leroy Jenkins and died as a result of his "curse."

She lost the case, but that story followed the reverend for the rest of his days in prison.

A HIT MAN CONFESSES

The kitchen has always been a special place for the Rev. Jenkins. Before prison, he did most of his entertaining in his own kitchen, laughing and chatting as he stirred up one of his favorite recipes. But the kitchen at Manning was a horror.

The first time he walked into the kitchen and flipped on the light, scores of cockroaches scattered across the grills and countertops. From that day forward, the Rev. Jenkins made sure the grills were scraped clean of encrusted grease, and the counters washed before meals were prepared.

When it was his turn to cook, the food was hot and appetizing.

"You cookin' again today, Rev?" one inmate, a big hardy fellow, said. "You cookin', I'm eatin.' You sure do know how to dish it up."

One day, as the reverend served food to the men in the line, God showed him that one of them had been sent to kill him.

He went to the warden and pointed the inmate out. The warden called the prisoner into his office, and the man admitted he had been paid $500 to kill the reverend. Both the Rev. Jenkins and the potential hit man were placed in solitary confinement until the matter could be investigated. In the Rev. Jenkins' case, solitary confinement served as "protective custody."

AN ANGEL IN THE DARK

The reverend remained there for three days, despite frantic calls from his staff and his lawyer, demanding his release. It was as if *he* had been the hired killer.

While in solitary, he was not permitted to shower or to change his clothing. His cell, which was in the prison basement, turned ink black when the lights went out.

One night, lonely and miserable, the evangelist clutched his Bible, wishing he had enough light to read it. At that moment, a shaft of light broke the darkness, illuminating the pages of his Bible. He read, and when he finished reading, the light went out.

Another time, he lay on his bunk, thinking about his ministry and asking for God's guidance. Suddenly a magnificent creature materialized from the blackness and hovered over him, shining in its ethereal majesty. The Rev. Jenkins reached up, and his hands felt the angel's wings, as silky as cobwebs. Just then, the apparition faded away.

The reverend was so inspired that he wrote to his entire mailing list of 440,000 families, telling them of the heavenly visitation and urging them to write to him.

"If you are free in the spirit, you are free indeed. If you are depressed, you are in bondage. You can get out of bondage in the spirit, so that if you are bound, you are not bound," he reflected later.

God had let him know he was not forsaken, even in that gloomy cell in the basement of Manning prison.

Twenty-two thousand families responded to the mailing. Through a misunderstanding, those who did not respond were removed from the mailing list, and the names were lost forever. The ministry did not falter, as might be expected, thanks to those same 22,000 families who continued to support the ministry.

TAKE THESE CHAINS

Christmas is the loneliest time for prisoners. They long for their homes and families. Memories of past Christmases make the void almost unendurable. The Rev. Jenkins was determined to make the best of the Christmas of 1979. (see photo on page 257)

Cheery Christmas cards sent to him by friends and followers lined the corridors outside his cell at Manning. The cards were the only touch of Christmas the men were allowed, and it relieved the monotony to read and reread the messages of love inscribed within.

In addition to the cards, the reverend sent every inmate at Manning a Christmas greeting with a five-dollar gift inside. It was more than most of the men had received in years, and their response was gratifying.

Dear Mrs. Buckingham,

Praise the Lord!! My name is Thomas Stevens[88] and I'm a friend of Leroy Jenkins. I want to thank you for the time and effort that you put forth to get over the gifts from Leroy that he brought to us.

Christmas is a very busy holiday and I know you had a million other things to do, but you took the time to get the gifts to us. I really am thankful, but there's a few here who are not.

Remember that you did a kind deed for people who might not get anything for Christmas. God likes people to do kind things for others.

I know God is going to bless you for what you've done. I thank the Lord for such as you, who don't forget about the people who are in prison. I sure hope you had a very Merry Christmas and thank you once again. I'd appreciate it very much if you would pray for me. May God bless you and keep you in His tender care.

Thank you very much,
Thomas Stevens

The Rev. Jenkins received his own special gift that Christmas. One morning he opened his eyes to see a little bird making its nest on the window sill of his cell. Day after day that little bird flew off to the pine forests beyond the prison walls and brought back bits of twigs, pine needles, and grass for her bed. Then she settled down to lay her eggs and warm them until they hatched.

---

[88] Not his real name.

Little bird, the Rev. Jenkins asked himself, *with this whole beautiful world outside, why did you come into this terrible place to make your home?* Inspired, he wrote a poem:

> Inside this prison wall,
> When there are trees beyond
> So green and tall?
> I see you each morning
> And I see you when the dusk begins to fall.
> You work all day
> Carrying mud and straw.
> When you could build your nest
> In the trees so nice and tall,
> Why did you choose your home
> Behind this prison wall?
> In a few weeks your eggs will hatch.
> Your family will grow and fly away.
> While I must stay,
> While I must stay.

A message came to him just then and comforted him: No one can imprison the soul. He knew his heart could fly beyond those walls just as the little bird had, and he could be free in his spirit. After that message lodged in his heart, the dreadful burden of the prison no longer had the same hold on him. He was free to serve his time in prison with the same joy of living and optimism that had always been a part of his personality.

JENKINS HOSPITALIZED AFTER "SEIZURE"

Anderson Independent, January 29, 1980

Steven Smith

COLUMBIA - Imprisoned evangelist, Leroy Jenkins was rushed Friday to Richland County Memorial Hospital here after he suffered a "seizure" of undetermined nature, a prison official said Monday.

Jenkins, serving a 12-year sentence for conspiracy, was practicing with a gospel group at Manning Correctional Institute when he complained to officials his right arm and leg had become numb suddenly, said Sam McCuen, public information officer with the Department of Corrections.

The Greenwood evangelist who attained fame with his controversial faith-healing services across the country, then lapsed into a "fit" said McCuen, and was rushed by ambulance to Richland.

Jenkins remained under close watch through the weekend.

"We have a guard keeping an eye on him every hour of the day," said McCuen.

Hospital officials said Monday that doctors spent the weekend conducting a series of tests on Jenkins, but could not determine the cause of the numbness or apparent seizure.

Judy Cotchett, director of community relations at Richland, said Jenkins was admitted in good condition for diagnostic treatment relating to the numbness.

"He is in excellent spirits," she said. "We do not presume there will be any significant change in his condition."

Hospital officials are not sure when Jenkins will go home, although Ms. Cotchett said he might remain hospitalized through the week.

Copyright © Anderson Independent

SHACKLED

Prison authorities were terribly unfeeling in their treatment of the inmates, as the above-mentioned incident demonstrates.

After his seizure, the Rev. Jenkins waited with another group of inmates for transport to the hospital. They were all shackled, their wrists handcuffed to a chain around their waists, and their ankles chained together. This made the inmates helpless to steady themselves in the prison van as it went around corners or changed lanes. In the event of an accident, they would be unable to protect themselves.

Six of the inmates stood shackled at the wrists, their arms intertwined. They faced one another, nose to nose, in a most dehumanizing manner.

"What a disgrace and shame to treat these men in such an inhuman manner," Mrs. Buckingham, the co-author, said to Warden McKellar, who was standing in the lobby of the prison. "You don't have any right to shackle them this way. Do you think Rev. Jenkins, after becoming so ill he had to be taken to the hospital, will get up off that stretcher and escape? You ought to be ashamed of yourself.

"This is a terrible way to treat these men. They are here to be incarcerated at the orders of the court, not here for you to torture them."

The warden blew his stack. Red faced and furious, he shouted that his orders were to be followed, that he was in charge, and he would d____ well do what he wanted to do. The fact that, thanks to Jesse Strickland, the reverend was permitted visitors every day must have rankled. But the warden knew the eyes of the world were on him, and that whatever he did to the Rev. Jenkins would wind up in the newspapers immediately.

DON'T ROCK THE BOAT

At the same time, the Rev. Jenkins and his staff were under pressure to "keep quiet."

"We can do much more for him, if he isn't in the news every week," Commissioner Leeke said.

When the reverend's mother made statements to a television reporter that made it appear she was complaining about his treatment in prison, everyone was quick to assure the public that their pastor was well treated.

JENKINS BARBERING IN PRISON; AIDE SAYS HE'S WELL TREATED

Delaware Gazette, February 21, 1980

Leroy Jenkins, the Delaware-based faith healer serving a 12-year prison term for conspiring to commit arson and assault, is happy with the treatment he is receiving at a state prison, his personal secretary in Greenwood, S.C. told the United Press International today.

"Under the circumstances, everyone is being as nice to him as they could possibly be," said June Buckingham in a telephone interview from Greenwood with the UPI in Columbia, S.C.

"He is not getting any worse treatment than anyone else is," Ms. Buckingham said. "In fact, he has complimented the warden and the guards - if it was any different, you know I would tell you," she said.

Jenkins, who was convicted last May, is serving time at the Manning Correctional Institution in Columbia. Jenkins' mother made statements to a Channel 10 reporter Wednesday that made it appear she was complaining about his treatment in prison. She told the Gazette today that she did not mean to make that impression.

Mrs. Jenkins said her son is being well treated by prison officials. She said he had been "initiated" in each prison he had been in. She said the prisoners "roughed up" Jenkins, as they apparently do all new prisoners.

Jenkins is working in the prison barber shop where he is cutting hair, she said. She said cutting hair used to be Jenkins' hobby.

"He's keeping the inmates' hair washed and curled," she said.

Jenkins receives visits from a select group of approved people, she said.

Ms. Buckingham, who is also secretary-treasurer of the Leroy Jenkins Evangelistic Association, said that although the group has moved its headquarters back to Delaware about four staffers will remain in Greenwood to handle Jenkins' real estate properties and other matters.

Copyright © Delaware Gazette

FAITH HEALER GATHERING FLOCK INSIDE HIS PRISON, MOTHER SAYS

Columbus Citizen-Journal, February 22, 1980

Marilyn Greenwald

DELAWARE - *Convicted faith healer Leroy Jenkins has converted many of his fellow inmates at the Manning S.C. Correctional Institute to the ways of God, according to his mother, Willa Mae Jenkins.*

"They love him there," Mrs. Jenkins explained as she spoke Thursday from Holy Hill Cathedral, new headquarters of the Leroy Jenkins Evangelistic Association.

"When they (the inmates) found out who he was they said, 'You're not that fellow we see on TV are you? What have they done to you?" She said about 300 inmates are now Jenkins followers.

Mrs. Jenkins, 74, believes her son was unjustly convicted in May 1979 of conspiring to commit arson and assault. Jenkins, 45, is now serving the second year of a 12-year term in the South Carolina state prison, where, his mother said, he is being treated well.

Although Jenkins and attorney F. Lee Bailey have been unable to obtain bail, Mrs. Jenkins says she expects her son to return to Delaware "before too long" and once again head the Leroy Jenkins Evangelistic Association at Holy Hill.

"God can unlock the door, I know He will," Mrs. Jenkins said.

As she spoke from her son's red and blue carpeted office at the Holy Hill complex on Ohio Rt. 23, Mrs. Jenkins explained that for the last few months she has flown in each weekend from her home in Tampa, Fla., to conduct services from the cathedral.

"When I get into that chair," she said referring to Jenkins' circular wooden desk, "I know I'm just taking his place until he gets back."

Jenkins' Delaware office is complete with one mirrored wall and a deep blue mural of the parting of the waters on the south wall. Immediately above the desk is a large framed photograph of Jenkins shaking hands with Jimmy Carter.

The picture was taken several years ago in Atlanta when Carter was still governor, Mrs. Jenkins explained, adding that Jenkins told Carter he was destined to be president "even before he (Carter) knew it."

Mrs. Jenkins said her son's gift of prophecy has apparently rubbed off on her; when she first visited Jenkins last year in the South Carolina state prison, she remembered a vision she had of the prison nine years ago. "When we went to visit him, I told him I knew exactly what the prison would be like. I had seen it," she said.

Yet she admitted she was not an evangelist until she realized the power of her son. She was not overly religious, she said, although she could not afford doctors and "I used to pray when one of mine was sick for them to heal."

And Jenkins father, who died seven years ago, was anything but an evangelist. The older Jenkins would periodically abandon the family in South Carolina, and did not accept the Lord until he was on his deathbed, she said.

Copyright © Columbus Citizen-Journal

PRISON CAN'T STOP JENKINS' GOSPEL

The State of Columbia, South Carolina, May 8, 1980

DELAWARE, Ohio (AP) - *The walls of a South Carolina prison can't stop faith healer Leroy Jenkins from spreading his gospel.*

Jenkins, convicted of conspiracy to commit assault and arson last year, has been preaching his word via long-distance telephone.

A spokesman for the Holy Hill Cathedral in Delaware, where the evangelist's Association is now headquartered, said Jenkins has been calling almost every Sunday since February. The telephone conversation is patched into the cathedral's public address system.

Jenkins, who was moved from a medium-security cell to a minimum-security cell at Manning Correctional Institution in Columbia on Monday, has served nearly one year of a 12-year sentence.

Copyright © The State

A GLIMPSE OF FREEDOM

Finally, after serving almost a year at Manning, and earning his "AA trusty"[89] status, the Rev. Jenkins received an offer to transfer to Walden Farm, a minimum-security prison. It was an open institution, with no fences or guard dogs.

Despite the benefits, the Rev. Jenkins was not sure that he wanted to be transferred there. He had mastered the system at Manning, knew all the men well, and had their respect. He was unsure about the move and asked his staff to go to Walden and see what it looked like.

Though the name might invoke images of Henry David Thoreau's idyll, Walden Farm consisted of a pitiful cluster of buildings and barns coated with red-brown dust, it was close to the road and eventual freedom.

When he first went to prison at Kirkland, God had told the Rev. Jenkins he would be moved seven times, the last time closer to the road, and then he would be released. He felt this move was in God's plan.

"You really ought to go," Jesse Strickland urged. "It is just one more positive move to freedom."

"If I do go," said the Rev. Jenkins, "I'll never call it Walden Farm. From now on it will be Walden Ranch."

And so it was that the thirty thousand people on Rev. Jenkins' mailing list soon received letters from him at "Walden Ranch."

When he left Manning, the men crowded around, happy for him, but knowing that a wonderful presence was leaving their midst. One of the group said to a staff member, "When Rev leaves here, it is just like a light is going out. It will never be as good here again."

---

[89]   A status given to prisoners who had demonstrated the greatest improvement and earned the trust of prison officials.

CLOSER TO THE ROAD

The Rev. Jenkins arrived at Walden Farm with mixed emotions. The dusty grounds and dilapidated quarters were dismal and discouraging.

On the other hand, Broad River Road ran alongside the prison just a few hundred feet away. For convicts, being closer to the road held much symbolism. The road led to freedom and home.

Commissioner Leeke had urged the Rev. Jenkins to accept a transfer to a newly opened institution in Greenville, some ninety miles north of Columbia. The facility was said to be the latest in prison design, well planned, and well maintained.

It didn't matter. God told the Rev. Jenkins not to leave Columbia, but to stay right under the noses of the administration. This was easy to do, because the department of corrections offices stood adjacent to the minimum-security prison. Jesse Strickland's office overlooked the prison yard. As long as he was incarcerated, the reverend intended to make his presence known. Maybe then they would be more interested in letting him go.

His arrival at the prison's "dormitory" was not entirely welcomed by the other men.

At Walden, the prisoners had heard the Rev had made his mark at Manning, and they did not want him to think he was going to come in and "take over things" at Walden. For the reverend's first night at Walden Ranch, fellow inmates wired his metal bed to an electrical socket. It was their way of showing him who was in charge. If it had not been for a convict named Coley Bryant, this unorthodox welcoming committee might have succeeded with their cruel plan.

I HAVE FOUND MY SHEEP THAT WAS LOST

In prison, reputation is everything. It can assure a man of a measure of respect from the other prisoners. Or it can get him killed. Coley Bryant had a bad reputation. A convicted murderer, he boasted of killing thirteen people, including lawmen. Fellow inmates figured the lifer wouldn't hesitate to add another corpse to the body count, so they gave this tough misanthrope a lot of space.

The Rev. Leroy Jenkins, on the other hand, was somewhat of an enigma to his fellow prisoners. He wasn't a murderer or even an armed robber. His conviction was based on a murky conspiracy charge. And he was a preacher—how tough could he be?

News of the plan to electrify Rev's bed somehow made it back to Jesse Strickland. Immediately, Strickland thought of a way to use Coley Bryant's bad reputation to save the Rev. Jenkins from not only a rough night's sleep but also what could prove to be years of torment by inmates.

It is no secret that inmates often control prison life. Otherwise, it would be virtually impossible to manage a population of largely antisocial men forced to live together day after day in cramped quarters. No small contingent of guards can expect to stand up to a riot by desperate men, most of whom have nothing more to lose. It is not unusual for a warden or an officer to encourage stronger inmates to use their influence to keep things running smoothly.

Strickland had developed, if not a friendship, a working relationship with Bryant when they were both at the notorious Central Correctional Institution. Coley had been the "big man" at

CCI, the toughest, most feared man in the prison. Strickland was CCI's young, brave, fair-minded, and highly respected warden at the time. It was Strickland who got the aging convict a job as supervisor of the gas station at Walden, where he was content to be alone.

Now, Strickland asked Bryant to return a favor.

"Coley," he said, "this is Rev. Leroy Jenkins. I want you to look out for him, okay?"

Bryant glared at the newcomer from under his bushy, white eyebrows and cursed, taking the Lord's name in vain. He warned the reverend that he kept an ax handle on the property and would not hesitate to use it.

Preferring to take his chances with Bryant rather than the "hot bed," the reverend persisted.

"Coley," he said, "I'm going to help you here in the gas station and pump gas."

Red-faced, Bryant cursed until every hair on his crew cut head stood on end. "The hell you are," he snorted.

"Nobody stays here at the gas station but me," he said. "That's the way I want it. That's the way it's going to be."

The reverend didn't flinch. Bryant did not know it, but he had met his match. Over Bryant's curses and howls of protest, the Rev. Jenkins spent his first night at Walden on a cot in the gas station office drifting off to the bitter aroma of gasoline and axle grease.

The gas station job was not a cushy one. At any hour of the day or night, prison guards, policemen, or Department of Corrections officials might pull up to the gas pumps. Escapes or other emergencies did not conform to banker's hours. Still, the reverend preferred it to sleeping in a dorm with thirty or forty other men.

Through the coming months, the preacher and the killer became friends. In time, Bryant accompanied the Rev. Jenkins on visitors' day where he picnicked with the reverend's family and some of his employees. Between bites of fried chicken, okra, and sweet potato pie, he began to open up to the visitors, speaking of his youth and the rare happy memories he had of the world beyond prison bars. The visitors winced at, but overlooked, his salty tongue. Slowly, he became a welcome presence at these gatherings. He was even heard to laugh. And eventually the curses softened.

Bryant's new attitude earned him a weekend furlough—his first outing in forty-five years. He had heard a great deal about the reverend's Holy Hill Cathedral in Delaware, Ohio. He now longed to meet the reverend's mother and sister and the rest of the congregation. One day, he got his wish. Prison officials pooled their own money to buy him a plane ticket and arranged a weeklong pass.

Coley Bryant stood before the Ohio congregation, as the Rev. Jenkins, through an amplified telephone call from the prison, told church members about how Bryant had been his protector and friend, keeping would-be troublemakers at bay with his infamous ax handle. The congregation stood as one to applaud Bryant, and his eyes filled with tears, proving that even the most hardened of hearts could be touched and transformed by the saving grace of the Lord Jesus Christ.

Bryant did not mind the dirt or the gas station's shabby appearance and fought all attempts to improve the place. When he returned from Ohio, he gaped at his room in the gas station office. His belongings had vanished. The walls bore fresh paint, and the greasy floors had been bleached and scrubbed. A humble chair and table sat next to the cot where the Rev. Jenkins now slept.

"Where am I going to sleep?" Bryant thundered.

"Coley, I sent your things over to the white house," the Rev. Jenkins said, referring to a small house on Broad River Road shared by some of the trusties.

"There's a porch there, and you can sit and watch the road. There's a kitchen where you can cook," he said.

For once, Bryant didn't put up a fuss. He was old now and weary. He went peacefully to his new home.

WALDEN GARDEN

For someone who loved flowers and greenery as much as the Rev. Jenkins did, Walden Farm was a distressing sight. Years later, he told his church in Delaware about his first project there.

"Walden was a miserable place. The hot Carolina sun shone down on a dusty yard, with a weedy, rock-strewn lawn. I was determined to make it a showplace. One day I sent for one of my enormous flagpoles that I had put up in Greenwood and an American flag to go on it.

"I told June all that I needed—fountains, hoses, cement, shovels, and pickaxes. That afternoon, I asked Warden [Willie] Portee if it would be all right if I fixed up the yard a little bit, and he agreed.

"I said, 'I want to put a little pond there.' And he said, 'Go ahead.' He didn't know that at five o'clock when he left, our truck pulled in loaded with everything—flowers, bushes, fountains—the works.

"I told the men if they would help to fix up the yard, at Christmastime I would bring in a tree and decorate it for them. They really worked, enjoying the prospect of surprising Warden Portee.

"That afternoon when Warden Portee left, there was nothing in the yard but mud. But when he drove up the next morning, there were flowers, trees, and shrubs everywhere. And a tall flagpole with an American flag waving in the breeze. We had worked most of the night to transform the place.

"He gasped and took a long time looking. He couldn't believe his eyes. We had built a pond and put in a fountain and cemented it in with rocks all around it, and had bought goldfish at the mall, and they were swimming around in it. (see photo on page 273)

"He said, 'My God, Mr. Leeke will fire me!' I said, 'Mr. Leeke likes it. He looked out from his office window and called over here and said that he really liked what we had done over here. He told us we had done a tremendous job!'

"He also said he knew that Leroy Jenkins was behind the whole thing."

A BODY RESTORED

Warden Portee was sitting in his office one day in conference with Greenwood attorney Hugh Beasley. Beasley had come to admire and respect the Rev. Jenkins.

"Leroy, son," he once said, "I can truly say that I love you, and I've never even told that to my own son, though I love him also."

A dignified, white-haired Southern gentleman from the old school, he faithfully kept in touch with his client and frequently visited the prison to see that he was being well treated.

As he spoke with Warden Portee, they looked out over the prison yard and saw the Rev. Jenkins standing in a group of inmates, conversing.

Across the yard came a tall, well-built man hobbling on a cane. Jack Elliott[90] had been injured when a printing press in the prison print shop fell on his feet.

"Come here, young man," said the evangelist, motioning him over. "How would you like to throw that cane away and walk freely?"

"I'd like it just fine," Elliott said, his face lighting up in a grin from ear to ear.

"Well, throw it down. Go on and walk," said the reverend. With a whoop of joy, Elliott dropped the cane and began to jump and run around the yard.

"Did you see that?" said Warden Portee. "That man just threw away his cane!"

---

[90] Not his real name.

The warden and Beasley went outside to join the men who were hugging Elliott and rejoicing over his healing.

EVANGELIST HEALS SICK DESPITE JAIL

Columbus Citizen-Journal, July 15, 1980

COLUMBIA, S.C. (UPI) - Evangelist Leroy Jenkins, formerly of Delaware, Ohio, has tried to continue his ministry and faith healing while in a minimum-security prison where he is serving a 12-year term.

He also says prison life is depressing, and he misses his family.

Jenkins works as a trusty in charge of beautifying the prison grounds.

"I've been able to minister to some people," he said. "One guy here was crippled. He was using a cane. I prayed for him, and he ran into the warden's office without his cane. Now he jogs around the field here.

"It's helped me understand people," Jenkins told the Charlotte (N.C.) Observer in a telephone interview." But there's a lot that isn't pleasant.

"The way they mix people up - the hard core criminals with the kids - and every prison I've been in has been overcrowded. That doesn't help."

When asked about the worst part of prison, Jenkins said," Just about everything."

He said he misses his family. "I was always pretty much a private person when I wasn't in my crusades," he said. "I was always with my family, my kids. This has caused my family a lot of grief, a lot of heartaches. Especially my mother.

"She came down to see me the day before yesterday. She cried very hard."

MORE PLEAS FOR RELEASE

During the Rev. Jenkins' stay at Walden Farm, Dr. Ralph Davis, president of the National Ministers Association, had learned of the court proceedings that had sent the pastor to prison. He headlined the story in his publication that reached over seven hundred thousand Christians.

Defiantly, they elected the reverend "Minister of the Year" and signed petitions requesting his release on bond while his appeal to the Supreme Court of South Carolina was pending.

MINISTERS ASSOCIATION PLANS TO FILE PETITIONS SEEKING RELEASE OF EVANGELIST LEROY JENKINS

Columbus Citizen-Journal, September 3, 1980

GREENWOOD, S.C. (UPI) - A pastor representing the National Ministers Association said he plans to present a petition with 7,000 signatures to the state Supreme Court Wednesday, asking for the release of faith-healer Leroy Jenkins, now in a state prison.

The Rev. Ralph Davis of Tujunga, Calif. said Tuesday he will visit the state Supreme Court offices in Columbia, "sometime shortly before noon tomorrow" to present the petition.

"We feel since he has served 15 months already, and the punishment was far in excess of the crime, he should be released, or his sentence commuted to time already served," said Davis.

Davis said the signatures on Jenkins' behalf came from all over the nation. "We've found that being silent has not helped, so now we're going to seek publicity," said Davis.

"He has served 15 months, and we think that's long enough for something like this. He never touched anyone," said Davis.

"We have convicted murderers who are released in five years, and he was sentenced to 12 years for only saying he would do something," said Davis.

Davis, who is pastor of the 600-member non-denominational Church of God in Tujunga, said Jenkins deserves some consideration because he "practically rebuilt the town of Greenwood at his own expense."

Davis said he brought the petition on behalf of the ministers Association with members' approval and knowledge, and he added that many of the names are from the membership.

He said the decision was made by the organization 30 days ago to try and seek Jenkins' release.

Davis said he would be accompanied to the court by June Buckingham, Jenkins' secretary, "and possibly one local attorney."

PASTOR'S QUEST TO FREE JENKINS IGNORED IN COURT

Columbus Citizen-Journal, September 5, 1980

COLUMBIA, S.C. (UPI) - *A California pastor, who carried 8,000 petitions to the South Carolina Supreme Court Thursday seeking Leroy Jenkins' release from prison, said Christians all over the country want the convicted faith-healer freed.*

Supreme Court Clerk Frances Smith accepted the petitions, but said the justices would not read them because the case is still under appeal.

Dr. Ralph Davis of Tujunga, California, President of the National Ministers Association, said the 8,000 slips of paper bearing the petition message were only a "token" of the amount of support for Jenkins.....

Miss Smith told Davis he could put the boxes in her office. But under South Carolina law, the justices are not allowed

to view anything unless it is part of the official case record,
she said.

Davis said he wants to see Jenkins' sentenced commuted to
the 15 months he has served.

Copyright © Columbus Citizen-Journal

PHOTO SECTION

The inside of Rev. Jenkins' Holy Hill Cathedral in Delaware, Ohio.
Holy Hill Cathedral was filled to capacity with
seating for 4,000 people every Sunday.
(see page 105)

A young Rev. Jenkins. This picture is taken around
the age he quit attending school to pursue the Calling
he had received from God to be a Preacher.
(see page 76)

A family portrait taken at Christmas time. Front row starting
left: Daniel, Ricky, Rev. Jenkins holding Devon on his lap, Inmate
Lee Vaught, Lisa, Candy. Back row: Scotty, Donna, Dennis,
Sharon, Candace, Manet, Danny, Theresa and David.
(see page 235)

Rev. Jenkins and "Bobby" the bird. Rev. Jenkins and
Bobby would perform on stage while on crusade. The Rev
has a huge heart and a big soft spot for animals!
(see page 62)

A decrepit old home on Stockman Street prior to renovation.
(see page 14)

From left to right: Beck Steel, Rev. Leroy Jenkins, and Deane Tatum
standing outside one of the many homes on Stockman Street that was
part of the renovation project completed by Rev. Jenkins.
(see page 31)

This was June Buckingham's home on Stockman
Street after renovation was completed.
(see page 32)

Rev. Jenkins' refurbished home on Stockman Street.
(see page 37)

LAST WILL AND TESTAMENT OF

MAUDIE BARTZ

THE STATE OF TEXAS

COUNTY OF ECTOR   KNOW ALL MEN BY THESE PRESENTS:

THAT I, MAUDIE BARTZ, a resident of Ector County, Texas, being
of sound and disposing mind and memory, and above the age of nineteen
years, do make and publish this my Last Will and Testament hereby expressly
revoking any and all Wills and Codicils by me at any time heretofore
made.

1.

I direct that all of my just debts shall be paid.

2.

I give, devise and bequeath the sum of $500.00 in cash to my
adopted son, LEROY JENKINS BARTZ.

3.

The rest and residue of my estate, I give, devise and bequeath
to MISSIONS THRU-FAITH, INC., a non-profit corporation, organized under
the laws of the State of Florida (Don Powell being its current president).
Without limiting such general gift, devise and bequest, it is my intention that such gift, devise and bequest to MISSIONS THRU-FAITH, INC.,
shall include all of the property which I own at the time of my death,
including, but not limited to, the flower shop business, my home place,
what money I have in banks and in my savings account at Odessa Savings
and Loan Association, Odessa, Texas, and in my savings account in
Tulsa, Oklahoma.

4.

I hereby nominate and appoint the said Don Powell, of Daytona
Beach, Florida, as sole and Independent Executor of my estate and of

Page one of Maudie Bartz's last will and testament, which both explains
and proves that she left only $500.00 to Rev. Jenkins at her death.
(see page 130)

4726

SOUTH CAROLINA
DEPARTMENT OF PROBATION, PAROLE,
AND PARDON SERVICES
COLUMBIA, SC

CERTIFICATE OF PARDON

KNOW ALL MEN BY THESE PRESENTS:

It having been made to appear to the SOUTH CAROLINA BOARD OF PROBATION,

PAROLE, AND PARDON SERVICES *that* _____ Leroy Jenkins _____

SCDC No. SS# 250-46-6794 *and* SID No. 236922 _____ *who was convicted of*
Conspiracy to Commit Arson (2 cts); Conspiracy to Commit ABHAN (2 cts) on 5/22/79; Obtaining
Prop. Under False Pretense on 12/29/53; Breach of Trust on 9/4/53 xxxxxxxxxxxxxxxxxxxxxxxx

xxxxxxxxxxxxxxxxxxxxxxxxxxxxxxxxxxxxxxxxxxxxxxxxxxxxxxxxxxx *in the County of* _____ Greenwood _____

has lived as a law abiding citizen since satisfactory completion of

parole and probation supervision
*and it being the opinion of the said South Carolina Board of Probation, Parole, and Pardon
Services that the pardoning of this prisoner is not incompatible with the welfare of society, and it*

appearing further that the Board is satisfied _____ he _____
will abide by all laws of this State.

It is therefore ORDERED that said _____ Leroy Jenkins _____

BE PARDONED, *effective this* 28th *day of* September _____ 19 93 _____
*and by this action, is absolved from all legal consequences of his above stated crime and
conviction, and all his civil rights are restored.*

In witness whereof this Certificate bearing the approval of the South Carolina Board of

Probation, Parole, and Pardon Services is issued this 28th *day of* September _____

19 93 _____

By order of:
SOUTH CAROLINA BOARD OF PROBATION,
PAROLE, AND PARDON SERVICES

By: *Michael J Cavanaugh*
 Commissioner

The original pardon issued to Rev. Jenkins on September 28, 1993, which
granted full and unconditional absolution and restored all civil liberties!
(see page 387)

Rev. Jenkins with Senator Marshall Williams and Mrs. Williams. Senator
Williams was the man who pardoned Rev. Jenkins September 28, 1993.
(see page 387)

Rev. Jenkins and Jesse Strickland, Deputy Commissioner,
Department of Corrections, South Carolina. The
Commissioner became one of his dearest friends.
(see pages 290-291)

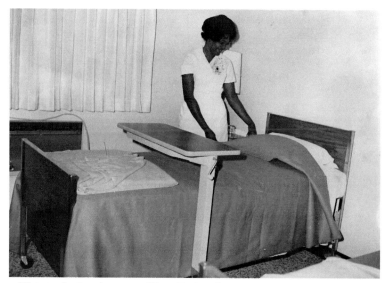

This is the head nurse of Rev. Jenkins' nursing home. This nursing
home received the award for "Nursing Home of the Year."
(see page 87)

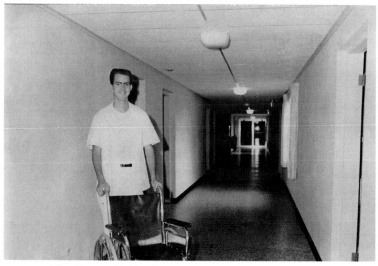

The former Sulfur Springs Hotel, which Rev. Jenkins
successfully managed to transform into a nursing home.
Shown here is an employee performing his daily work.
(see page 87)

The State Penitentiary of South Carolina, or CCI. (Courtesy
of *www.palmettohistory.org*.) Rev. Jenkins traveled to
this maximum security prison to preach to the inmates
during the time he was serving in prison himself.
(see page 292)

The new Boy's Ranch Building on Pollock Road in
Delaware ablaze. This was typical of several other fires that
followed Rev. Jenkins during this time in his life.
(see page 110)

The Rev's arrival at Kirkland Correctional Institution pictured
with inmates. Many of these inmates knew and loved the Reverend
because some of them, their mothers and family members
had attended his crusades. (Notice the picture of Governor
Jimmy Carter and the Reverend being held up in front.)
(see page 199)

An actual photograph of Rev. Jenkins in prison. He had all of his shirts
embroidered with the name "REV" in the upper left hand corner.
(see page 70)

Daily mail Rev. Jenkins received while in prison.
(see pages 202 and 282)

Mrs. June Buckingham
(see page 10)

Rev. Jenkins clothed in one of the costumes given to him by Elvis Presley.
(see page 342)

Rev. Jenkins and the car, 450SL Mercedes, Jim Whittington
gave him as a gift while he was in prison.
(see page 339)

Linda Evans and Rev. Jenkins on the set at Four Star
Productions. Rev. Jenkins has on Lee Majors' hat, who
starred on the television program "The Big Valley."
(see pages 16 and 317)

Al Green and Rev. Jenkins in his office on a Sunday morning
in Delaware, Ohio. He came to sing and have dinner with
the Rev afterwards. Al was converted at this crusade, began
preaching and later built a church in Memphis, Tennessee.
(see pages 16 and 317)

John Derek and Rev. Jenkins in the parking lot of
Healing Waters Cathedral, Delaware, Ohio.
(see pages 16 and 317)

Telly Savalez and Mike Mazurki with Rev. Jenkins back
stage at Madison Square Gardens, New York.
(see pages 16, 316-317)

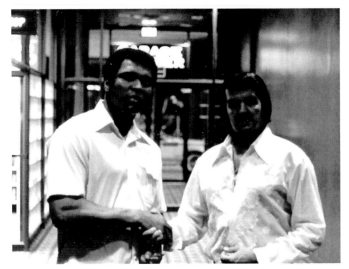

Muhammed Ali and Rev. Jenkins meet in Chicago.
(see pages 16 and 317)

Sugar Ray Leonard and Rev. Jenkins at a tent crusade in Columbus,
Ohio. He came all the way from Concord, CA, where he was training
for a boxing match to attend this crusade. Rev. Jenkins prophesied he
would win an upcoming match and he did so, winning $40 million!
(see pages 16 and 317)

Robert Wagner and Rev. Jenkins are on the set of the film
"The Calling." They are by the baptism waters where
Rev. Jenkins baptized the inmates in this movie.
(see pages 16 and 317)

Willie Nelson and Rev. Jenkins at a concert in Columbus, Ohio.
(see pages 16 and 317)

Mae West and Rev. Jenkins. The Reverend was influential in bringing
Mae West out of retirement to make the movie "Myra Breckenridge."
(see pages 16, 316-317)

Dale Evans and Rev. Jenkins in Madison Square Garden,
New York. This crusade had 22,000 in attendance
and tens of thousands had to be turned away.
(see pages 16, 316-317)

Rev. Jenkins headed up a landscaping project with the inmates at Walden Correctional Institution. This project resulted in a beautiful place for the community and improved relationships between the prisoners.
(see pages 249 and 312)

Rev. Jenkins and "The Crusade Team Band" performing at church services held inside the Kirkland Correctional Institution.
(see page 317)

Candy and Theresa Jenkins, Rev. Jenkins' daughters, and a crew
of followers spread sawdust and prepare for a tent revival on
Broad River Road down the street from the Walden Ranch
Correctional Institute and the Campbell Work Release Center.
(see page 356)

Rev. Jenkins and Lester Maddox exchange comments after the address to the Senate (Top Picture) where Rev. Jenkins was invited to give his testimony (Bottom Picture). This is where he met Governor Jimmy Carter and was invited to come to his office for a visit.

(see page 166)

Rev. Jenkins and Lester Maddox, reformed segregationist,
who invited the Reverend to speak to the Senate.
(see page 166)

Governor Jimmy Carter and Rev. Jenkins in the governor's office. Rev.
Jenkins prophesied to the young Governor Carter that he would become
the next President of the United States and it came to pass.
(see page 166)

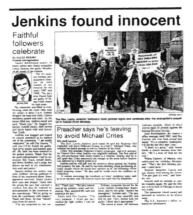

Jenkins found innocent

Faithful followers celebrate

Preacher says he's leaving to avoid Michael Crites

A copy of an article from the *Delaware Gazette,* March 30, 1993. Rev. Jenkins is victorious in an unjust trial against the IRS. About 100 people, including Rev's staff and many supporters, cheer Rev and his lawyers as he exits the courtrooms. Not only did the IRS wrongly accuse the Reverend of tax evasion, but they have managed to lose massive amounts of money that have just disappeared without a trace. Like the sign in the photo states – Who checks on the IRS? In 1993 this was the first time in history the IRS had lost a case. This case was later mentioned in law books as an example for educating future attorneys.

(see page 60)

Chubby Checker and Rev. Jenkins in the Rev's home in Delaware, Ohio. Chubby, who popularized the "Twist" dance craze, was actually beaten in a "Twist Dance Contest" by the Reverend! This loyal friendship spans 40 years and together they have many fun and lasting memories.

(see pages 16 and 317)

June Buckingham is on a visit with the Rev while he shares his barber talents and cuts the hair of his fellow inmates. Inmates were not usually permitted to have scissors in their possession, but Rev. Jenkins was. This was the very shack where the alcohol bottles were hidden to frame the Rev as well.
(see page 364)

Rev. Jenkins performs a baptism complete with a fountain and his manmade pond at Spirit of Truth Church, South Carolina. This is the same pond where both Jesse Strickland and Coley Bryant were baptized.
(see page 355)

Rev. Leroy Jenkins' South Carolina mansion. When delivering newspapers as a boy he threw the newspaper on the lawn one day and was reprimanded by the owners who lived in this mansion. Young Leroy proceeded to say he would come back one day and buy this place and they would have to move! He did it!
(see page 15)

(1) Rev. Jenkins conducting the funeral services for his son, Scotty Jenkins, who was killed in a car accident. [Note: This is the crystal chandelier given to Rev. Jenkins by Mae West. This chandelier hung in the Spirit of Truth Church in Columbia, South Carolina.]
(2) School friends carry Scotty's casket to his final resting place.
(3) The crypt where Scotty said he wanted to be buried someday.
(see page 381)

THE SHAKEDOWN

The flurry of news in the press about thousands of Christians seeking the Rev. Jenkins' release must have been too much to bear for those who sought to keep him in prison. There was a real danger that South Carolina's Supreme Court would grant the appeal and a new trial—a fair trial— would surely free him.

A plot was hatched to discredit him, and the timing couldn't have been better.

JENKINS IN DUTCH OVER SCOTCH

Greenville News, September 18, 1980

COLUMBIA (UPI) - Convicted evangelist Leroy Jenkins has been transferred from a minimum-security prison facility because two half-filled bottles of Scotch whisky were found in a room he supervised, authorities said Wednesday.

Jenkins, serving a 12-year prison term for conspiracy to commit assault and arson, has been moved from Walden Correctional Institution, a facility for low-risk prisoners, to Kirkland Institution, a medium-maximum facility.

A spokesman for the Department of Corrections, Sam McCuen, said the two bottles of Scotch whisky were found on a routine spot check at Walden Monday.

McCuen said the liquor was found in a room to which Jenkins has the key. He said Jenkins, who is in charge of cleaning up the yard at Walden, supervises the building in which the liquor was discovered.

He said Jenkins is the "one who is blamed." He said Jenkins will appear at a disciplinary hearing within two weeks, and the panel could invoke a "whole range of things" as punishment.

McCuen said punishment could range from a loss of up to 18 months of "good time" to a transfer to a high-security institution such as the Central Correctional Institution.

In August 1979, the evangelist was moved from Kirkland to a minimum-security facility after he told authorities about a prison guard's offer to help him escape for $6.000. The guard was later sentenced to three years in prison.

Earlier this month, the Rev. Ralph Davis of California delivered to the South Carolina Supreme Court 8,000 petitions from people who think Jenkins should be given an early release from prison.

The petitioners, said Davis, believe that Jenkins has been punished far out of proportion to the nature of his crime.

Copyright © Greenville News

THE SHAKEDOWN

This latest news about the embattled evangelist again put him in headlines all across the nation.

While the Supreme Court was considering his appeal for a new trial, he was branded a drunk, with claims that "half-filled" bottles of scotch were found in his quarters.

The reverend's Greenwood attorney, Hugh Beasley, immediately demanded a hearing on the charges. Upon investigation, it was determined that the "half-filled" bottles of scotch were, in fact, empty except for a half-teaspoon of liquid in one of them apparently caused by condensation from the bottles having been hidden for so long. The labels were old and deteriorating. Obviously, someone had lied about the scotch.

The Rev. Jenkins was cleared of having anything to do with the bottles, and the charges brought against him were dismissed. Nevertheless, stories given to the press by the prison authorities lasted just long enough to spoil his chances for a new trial.

Most believed the shakedown had been engineered by Thomas Lescene. A former secretary to Jesse Strickland, Lescene had been overwhelmed by mail from the reverend's supporters. (see photo on page 266) Many of those who worked in the prison system felt prisoners should be punished in addition to being locked behind bars. The letters must have rankled Lescene. Now, he was assistant warden at Walden, where his attitude toward the Rev. Jenkins became obvious.

"Mr. Lescene didn't like any of the inmates," the Rev. Jenkins said later. "He thought he was better than all of us, and he wouldn't do a thing to help anybody if he could help it."

"One day I saw him going across the yard with that cocky walk of his, and I asked him if I could talk to him a minute.

"He said, 'Not now, I'm very busy.'

"I said, 'So am I, but you are supposed to talk to me when I am having a problem, and I am having one right now.'

"He said, 'I'm busy, I'll talk to you tomorrow.' I said, 'Forget it.' I knew that I was going to have trouble with him.

"Sure enough, one day they took some nine-year-old liquor bottles and put them up in the ceiling over a place in the toolshed where I was the only one that had a key. They had a shakedown and went right to that place in the toolshed and pulled out the bottles.

"They called me to the office, and Lescene slapped the cuffs on me and sent me away to lockup in maximum security and would not even tell me what they were arresting me for. He said, 'Get in that van, and shut up.'

"I turned around and looked him in the eye and said, 'Mr. Lescene, you're going to be sorry you ever did this,' as they shoved me into the van and took me away."

Even the most cursory observation by Lescene could have determined the bottles were empty and old, as the labels were rotting and peeling off. Why then was the news given to the press that the bottles were "half-filled"?

Along with the bottles, officials "discovered" a knife in the shed. Commissioner Leeke told the *Greenville News*, "It's not that he [Jenkins] was going to do anything with it, but we can't allow knives to be lying around a prison."

Actually, the rusty old knife had been hanging on the wall long before the Rev. Jenkins first set foot in the shed. AA trusty inmates—those who had proved themselves the most trustworthy and were given more privileges—used it to cut up cardboard boxes and make shelters or room dividers for themselves when they met with their wives in the shed. Prison officials knew this and allowed it.

Before the shakedown, the Rev. Jenkins had made every effort to secure "good time" to increase his chances for early release. He had taken on the hardest jobs at Walden, taking care of the grounds and manning the gas pumps with Coley Bryant.

The men at Walden had come to respect him and to come to him for counsel. None of this mattered, now.

As expected, in the midst of all the unfavorable publicity directed at the reverend, the South Carolina Supreme Court denied the Rev. Jenkins a new trial.

HIGH COURT REJECTS EVANGELIST'S APPEAL

Anderson Independent, September 27, 1980

COLUMBIA - Leroy Jenkins, the flamboyant Greenwood faith healer sent to prison last year for four conspiracy convictions, on Friday lost his appeal to the South Carolina Supreme Court.

Jenkins, who led a $3 million-per-year religious Association, had asked the high court to overturn his May 1979 conviction on two counts of conspiracy to commit assault and battery and two counts of conspiracy to commit arson.

He was accused of scheming to burn the homes of a highway patrolman and a Belton man, and of plotting to assault the same highway patrolman and a reporter for The Anderson Independent.

He was sentenced to 12 years in prison after his controversial trial.

There was no immediate word on whether Jenkins' current attorney, famed defense lawyer F. Lee Bailey, would appeal the Supreme Court's decision to the federal courts.

The Supreme Court's action was the second round of bad luck in as many weeks for the 46-year old former television evangelist, who has kept up contact with his remaining flock in Greenwood and Delaware, Ohio.

Last week, Jenkins, who had been described as a model prisoner, was charged with having liquor in an area he was responsible for supervising. And corrections officials said Thursday they also found a knife in Jenkins' area.

Jenkins' longtime personal secretary, June Buckingham, has said the faith healer has been exonerated of the liquor-related charges.

But Corrections Commissioner William Leeke has denied her claim, saying the issue is "still in the office of the assistant deputy commissioner" on appeal.

Jenkins was transferred from the minimum security Manning Correctional Institution last week after the prison disciplinary committee ruled he violated rules.

Leeke said the assistant commissioner "has told me in a casual conversation that he thinks at this point there might not be sufficient evidence concerning the allegation of possession of some form of liquor, but there has been no formal action taken at this point."

Before the liquor and knife charges, Jenkins had apparently obeyed the rules, and once helped catch a prison guard who allegedly offered to let him escape in exchange for money.

Followers of the evangelist had flooded Gov. Dick Riley's office with letters and phone calls asking for Jenkins' release. But Riley insisted he had no control over courts.

Also intervening on Jenkins' behalf was the National Ministers' Association, which submitted to the Supreme Court 8,000 signatures on petitions seeking his release.

The state's high court had refused to set bond for Jenkins after hearing arguments from representatives of the Attorney General's office, who said Jenkins is dangerous and might seek reprisals against witnesses in his trial.

THE TRUTH EMERGES

The press snapped up every morsel of information fed them by prison public relations personnel. Within a week after the South Carolina Supreme Court turned down the Rev. Jenkins' appeal, the truth about the liquor bottles finally emerged. Sadly, it was too late. The damage had been done.

The press, so eager to print the bad news, had once again passed up a prime opportunity to shine the light of day on the evasive answers and questionable behavior of some prison officials.

JENKINS CLEARED OF LIQUOR CHARGE

The State, October 4, 1980

A S.C. Department of Corrections disciplinary committee has cleared evangelist Leroy Jenkins of having contraband liquor in a room he supervised at a minimum-security prison.

But charges that Jenkins permitted a knife to be in a room he was in charge of still stand, according to Corrections Department spokesman, Sam McCuen.

The nearly empty liquor bottles, knife and other contraband were found in the room last month. He was transferred from the minimum-security Walden Correctional Institution to the Manning Correctional Institution after the discoveries.

As a result of the committee's decision on the knife, Jenkins will remain in the Manning prison and also loses three months of good behavior time that would have been knocked off his sentence.

McCuen said the committee decided Jenkins probably didn't know about the liquor because it had apparently been stuck in its hiding spot above some ceiling tiles for several years. The liquor content in the bottles was diluted, indicating it had aged considerably. The labels on the bottles also indicated they were several years old.

Copyright © The State

SOWING AND REAPING

Amazingly, on the same day, on the same page of the newspaper that ran the preceding article, there was another story about a top man in the Department of Corrections being arrested for drunken driving.

Many men serving time for the very same offense committed by the corrections official had a good laugh at the expense of the department, and Rev. Jenkins' staff sent out copies of the two adjacent articles, along with a letter to his followers:

> FRIENDS - SEE HOW GOD WORKS!! The Bible says, "Touch not my anointed and do my prophets no harm." After Rev. Jenkins was unfairly accused by the Department of Corrections, see what happened to ONE OF THEIR OWN!!
>
> We do not glory in [the official's] embarrassment, we pray for him, but thank God that He is just (and merciful).

CORRECTIONS OFFICIAL CHARGED WITH DUI

The State, October 4, 1980

Peter O'Boyle III

A deputy commissioner for the S.C. Department of Corrections, who will take office today as president of the S.C. Correctional Association, was charged Wednesday night with driving under the influence of alcohol.

Charles A. Leath, who heads the prison administration's operations department, was charged with DUI First Offense while in a state car.

Leath will be sworn in this morning as president of the 650-member Association made up of prison officials and others interested in criminal justice. The group has been meeting at the Carolina Inn in Columbia since Wednesday.

Leath was stopped after a motorist notified the Highway Patrol by citizens band radio that he saw a car moving erratically. The motorist said the car nearly hit the retaining wall on the westbound lane of Interstate 26 about 10:30 p.m.

Patrolman H.L. Cumbie heard the report and stopped the state vehicle driven by Leath. Leath was arrested and given a Breathalyzer test, which registered .23 and was then charged with DUI.

A Breathalyzer reading of .1 is considered evidence of intoxication under South Carolina law.

"HOME" AGAIN

Following the Rev. Jenkins' exoneration, fifty-five Walden inmates petitioned the Department of Corrections for the Rev. Jenkins' return. Finally, he was restored to his position as an AA trusty at Walden Farm. He told his church about his experience:

> After they charged me with contraband, I fought it, and went as high as I could go. I took it to [Department of Corrections Commissioner] Mr. Leeke, and the board, and I won.
>
> I also insisted on going back to the same place I had come from.
>
> Once again I saw Mr. Lescene going across the yard, and once again I asked to talk to him. I said, "Come here, and this time you are going to talk to me. If I have to wrestle you to the ground, you are going to talk to me!"
>
> He said, "Well, what do you want?"
>
> I said, "You remember what you did to me? You had me handcuffed and locked up on that trumped-up liquor charge, and SLED found that the residue in the bottles was nine years old. You set me back nine months with that charge."
>
> I said, "I had been doing everything right so I could get out of here early. Furthermore, now they are going to do the same thing to you! They are going to handcuff you and lock you up.
>
> "You are going to go home one night and go crazy, and beat the bathroom door down and try to kill your wife. And they are going to lock you up."
>
> [Speaking to the members of his congregation at Holy Hill Cathedral, the Rev. Jenkins marveled.] Can you believe that God told me all that?

So he went home one night, tore the door off the bathroom with a hatchet and tried to kill his wife. The police came and handcuffed him and locked him up - just exactly like I told him they would do.

His wife divorced him, and came to work in my office.

One day the phone rang [at the Association office] and Mr. Lescene's wife answered the phone. Mr. Lescene could not believe it was her.

He said he wanted to talk to Rev. Jenkins. I got on the phone and he said, "I want to ask your forgiveness for what I did to you. Everything happened to me exactly the way you told me and you have made a believer out of me."

He cried, too.

I said, "What I was going to tell you that day could have helped you avoid all this. Mr. Lescsene, the Bible says touch not my anointed and do my prophets no harm. In the rest of your days at the penitentiary, don't do anybody wrong, or it will come back on you."

"Mr. Lescene had made his peace with me and with God, and he was restored to his job shortly after that," I said.

"You don't walk on God's people to depress them and keep them from doing what God wants. The gift I have is supernatural and the same gift Jesus had.

"Greater works than these will you do, because I go to the Father.

"You can't stop it, and I'm not trying to. I know I am the most different person you know, because I listen to God, and do things His way.

"I have tried to change to please people, but the Lord said to me, 'If you are satisfying me, you don't have to worry about anybody else. You have done well with what you had to work with. I promise you a place in heaven that you can't stop me from giving you.'"

FRIENDS INDEED

The Rev. Jenkins could not have survived his prison experience without the help of friends, men who were willing to go out on a limb for him, to believe in him when no one else did, and to cover his back.

Their shared experiences would forge bonds that endure to this day. The following are the stories of two of these men, each on opposite sides of the law.

JESSE STRICKLAND—THEY CALLED HIM "BOSS"

Jesse Strickland and the Rev. Jenkins had a lot in common. Both were born without a break. And both had a tendency to write their own rules, a trait that frequently got them into tangles with bureaucrats. (see photo on page 262)

Old-timers still talk about Jesse Strickland in South Carolina's prisons. One of the most powerful men in the system, Strickland's rise from guard to warden to deputy commissioner in charge of the state's fourteen institutions became a legend of sorts.

Stories, some apocryphal, tell of a handsome, swaggering, gun-toting warden who single-handedly dispersed rioting mobs, who threw the rule book out the window, who knew his inmates by name, and who walked among them fearlessly. The stories depict a man who wielded the power of the Almighty and whose personal motto—"Prisoners should be treated like human beings"—gained him the loyalty of scorned and forgotten men.

His efforts on behalf of inmates won him many awards, among them, a national honor presented by the Jaycees for "outstanding contributions toward improving and modernizing corrections." The Department of Corrections even created an award in Strickland's honor. The Jesse W. Strickland Memorial Award was given first to Strickland in 1982 and every year thereafter to an outstanding corrections employee.

Born in the South Carolina Lowcountry, Strickland grew up among people whose homesteads were devoted to two occupations: tobacco farming or bootlegging. His daddy, Dayton Strickland, practiced both.

As a child, he remembers living in dread that his soft-spoken, smiling father—known as Mr. Dayton—might one day be arrested or even killed while tending his still deep in the woods. It was an all-too-common occurrence in those days.

His dark fantasy nearly came true years later when federal agents swarmed over the farm, demolished the still, and took Mr. Dayton away to serve a year in the federal penitentiary in Tallahassee, Florida.

Stung by small-town gossip, the seventeen-year-old dropped out of school and joined the army. While serving in Japan, he received another shock. His closest friend, a young black man, was executed in the electric chair after having been convicted of an ax murder in the South Carolina Lowcountry town of Orangeburg.

From these two incidents, Strickland developed a philosophy that was reflected in his career: "Crime is no respecter of persons."

LOCAL HERO

Strickland studied sociology at the University of South Carolina in Columbia and worked as a police officer to supplement his income. One Saturday night, he was called from his usual beat in the Combat Zone, a downtown district so named for its weekend influx of rowdy soldiers from nearby Fort Jackson. He was told to rush to the Blossom Street Bridge where a man was threatening to jump into the rushing Congaree River below.

The man jumped, and Strickland took the plunge as well, pausing only to drop his belt and gun on the way. The sensational feat made headlines, and the new warden at the Central Correctional Institute hired him on as a guard. CCI was the very same prison in which his childhood friend had been executed a few years earlier.

His duties consisted of "walking the clock"—patrolling the cell-block areas and inserting keys into clocks stationed at checkpoints along the patrol route. He also participated in shakedowns, where his only instruction was to see that "nothin' comes in and nothin' goes out."

CCI at that time was *the* state penitentiary, a hundred-year-old collection of brick-and-granite buildings on the city's back side and bordered by a river. The dreary yard was enclosed by double chain-link fences and patrolled by guard dogs. Towers manned by shotgun-toting guards surrounded the stockade. (see photo on page 264)

Strickland was issued a uniform and a billy club, which he promptly handed back, for fear it would be taken from him and used against him. Only the tower guards carried guns. His first week in prison was terrifying. The main prison rose up in five tiers called Cell Block One. It was connected to the administration building and cafeteria by a tunnel that looked to Strickland like it was five miles long. He had to walk that tunnel every day.

Strickland had seen police brutality as a patrolman. "Those sadistic cops thought you really had to hit people with that nightstick," he says. Still, he was not prepared for the brutal kicking that he saw a captain deliver to an inmate sitting in that tunnel when he failed to stand and doff his hat to the captain.

"If I could have found my way out, I would have left right then," he says.

He stayed, and his career soared. He was soon promoted to the position of deputy warden of Wateree River Correctional Institution, where he remembers spending most of his time running bloodhounds through the dense Lowcountry underbrush and black-water swamps in search of escapees.

"YOU TALK TO 'EM, BOSS— I'LL HOLD THE TABLE"

Within five years, he returned to CCI as the state's youngest prison warden. Times had changed. The emphasis was on reform, and the former warden had installed a sign over the door, "Prison is a highway—not a dead end."

Strickland took that admonition literally, initiating reforms, breaking rules, and offending some officials who thought he was too "pro-inmate."

While he was at CCI, he helped establish the work-release program, which offered AA trusties to secure jobs outside the prison and return at night, preparing them for gainful employment when they were paroled.

"Where could a man get a job makin' license tags?" he scoffs.

The "hole"—a small cell located beneath the maximum-security building where a recalcitrant prisoner could spend up to twenty-eight days with nothing but a mattress and a full meal every third day—was done away with.

He ordered a wall torn down in the cafeteria that separated blacks from whites. "I figured if they could work together, they could eat together," he says.

"The whites still ate on one side, and the blacks the other," Strickland says with a laugh. But there were no riots.

He started baseball and boxing teams in the prison and recruited the best musicians to play in prison bands. On occasion, he could be found with one of the bands, strumming a six-string guitar and singing the Merle Haggard favorite "Today I Started Loving You Again."

Strickland had absolute control over the day-to-day lives of more than 1,500 inmates. Perhaps his greatest power came through prisoner classification—determining where inmates would live, whether they could leave the prison grounds and whether their time would be shortened or lengthened.

This he did with great aplomb, often circumventing department policy. One official remarked, "There's the Department of Corrections classification system and Jesse Strickland's classification system."

Former assistants remember the warden saying, "Forget the paperwork, get down in the yard, and learn those inmates."

The yard is where Strickland could be found, walking among the inmates, discussing problems, listening to complaints, sniffing the air for trouble, cultivating informants.

They never got too familiar, calling him "Mr." or "Warden." Mostly they called him "Boss."

He learned who needed to be watched, who could be relied on for information, who would back him up when trouble came. Once, he waded into a fight in the cafeteria. When he jumped up on a table to talk to the men, the table started to fall. A hulking, much-feared prisoner steadied it and said, "You talk to 'em, Boss, I'll hold the table."

Another time he faced a mob of enraged inmates in the tunnel. The guards had fled in panic. Standing there, hands on hips, he ordered them to lay down their weapons—chair legs, saws, chains, knives fashioned from sheet metal used in the shops—and after a tense moment or two, the angry men complied.

"I was hard on them when I had to be," Strickland says. "You couldn't be wishy-washy."

"I DON'T TALK TO A MAN IN CHAINS"

Having written the state's death penalty, he submits, "For some crimes, society ought to be rid of a fella." Yet if a man asked Strickland for a break, more often than not, he got it.

Take the case of Zeb Osborne. An eleven-year veteran of the federal prisons, including Alcatraz, he had a reputation as being "as dangerous as a rattlesnake." He was in CCI for killing a man during a robbery.

"Life didn't mean anything to me," Osborne said later when asked to reflect on his experiences. "I once killed another inmate, and they gave me shock treatments and drug therapy for antisocial behavior."

At CCI, he became involved in drugs and other unsavory activities. Strickland sent him to solitary confinement more than once. "[Strickland] showed you where the tire hit the road," Osborne says.

During one of these lonely interludes, Osborne experienced a religious conversion and requested an interview with the warden.

Strickland agreed to see him, and he was brought in to the office, shackled hand and foot. The warden glared at the guards and said, "I don't talk to a man in chains." The chains were promptly removed.

"That was a trust that had never been shown me," Osborne said later. Jesse listened to the story of his conversion, and his desire to mend his ways. Thereafter he watched the small, wiry prisoner whose almond eyes and high cheekbones reflected his Cherokee blood, whose nose was flattened and scarred from having been bitten off in a fight with an inmate.

Strickland decided Osborne meant what he said and arranged for him to attend classes at Erskine Theological Seminary. "It was probably illegal," Strickland admits.

The gamble with Osborne paid off. The once-incorrigible prisoner earned a master of divinity degree, graduating at the head of his class. He dedicated his life to the community as chaplain of

Christian Prison Ministries and could often be seen in the Rev. Jenkins' crusades, escorting other prisoners to the meetings.

"I'VE BEEN IN THE JAIL HOUSE LONG ENOUGH"

As deputy commissioner, Strickland was at one time in charge of all South Carolina prison operations. "There were people over him in name," said one official, "but he ran the institutions."

A former inmate echoed the sentiment of many of the prisoners.

"He was a man's man. Most of them [officials] don't have the guts to walk down in the yard. He did, and he was not afraid to be human. If you went to him with a problem, he would help you. If you were wrong, he would tell you so. You have to be down to understand, and I was down."

The South Carolina prison system has changed considerably since a nervous, idealistic young guard walked the clock. CCI has been torn down. Inmate councils, such as the one the Rev. Jenkins headed up, served as a way for inmates to voice their complaints.

At the same time, the Department of Corrections has become more bureaucratic. "Policies have replaced personalities," says one former inmate. "They're [the officials] like IBM executives running around, saying, 'Take a memo.'"

Some prisoners say they have never even seen their warden. There is no longer room for individualists such as Strickland, whose tenure ended after butting heads with the prison system once too often.

"I've been in the jailhouse long enough," he says. "The system outgrew me." But he was there with understanding and compassion when the Rev. Jenkins needed him.

Strickland now lives in the idyllic Lowcountry of South Carolina where he grew up. But among many prisoners a memory lingers. "The old-timers, they remember Jesse Strickland," one says. "They knew the man they called the Boss, and they know they've lost a friend."

COLEY BRYANT'S STORY

First of all, his name wasn't really Coley, but Robert. His brother's name was Coley, and how he acquired his brother's name is a story in itself.

Almost everything in Bryant's life seems more like fiction than truth, even though much of it is documented. As for the rest, the reader will just have to take it on faith.

Jailed for the crime of murder, Bryant figured the more men he had sent to their reward, the more he would be feared by his fellow inmates. As the body count grew, so did his reputation.

Nobody fooled around with Bryant. His word was law in the most infamous prison in the state of South Carolina, the forbidding Central Correctional Institute. Sprawled along the river near downtown Columbia, the old prison's high walls, guard towers, and closely barred windows presented a dismal sight to passersby.

Housed there were the most serious offenders, those the system decided had little or no chance for rehabilitation. Coley Bryant was one of these men. For the sake of authenticity, the following story is repeated exactly as he told it. It is hoped the reader will forgive any offensive details, including references to race.

MURDER IN THE PINEY WOODS

I was born in nineteen-ought-nine on a farm in Trenton, South Carolina. I loved my mamma. She was a good woman. Never had much to work with, but she did the best she could with us boys. I got her old Bible right here with me today.

I was the youngest, but as soon as I got my growth, about sixteen or seventeen, I let my daddy and brothers know that I wasn't goin' to let them treat Mamma bad while I was around.

"You do that once more, and I'll blow you all away," I said the last time they come in from huntin' and rousted her out of bed in the middle of the night to cook for 'em. I had a 30/30, and I knew how to use it.

They didn't do that again whiles I was around, I can tell you that.

But you want to know how I got in this prison. Well, honey, let me tell you how it happened.

One day some young girls was coming home from a country school, Mt. Zion it was, way back in the woods outside of Edgefield, South Carolina.

These black sawmillers attacked 'em and stripped their clothes off 'em. They was white girls. There were thirteen black men in the group, and they tore their clothes off.

Mr. Hit's daughter was in the group. He was one of my neighbors, so I went with him down to Sheriff Howard's office.

I told him, "Now listen, get out there and do somethin' about it." I said, "If they attack one of mine, I ain't goin' to come back and ask you to do somethin', I'm goin' to do it myself."

I told the sheriff and his deputy, Jones, "Now listen, if they attack one of mine, that's the last thing they'll do on this earth."

Well, they never did nothin' about it.

Shortly after that, on a Friday afternoon, I was at the house about a hundred yards from the old well. I heard this kid screamin' and yell, "Daddy!"

I went runnin' down there, and my little seven-year-old girl was lyin' on the ground, bloody. I assumed she was dead.

Her name was Connie. I called her Little Connie. So I took off my white shirt, and I wrapped it around her.

She said, "Daddy, I hurt all over!"

I turned to them black bastards and said, "Which one of you rats did this?"

They said, "Wouldn't you like to know?"

I said, "I will know, if you'll wait a minute."

So I went back to the house and got a Winchester rifle. It was automatic. I said, "Now *you'll* know!" And I started shooting, and I didn't stop shooting 'til all thirteen of them blacks went down.

My poor girl was lyin' there in a pool of blood, and she'd been raped.

That night the law came out there—Deputy Jones and Sheriff Howard. I heard Deputy Jones say, "Let's get out of here and let that man alone. That man will kill you, now. You should have come out here before, and this wouldn't have happened."

I had switched rifles, and I had a 30/30.

Sheriff Howard said, "Come on, Robert [Coley's given name], you know we got to take you in. We are goin' to get you if we have to kill you."

I said, "Well, I've got news for you. I've got somethin' to shoot with too."

The sheriff was standing behind the car. He was drivin' an old high-wheel blue Buick. His leg was all I could get a view of. I didn't get a chance to see which of 'em fired at me, but him or Jones—one of 'em—fired at me.

I fired back and busted the sheriff's knee, and he bled to death before they could get him to the doctor.

Then I shot Jones in the right shoulder, and that big bullet from my 30/30 took his arm apart. He died that night too.

They had beat her up. She was about a quarter of a mile from the house when they beat her up and raped her.

When I got to where she was, I picked her up in my arms and wrapped her in my white shirt and took her back to the house and laid her on the porch.

I called a friend of mine, London Green, to take her to the hospital, but it didn't do no good. She had done died.

I stayed around until after Connie's funeral. My aunt came from California and got the other two girls and took them back with her, 'cause she knowed there was goin' to be plenty of trouble.

See, my wife died when Connie was born. She was the baby. She's buried at Mt. Zion church out on Highway 25 about twenty-five miles this side of Augusta, Georgia. I named her Connie after Connie Francis.

"ANY TIME YOU SEND SOMEBODY AFTER ME, YOU SEND THE UNDERTAKER TO BRING 'EM BACK"

After the funeral, the law began hounding me, so I went to dodging. Dodging is what people call it to keep from being picked up.

One of [the dead men's] grandmother's was Savannah Lindsey, and she showed kindness to me. She said, "They never should have done that. I raised my boy better than that. They should have known if they bothered a man's children that man would hurt 'em."

I heard tell that she said, "That's a good man. He don't bother nothin'. You know he lent us money to run the farm on several times."

It wasn't too long before J. Dewey Oxner, the judge, put a blanket warrant on my head, for dead or alive.

I told them that works two ways. I said, "From now on, any time you send somebody after me, you send the undertaker to bring 'em back, 'cause somebody ain't comin' back."

But they sent a posse after me. They was about thirty of 'em in the posse. I run some of 'em down in the quicksand down there, so some of 'em backed off.

Tricked 'em, I did. I threw my coat over in the shallow water and in the quicksand, which was white. I just ran around and jumped over on the other side. They come runnin' in after me.

That pond of water was 'bout as big as a baptizin' hole, about thirty-five to forty feet.

They thought I had run through the water, see, but I had run around the other side and jumped over. Some of them posses went down in the quicksand. They was a bunch of 'em that got in it, but just two or three of 'em went out of sight.

Yeah, that quicksand just swallered 'em up.

I fired a couple of warnin' shots from the other side of the pond and put a bullet through one of 'ems hat, and the rest of 'em turned and went back.

They seen they wasn't goin' to make any headway with me. Not one. Yeah, that was on John Henry Mealing's property.

SLEEPING IN THE GRAVEYARD

I kept on runnin' from the law for about two years until they caught up with me. I was a "spook" in the Edgefield cemetery for about a year.

My muvver died in 1936, and I used to slip in there and spend the night. I lay my head on the mound of dirt where she was buried at. I would sleep there, because I knew nobody would come in there.

Yeah, I stayed in that cemetery for about a year. I warn't afraid. I figured them that had gone to hell couldn't come back, and I figured them that had gone to Heaven didn't want to, so I slept just as peaceful as a lamb at my muvver's grave.

I stayed there no matter what the weather was. If it rained, it rained. It didn't make no difference. I had a part of an old canvas tent I slept in. You know, it'll keep you dry.

John Delawter give me the tent. I saw some of 'em like it down by the Savannah River, down by what they call the Black Water.

You know what I put on my momma's tombstone? "Jesus took the sunshine out of our home."

She died while I was on the dodge. I called the sheriff in Edgefield and told him, "I am comin' to my muvver's funeral in Lamar."

And I said, "Better not nobody that looks like lawmen be there. I will be there tomorrow. I'll be lookin' for bear."

See, I had all the guns and ammunition I needed. I got it at Hugh Gardner's country store. He give me all I wanted.

I had to be keerful, 'cause I didn't want any of my friends to get in trouble for hidin' a fugitive. So I didn't stay with any of 'em, but they give me food every day.

Some of the guards were fool enough to get some dogs and come down there and try to have 'em run me. I stayed on a stump and taken my rifle and killed everyone of them dogs.

Well, I finally give myself up. About two years after my muvver died. My sisters kept telling me, "They ain't goin' to be nothin' to it." So I went and give myself up.

I surrendered to Lonnie Robinson; he was the sheriff that had been elected in Aiken County. I called him and told him to meet me at four o'clock in Graniteville, South Carolina.

I said, "You come alone too. Don't bring nobody with you, because," I said, "I ain't giving nobody up my gun until we get to the jailhouse."

I was carrying a rifle, a sawed-off shotgun and two German Luger pistols and a .38 pistol. To tell you the truth, I was a walking army.

At four o'clock, I went up there, and people was hid all around behind cars, and some come runnin' out and the sheriff told 'em, he said, "Back up." He said, "He ain't unarmed."

He said, "I'm backin' him up. He called me and give himself up to me. Any of you try to run up and try to fire a shot, I am goin' to open with my gun too."

The trial was in Aiken County. They give me three life sentences and twenty-five years. It took the jury about four and one half hours. I got up and started fightin' in the courtroom and slapped the solicitor over the table.

That was D. D. Carter of Bamberg, South Carolina. See, the judge had told him one time not to say anything to me. He smarted off to me when I wanted to talk to my lawyer. The judge told him, "Don't say no more to that man."

I said, "Well, Your Honor, if he points his finger at me again," I said, "you may not stop him." But I said, "It is one thing for sure,

I will!" So when he run over and tried to grab me and pointed his finger at me, that is when I laid it on 'im.

They had to give a thirty-minute recess then to get the courtroom quietened down.

I hired them attorneys to represent me. I might as well have tied the money to a hog's leg and hollered "suie"; it would have done just as good.

See, they sold me out. Money passed under the table.

HOW COLEY GOT HIS BROTHER'S NAME

So I served my time at CCI, until they made a mistake and let me out. That was in 1940.

See, they come to let my brother out; his time was up. My brother's name was Coley, and I was Robert Blease Bryant.

They had us lined up, and they called for Coley Bryant. I looked around, and Coley wasn't anywhere in sight, so I stepped up and took the papers. Said I was Coley, and the fools believed me.

I hadn't been gone over half an hour when they found out they had made a mistake, but they couldn't find the way I went.

I outfoxed 'em. I went to the Farmer's Market on Huger Street, and there was a truck parked. I asked the man, "What about giving me a lift? I ain't got but ten dollars, because they give that to you."

He said, "Crawl on that haystack back there in back."

When they found out they had made a mistake, they called all the bus stations and all the railroad stations, but I had done gone.

The truck was goin' to Florida, an' I had a nephew worked on the police force there, and he give me two .38s. That was John Moore give me them guns.

So I caught another ride and went to Alabama on a truck—an old oil tanker. I went to see my first cousin Bear Bryant, and he give me enough money to go to California.

Bear was a football coach at Alabama. He was my daddy's brother's son. When I told him what happened, he said, "Well, don't hang around here, because they will be hot after you. Do you need some money?"

So he give me $750, and I went on to California.

See, he was tied up with this football thing, you know, and the football people didn't want him being associated with any known criminal. I don't blame him. I can understand his views.

I stayed on the dodge a couple of years in California and round about. Then I come home to see my muvver's grave. You know how it is.

I lived in the caves down there. There's lots of 'em, and folks don't come around the Black Water. Think it full of haints.

Folks come down to the Black Water, they're never seen again. They's no bottom to that hole. Didn't scare me none.

One day the sheriff told my friends if I give myself up, it would go easy on me, so I got tired of runnin', and I did it.

They never caught me—no, sir, I give myself up. Got tired of runnin', that's all.

FREE, INDEED

How did I meet Rev. Jenkins? Well, see, he come down to the gas station where I was workin'. I knowed him from TV. First time I saw him, I knowed he was a man of God. You know you feel it right here, in your heart.

I wasn't a Christian then, but see, when that feeling comes in, it's real. I used to feel that with my muvver. When Leroy baptized me, I'll never forget how I felt. I done a lot in my life, but I know the power when I feel it.

He come down to the gas station that first day they brought him to Walden. He said, "They told me it was off limits, and I couldn't come down here."

I said, "You can come down here any time you want to, and nobody's goin' to bother you."[91]

He said, "From what I hear about you, I don't believe they'll bother me, either."

See, before I got baptized, I was rough. I carried a pocketknife all the time, called it the Red Dragon. Had a picture on either side of the handle of a dragon. I'd use it too, and everybody knew it.

They made it hard on Rev, tried to keep June from comin' into the gas station, and lots of other things. See, she would come and bring him lunch and cakes and things.

One day that redhead lady guard comes down and says, "Time's up."

June says, "I will go when Coley feels better." See, I was sick out there.

"Well, let me tell you one thing," I said. "You've got diamonds that shine better goin' away from here than they do comin' down here," I said. "Get the hell out of here."

See, I didn't take nothin' from nobody. I let Rev have his visitors down here at the gas station. Jim Whittington,[92] he come, and we had a good time, playin' and singin'. I tell you we had a good time. They was fine people, Rev's friends.

They wasn't ever goin' to let me out of that joint, but Jesse[93] and Rev, they talked it up to the Man. They said, "Now look here, Coley done enough time, let him go." So they let me out.

I got this little trailer here, out in the woods, and I help these folks out, live here near me. They looks after me, cooks for me sometimes.

---

[91]   This account of the meeting between Bryant and the Rev. Jenkins varies considerably from the reverend's recollections. See chapter "Closer To The Road."

[92]   A North Carolina evangelist who came to visit the Rev. Jenkins while he was in prison.

[93]   Deputy [prison] Commissioner Jesse Strickland.

June comes out and takes me to church. Fine church there in Columbia. Rev's church. I got it made.

Took me to the hospital couple months ago. Doctor said, "When you go on that operating table, you ain't goin' to make it." They said to me, "What undertaker you want to have your remains?"

I said, "I got a lot of good friends prayin' for me." And I said, "I got the Lord on my side. I'm seventy-four years old. I'll be around to see the next seventy-four. I don't want no undertaker. If you want one, you get him, but I don't need him."

When I got up from that hospital bed, June picked me up and said, "Coley, you'll be around for a while yet."

Yeah, I aint' ready to cash in yet.

On May 25, 1983, just two months later, Robert "Coley" Bryant died of a cerebral hemorrhage.

"AFTER FORTY-THREE YEARS YOU SET HIM FREE"

None of Bryant's kin claimed his body, so the Rev. Jenkins paid for the finest funeral anyone could have. A silver-gray casket covered with flowers held Bryant's earthly remains and stood in honor on the platform of the reverend's church in Columbia.

The Rev. Jim Whittington assisted his friend in the service before a packed church as they said their last good-bye to one who loved them so.

"I never before preached a funeral," said the Rev. Jenkins. "But I owe this one to Coley.

"I don't know how to preach death. I preach love, but today we are here to honor a man who showed me love in prison, where he became one of my dearest friends.

"Walden was no Boy Scout camp. He watched over me and made sure I was safe and that I had what I needed. Coley once said to me, 'You are the only man that I ever told that I love.' I believe that.

"'If anybody ever bothers you, I'll kill them,' Coley said. I believe he would have done that too.

"He was a man who held my attention. I watched him change from a cursing, knife-toting man to a humble, smiling Christian.

"I thank God I had something to do with that.

"I remember I told him once, 'When I get out of here, I am going to have a church, and you are going to come.'

"Know what he said? He said, 'You will never catch me going to church.' That's what he said.

"But when I opened the church on Marley Drive,[94] Coley Bryant was one of the very first ones there. And he popped up to testify every time.

"I'm going to miss Coley Bryant. He was like my own father, and I'm going to miss him.

"He's in a place now he won't ever have to worry about another chain or shackle, where he will get his next meal, or who his friends are, because he is right up there where I knew he would wind up.

"This body here is not Coley Bryant. Coley Bryant is with God."

The funeral cortege, led by several limousines, wound slowly to Lexington cemetery, and there, close to the piney woods, he was laid to rest.

"God, we thank you for the memory of Coley Bryant," said the Rev. Jenkins. "He did his time, and he paid his debts. He did what you told him to do and got baptized. After forty-three years, you set him free. Amen."

---

[94]   While on work release, the Rev. Jenkins bought an old school on the outskirts of Columbia and converted it to the Spirit of Truth Church.

THE GREENWOOD
FIRESTORM CONTINUES

Spring 1981 found the Rev. Jenkins back in court, but this time he wasn't the defendant. He was suing the Aetna Insurance Company to try to force them to pay for personal items lost in the fire at his home in 1978.

It had taken more than a year to gather together the proof of claim the insurance company required. Many of the lost items were irreplaceable antiques, and it was difficult to arrive at an acceptable estimate of their value. A prominent antique dealer and auctioneer, who had visited the Calhoun Street home before the fire, testified as to the value of the furnishings, china, glassware, and chandeliers.

The Rev. Jenkins' conviction on charges of conspiring to commit arson had given the insurance company a way to avoid paying. They simply claimed that the reverend was guilty of setting the fire.

Testimony proved that at the time of the fire, the Rev. Jenkins was at a Greenwood Braves baseball game giving the invocation and throwing out the first ball in full sight of hundreds of fans.

WITNESSES SAY MAN THREATENED TO BURN JENKINS' HOME

Greenville News, April 23, 1981

Duncan Mansfield

GREENWOOD—*A Greenwood policeman and a gasoline station operator testified Wednesday that a Greenwood man threatened to kill Evangelist Leroy Jenkins and burn his house just days before Jenkins' house was destroyed by fire.*

The testimony came in the third day of a jury trial in Greenwood civil court about an $86,250 insurance claim Jenkins filed to collect from Aetna Insurance and Casualty Co.

The insurance company has refused payment, contending that Jenkins was involved in setting the April 29, 1978 fire that destroyed his 322 Calhoun Ave. home in Greenwood.

"I did not pay anyone to do it," Jenkins testified. "If anything, I paid people to prevent it from happening."

The evangelist said he hired five bodyguards in April of 1978 to protect him at crusades and in his Greenwood home.

Two bodyguards were at a minor league baseball game in Greenwood when the fire started at about 7 p.m., the evangelist testified. No one was at the house at the time of the fire.

As Jenkins' last witnesses, Greenwood Police Captain Ulysses Scott, and local gasoline station operator Clarence Owensby, testified about the alleged threats against Jenkins made by a man identified as Ernie Proctor.

Proctor has not been subpoenaed in the case because his residence is unknown, attorneys for Aetna said.

Shortly before Jenkins' Greenwood home burned, Proctor was placed on a bus and sent out of town by order of City Judge Ted Wyndham for repeatedly threatening Jenkins, Scott testified Wednesday.

While waiting for the bus, Scott recounted Proctor saying, "He was going to get Reverend Leroy Jenkins."

"I'm going to get him if it's the last thing I do," Scott recalled Proctor saying.

Owensby, who runs the Henderson Gulf Service Station next door to the bus station, testified he also heard Proctor's threats.

"I'm going to burn that house down and kill Leroy Jenkins," Owensby recalled Proctor saying.

COMMON SENSE PREVAILS

Two days later, Judge Francis Nicholson declared a mistrial because the jury panel was deadlocked 11-1 in favor of the reverend, and further deliberations were deemed fruitless.

In a subsequent trial held later that year, the jury didn't buy the accusations by Aetna and their attorneys that the Rev. Jenkins had anything to do with the fire in his home. They ignored sworn testimony by AFT agent Bruce Mirkin, who had successfully testified against the reverend in the trial that sent him to prison. The Rev. Jenkins' attorney, Hugh Beasley, asked the jury to disregard the fact that the reverend was serving a 12-year sentence for conspiracy to commit arson and assault.

"He's now paying that debt to society and don't let him go back down there, (to the Department of Corrections) and say there is no justice in Greenwood," Beasley said.

Beasley characterized Mirkin as a "trained liar." Apparently, the jury agreed.

On Oct. 1, 1981, they awarded the Rev. Jenkins $75,000.

Copyright © Greenville News

WORK RELEASE: HALFWAY HOME

"My Life Has Been Blessed by Knowing Leroy Jenkins"

Campbell Pre-release Center stood just across the field from Walden Farm, where the Rev. Jenkins was serving out his sentence. But it was much, much closer to home.

Inmates who lived at Campbell had real jobs in the community. They left the prison each day to go to work and then came back each night.

The Rev. Jenkins had done well at Walden and in June 1981; after more than two years behind bars, he earned a transfer to Campbell. Inmates and officers alike were happy to see him take another step toward freedom, though many were sorry to see him go.

Corrections Officer Elly Manning, wrote the following:

There has been a remarkable improvement in the landscaping and grounds due to the work and talent of Reverend Jenkins, who puts in long hours of volunteer work into making Walden a nicer and more beautiful place to be. For inmates and officers alike this has been a morale booster. (see photo on page 273)

Speaking for myself, my life has been blessed by knowing Leroy Jenkins. Reverend Jenkins has shown much-needed concern to me and to the inmates, and that I can certainly appreciate.

Corrections Officer Colene Thomas wrote the following:

I had occasion to supervise Leroy Jenkins on a day-to-day basis. He showed eagerness to help his fellow inmates. He understood their problems and tried to help them through reading the Bible and praying with them.

"Jenkins is always helping other inmates at the institution who have problems," another officer wrote. "His background in the ministry has benefited the institution. Many inmates go to him for advice about personal problems."

Corrections Officer Jerry Brody wrote the following: "I have found that there is one inmate who has the attention of all other inmates. This man has influenced inmates and officers alike to do their best."

A supervisor on the second shift, Richard Hefner, who was retired from the US Air Force after twenty-one years of service, wrote the most telling letter:

Prior to the arrival of Rev. Jenkins, Walden was drab and the grounds were unkempt. Shortly after his arrival, Rev. Jenkins was put in charge of the yard detail, and things began to happen immediately.

Rev. Jenkins, of his own volition, acquired shrubbery and placed it strategically in the most advantageous locations, which enhanced and beautified Walden's grounds. As long as Rev. Jenkins was in charge of the yard detail, the favorable comments continued to flow from visitors to the institution as well as employees who appreciated his efforts.

Rev. Jenkins, who took a personal interest in his work, would spend from 12 to 15 hours a day laboring in the hot sun, and long after dark. During my entire service career, and since then, I have never witnessed any person who strived so hard to make things better for his fellow men.

After being taken from the yard detail, Rev. Jenkins was assigned to work at the service station at Walden and immediately things began to happen. He cleaned and painted the inside of the gas station and made a show place of a cluttered and greasy service building.

Rev. Jenkins is a most competent individual who continually strives to improve and enhance the image of his surroundings. He is an acute and knowledgeable individual who is a credit to himself and his ministry. His behavior has been of the highest caliber.

"KEEP HIM UNDER YOUR THUMB"

Campbell's Warden, Olin Turner, found himself between a rock and a hard place. Jesse Strickland had asked him to keep a watchful eye on his friend, the Rev. Jenkins.

"He is in your custody, Olin, even though he should never have been in prison," Strickland told him. "Treat him right, and you'll never have any trouble out of him. Remember, he is a fine person, and he is my friend," Strickland said.

Turner received a far different order from another prison official.

"Olin, the "powers-that-be" don't want this man to have any more privileges than he has to have. The media will be on top of you; be sure to keep him under your thumb," the official warned. "It will be your neck if you let him get away with anything."

Turner's piercing, blue eyes scanned his newest prisoner.

"Rev. Jenkins, you will be assigned to securing supplies for the commissary, keeping inventory, and distributing what is needed," the white-haired warden said. "I hope that you do well here."

"Your biggest challenge here is winning over Assistant Superintendent Boyd Roberts," Turner said. "The first thing you better do is go see him."

A BELIEVER

Roberts was seated at his desk when the Rev. Jenkins found him. Leaning back in his chair, he regarded the notorious evangelist.

The reverend's heart beat faster as he met Roberts' steady gaze. The assistant superintendent was in charge of inmates' comings and goings. He was known as a strict disciplinarian, even a tyrant. Everyone agreed he would be the most formidable hurdle the reverend would face.

"Well, Rev. Jenkins, what can I do for you?" Roberts said.

"Mr. Roberts, I'm glad to meet you," the reverend said. "I've heard you are a fair man. You won't have any trouble with me. All I want is to be treated with respect as a human being. I promise you I'll do the best I can, and I mean to be a blessing to this place," he said.

The reverend noticed four Bibles piled on the desk next to four ashtrays, overflowing with cigarette butts.

"You must be a Christian," he said, looking meaningfully at the cigarettes.

"Yes, son, I've been saved forty years," Roberts confided. "The only thing I haven't been able to give up is these coffin nails. It's the pressure of the job, you know," he said.

Despite the dire warnings about Boyd Roberts, their love of the Lord led these two men to an enduring friendship. Roberts became a true believer in the ministry.

Shortly after they met, he asked the Rev. Jenkins to pray that a cancer on his neck would go away. The evangelist prayed, and overnight the lesion healed, never to return. After this miracle, much to the joy of his wife, Louise, Roberts gave up the smoking habit that had him bound for forty years.

THE WARDEN'S WIFE

Things went well for the Rev. Jenkins at Campbell Pre-Release Center. Inmates elected him Inmate Adviser. He spent most of his time in the warden's office seeking clemency for those caught in an infraction of the rules.

Many men owed the success of their time there to his intervention. He not only spoke on the inmates' behalf, but he also counseled them on the folly of sneaking drugs into the prison or getting drunk while on pass, infractions for which they often lost their "good time."

He also lobbied for the installation of telephones in all the wards at the prison. When he entered the system, inmates could make one call per week, if at all. One telephone in the lobby served all prisoners.

This irked the Rev. Jenkins, who managed by hook or crook to make as many calls as he wanted to. He resented having to scheme to do it, and he resented the fact that others were unable to make calls.

He and his willing sidekick, fellow trusty Coley Bryant, posed as prison officials and convinced the telephone company that it would be good business to install pay phones in the wards. Luckily, Jesse Strickland approved the plan, and soon the inmates could call their families much more often.

Meanwhile, the reverend made himself as comfortable as possible, furnishing his cubicle with plump cushions and a colorful bedspread. His newly won freedom allowed him to go on passes to the dentist and to the health spa, where he worked to restore the muscles in his back that had been damaged in the attack at Manning.

These indulgences prompted Warden Turner to call the Rev. Jenkins into his office for a private conference.

"Come in, son, and shut the door," Turner said. "Do you want to be sent back to Walden and have me get fired? You really must keep a lower profile," he said. "Everybody over at headquarters is watching you like a hawk."

It was hard for the warden to come down too hard on his prisoner because the Rev. Jenkins had a secret weapon. After he qualified for work release, he founded a church near the prison. Alice Turner, the warden's wife, was there every time the door opened. If the Rev. Jenkins felt he had been harshly or unfairly treated, he called Mrs. Turner. When Turner came home at night, he would have to justify his actions to her.

"If I'm too hard on him, he gets Alice on my case," he complained, playing down his own growing fondness for the preacher who had been placed in his custody.

In the long run, Warden Turner tolerated Rev's constant bids for relaxation of the rules, because he never caused any trouble. His influence on the residents made discipline problems a thing of the past. His enthusiasm for life gave the prisoners a much-needed morale boost.

CHRISTMAS AT CAMPBELL

"Hollywood Comes to Columbia" read the headline in the December 17, 1981, edition of *The State* newspaper.

Mike Mazurki, Hollywood actor and former bodyguard for Mae West, had come to town to help department of corrections inmates at Campbell Pre-release Center celebrate Christmas with their families. (see photos on pages 269 and 272)

"You might not recognize the name, but you'll recognize the face," the article said. It was true. Mazurki, a giant of a man, made a career for himself as a wonderful character actor, playing convincing gangster roles in a number of films. A tough guy in the movies, in real life he was a gentle man with a smile that took over his whole face. He and the Rev. Jenkins had been friends for years. The inmates were thrilled that he cared enough to come and visit them. Christmas at Campbell was the first real Christmas the Rev. Jenkins had celebrated in years. After a dinner catered by prison cooks at a local church, the reverend's crusade team band and vocalists put on a festive program, and Santa Claus presented all the children with gifts. (see photo on page 273)

It was quite a change from past Christmases at Manning, where there was no celebration of the birth of Christ. Walden hadn't been much of an improvement. There, the men had no Christmas tree. Instead, they strung lights on a live oak tree outside the prison dormitories where they stood singing carols, their faces numb from the wintry air.

At the Campbell Christmas, thanks to the participation of community volunteers, the Rev. Jenkins saw to it that every child got a Christmas present. The inmates got the best present of all—a night away from the prison, good food, a visit with a Hollywood celebrity (see photos on pages 268-272, 277), entertainment that could not be matched locally, and the joy of being with their wives and children to celebrate the birth of the Savior.

"REVEREND JENKINS SHOULD NEVER HAVE BEEN CONFINED"

Impressed with the Rev. Jenkins' achievements both in the prison and on work release, Warden Turner and other prison officials happily wrote letters on his behalf, recommending him for parole.

TO WHOM IT MAY CONCERN:

> I have been a Warden with the South Carolina Department of Corrections for the past fifteen years, working primarily with the Pre-Release and Work Release Programs. I have served as Warden at three different Centers including my present position as Warden of Campbell Work Release Center here in Columbia, South Carolina.

During this period of time I have had personal contact with hundreds of inmates and the opportunity to observe their performance on the work release program and successes, as well as some failures. I have come to respect and admire many of the contributions some of them have made to the program and continued success after leaving the program and returning to the community.

I mention the above only to help clarify my association with Rev. Leroy Jenkins since his assignment to Campbell Work Release Center, as member of inmate staff, on June 24, 1981.

I have never met a man in or out of prison who has demonstrated a more sincere love and compassion for his fellow man than Rev. Jenkins. He is more than self-sacrificing in his time, talent, and assets in helping his fellow man and he has accepted his responsibility as an inmate at Campbell Work Release Center, in giving the highest performance in assigned duties.

In addition, Rev. Jenkins is held in high respect by Officers and Inmates at CWRC and has been more than instrumental in helping to promote the programs now in effect, and has been a leader in the organizing and function of a Prayer Breakfast Club that was instituted in December 1981.

I personally feel Rev. Jenkins should have never been confined to a penal institution; however this is my personal opinion and is not intended to reflect on the courts of our state or my position as Warden. I further feel Rev. Jenkins will make a great contribution to our society when he is released, through his ministry and personal contacts with citizens of the community. There is no doubt but what he will succeed in whatever environment he is placed in.

Olin L. Turner, Warden I
Campbell Work Center
South Carolina Department of Corrections

"HE INSPIRED OTHERS TO FOLLOW IN HIS FOOTSTEPS"

TO WHOM IT MAY CONCERN:

Leroy Jenkins SCDC #96650 was assigned to the Campbell Work Release Center on June 24, 1981. He was in "AA" Custody, a trusted status in prison and I can honestly say his behavior has been above and beyond what is expected. Resident Jenkins was assigned to my caseload on the day of his arrival. It is now 10 months later and his behavior and attitude is still excellent.

My interest in Leroy is just as important as my interest in the others at Campbell Work Release Center. However, Leroy proved to me time and time again to be loyal, compassionate, honest and hard-working. I have seen Leroy on a day-to-day basis and believe this to be an accurate opinion.

Briefly, upon his arrival he was assigned to the resident staff position/commissary supervisor and then promoted to senior ward keeper. His production in these positions was overwhelming and inspired the others to follow in his footsteps. The Center looks terrific and all the residents take great pride in its appearance.

Leroy is now assigned to the work release program which entitles him to work in the community and return to the center in the evening. He is working at the Leroy Jenkins Evangelistic Association here in Columbia, South Carolina.

I would like to add that Leroy helped Warden Turner to form a Prayer Breakfast Club, which meets in a community restaurant. The residents operate the club in conjunction with Mr. Turner. Leroy Jenkins was nominated by his fellow prisoners to the position of Chairman, Inmate Advisory Council (an extracurricular position) and helped many residents out of their troubles.

I strongly recommend that Leroy Jenkins be returned to the community so he can again preach on a full-time basis.

Respectfully,
Charles D. Porter, Community Program Supervisor
Campbell Work Release Center

"LEROY HAS BEEN A MIRACLE TO ME"

TO WHOM IT MAY CONCERN:

It is with great pleasure that I write this letter of recommendation on behalf of Leroy Jenkins, resident at the Campbell Work Release Center.

Over ten months ago Leroy was assigned to the Campbell Work Release Center and I can say that it's been a miracle to me and the operation of our center. Personally, through his prayers to God I was healed of a neck infection and I've even given up cigarettes. It already has been about six months since I touched a cigarette. I've always wanted to quit smoking and finally my prayers were answered.

Leroy Jenkins was assigned to Campbell over ten months ago as a staff resident and based on his excellent adjustment he was promoted to senior ward keeper. Just recently Leroy became a participant on the work release program. So he now works in the community where I feel he belongs.

He is an example of what all men should be. Loyal, honest, sincere, helpful to all people. A true man of God. I recommend he return to the community where he can preach full-time and be with his family.

Respectfully,
Boyd P. Roberts, Deputy Superintendent
Campbell Work Release Center

"HE HAS REACHED BEYOND HUMAN CAPABILITIES"

WHOMEVER IT MAY CONCERN:

This is to certify that Mr. Leroy Jenkins #96650 has been under my supervision for the past ten months at Campbell Work Release Center. Resident Jenkins has adjusted extremely well to his prison environment and has been a model inmate in every way.

Since his arrival at Campbell he has shown a lot of initiative in the labor force here. He worked his way into the supervisor slot in the commissary and from that position he was voted as president of the Inmate Advisory Council. Considering the pressure this man had on him he has fared well in that capacity. He has reached beyond human capabilities and moved in compassion through the spirit to help others when he couldn't help himself.

In addition to these achievements he has refused to accept limits on his compassion. With the assistance of the Warden he has helped to form a Prayer Breakfast meeting every Saturday morning with the families of inmates and other noted citizens. This has been a tremendous success, and hopefully will continue after his dismissal.

Words cannot express the impact he has had on myself as well as others who have grown to understand and respect this fellow human being. I only hope that in someway the thoughts that I have conveyed to you have given the type of recommendation acceptable and commendable for a man of this stature.

Harvey Webster, Jr.
Supervisor COAS

"HE ENCOURAGED A POSITIVE ATTITUDE"

TO WHOM IT MAY CONCERN:

I take great pride in recommending Leroy Jenkins, SCDC#96650 to the community.

For the past ten months I've worked closely with him. He has always displayed an outstanding attitude, and his behavior is way above the standards asked for.

I know he worked very hard when he was commissary supervisor and since he did such a great job I promoted him to the senior ward keeper where he really showed what he was capable of.

He and his fellow inmates made the center sparkle and he encouraged all the other residents to display an attitude which was positive even though this type of work was not the work they did on the outside.

Leroy Jenkins is now on the work release program and I believe he will prove to the community that he belongs there instead of in jail. I highly recommend that he become a full-time community individual and that will allow him to return to his preaching and his family.

Marvin Wiggins, Building Supervisor
Campbell Work Release Center

A MURDERER PAROLED

The Rev. Jenkins' good record with prison officials gave him the influence to improve the lot of many other prisoners. One of these was a man nobody thought would see the outside of prison walls.

"What did you do that for?" roared the towering, muscular man. Fists clenched, veins bulging in his neck, his dark eyes shone menacingly as he glared at the Rev. Jenkins.

Unmoved, the reverend stood nose to nose with one of the most feared men in the prison, as his heel crushed James Alston's watch into the ground.

In prison for murder, Alston had long ago made a mark for himself because of his hatred of the white man and his world.

He was a Gullah, part of a unique group of descendants of West African slaves who live in small, isolated farming and fishing communities on the sea islands off the coast of South Carolina. Because of their isolation, the Gullah had been able to retain much of their native language, culture, and rice-farming skills.

Accustomed to open sky and fresh breezes sweeping over the island, the barefoot boy grew up unfettered, until a tragic event brought him into the incredibly dark and dank prison in a town far removed from his birthplace.

His burning hatred and physical strength put him at the fore in the brutal life at CCI. James Alston caused more trouble there for Warden Jesse Strickland than anybody else ever had.

"I finally had to put him in solitary for a year," Strickland said. "It gave him a chance to think things over. He came out of there a changed man."

Now he was an AA trusty—a powerful, quiet, lonely man, who held his emotions in check.

All at once his fury at the Rev. Jenkins subsided, his muscles relaxed, and his hands fell loosely to his sides. "Rev, what the hell did you do that for?" he asked.

"James, I wanted to see if you were ready," the reverend said. "Or if you would explode when somebody did you wrong. I'm going to ask Jesse to try to get you into the governor's mansion. That's the only way you'll ever get out of here," he said.

Gov. Dick Riley employed prisoners in the governor's mansion as cooks and butlers. Murderers were commonly chosen for the jobs, as they were considered the elite of the penitentiary. Unlike career felons, most murderers were otherwise decent and trustworthy people who had committed a terrible act in a moment of extreme passion.

Alston had gone up for parole a number of times, but his victim's family never failed to appear against him. If Alston could get the appointment as a butler, and if they liked him, his chances for release were very good.

Shortly after the watch incident, Alston was given the position of butler to the governor. He was so efficient and dependable he became a great favorite with the governor and his family. Eventually, Gov. Riley recommended him for parole, and he was set free.

But the hatred of the victim's family fanned the flames of the adverse publicity, and Alston suffered a heart attack.

The last anyone heard of Alston, he had moved away from Columbia and was trying to make a new life for himself in another part of the state.

PRISONER IN THE PULPIT

PRISON FAILS TO VANQUISH S.C. PREACHER

Charlotte Observer, March 22, 1982

COLUMBIA - The voice was imitation Elvis Presley: deep, strong, silky.

"Please release me from this place," the man sang to the standard old tune, "Release me, and put a smile back on my face."

It was show time for Leroy Jenkins - pentecostal preacher, faith healer, singer and convict.

He clearly relishes being back in action, hearing his faithful sing his praises.

In Columbia's Spirit of Truth Church, in an old red brick former school building that his Leroy Jenkins Evangelistic Association paid $300,000 for recently, God is the back-up act, Jenkins is the star.

"I told (Sen.) Strom Thurmond you've got God in jail," a teary June Holloway told the mostly working-class crowd after explaining that Jenkins healed a neck injury for her.

Dressed in a dark gray three-piece suit, Jenkins was in total control of the 100-person crowd for more than two hours Sunday.

He sang to them, laid his hands upon those who sought health and plied them with testimonials to his sterling character and faith-healing skills.

But more than anything else, he railed against the justice and prison systems in South Carolina.

He insisted time and again that he had been framed, that tape-recorded evidence against him had been doctored, that unnamed people were out to get him.

"I didn't go out looking for trouble," he said. "That bunch of devils came looking for me."

Now he lives with fear, he said.

"I worry about getting set up," he confided." Not everybody that works for the prison system is honest, and they might try to do something to frame me and throw me back in maximum security, where I can't do my work."

But several times he assured the noisily appreciative audience he would not be stopped.

"They haven't stopped me," he roared. "The only way they can stop me is to kill me."

Later on, he asked: "You think I'm going to sit back and be quiet just because some crooked people don't like me? To hell with them!"

Flashes of arrogance seemed only to endear him more to his listeners.

He told them he was framed in Greenwood, "because I was successful, good-looking, and had some money."

He said he was glad he had been chosen for this ill treatment because, unlike some other men, he was strong enough to withstand it.

"I'm glad that of all the ministers in the world they could have chosen, it was me," he said.

While in prison, he said, he had been a model inmate: "I'm a model for the Lord Jesus Christ."

Dropping the prison theme momentarily, he ridiculed "the cold, dead, dried-up atmosphere" at some other churches.

Then he turned his wrath upon the crowd.

"I don't care whether you like what I say," he told them. "You can just lump it. You can't put me in jail, I'm already in jail."

The bravado was unnecessary. The audience was primed and ready for the faith healings to begin.

One old woman raised her right arm above her head after her encounter with Jenkins, apparently cured of bursitis. Another swooned with convulsions after Jenkins' treatment for an unspecified ill.

Another woman sobbed all the way back to her gray steel folding chair after Jenkins told her, "You are healed from the top of your head to the soles of your feet."

Jenkins hasn't always worked out of makeshift churches. Before his legal troubles began, he ran a nationwide TV evangelism and faith-healing operation that brought in $3 million a year.

Now he appears ready to begin recouping his lost time and money and rebuilding his flock.

He becomes eligible for working in the community on April 5, though he'll still live at the Campbell Work Release Center, and he plans to resume preaching each Sunday.

A member of his audience is S.C. Senator Tom Turnipseed. Jenkins is a man itching to get on with his life.

"I believe we have not even scratched the surface," he told his listeners, "of what we are going to do for God."

Copyright © Charlotte Observer

A NEW CHURCH

The news that the Rev. Jenkins had made his way back into the pulpit was a top story all across the country. But few knew how it happened.

The reverend had been stabbed in the back during an attack at Manning. When he reported the incident, he was shackled hand and foot, loaded into a prison van, and transported to the doctor's office. It was during this unhappy excursion that he spied a lovely old-school building surrounded by acres of trees, just off Broad River Road near the prison.

He called his secretary, June Buckingham, at the Columbia office.

"I've found our new church," he said. "Call the realtor and see about it."

Mrs. Buckingham contacted Polly Osborne, one of Columbia's top realtors and Jesse Strickland's aunt.

This delightful little lady had conspired several times to get the Rev. Jenkins out of prison on a pass. Her dark eyes sparkling, Mrs. Osborne signed the reverend out and then drove him around in her Lincoln Continental, sightseeing and looking for a suitable place near the prison for the Association's Columbia office. She had already helped find a nice rental house on a secluded street for the Rev. Jenkins' sisters and younger children to live in.

Now, she would reap the benefits of a major property sale if it went through.

Out from under the guards' noses, the Rev. Jenkins relaxed and enjoyed these outings thoroughly. They often wound up at a popular log cabin restaurant on Lake Murray, where the menu included fish and barbecue and where they enjoyed the antics of a family of ducks swimming in a pond outside.

Mrs. Osborne arranged a meeting with the doctors who owned the Broad Street property. She signed the reverend out and drove him to a lawyer's office downtown. Everyone assembled around a large conference table. The Rev. Jenkins was impeccably dressed in a blue suit.

Members of the reverend's staff were a little apprehensive about what the doctors would think of the convict pastor. To everyone's relief, they seemed to be quite impressed with him. They were asking $400,000 for the property, but agreed to take his offer of $350,000.

The building had been a private school, with classrooms facing a small wooded area. The former classrooms were converted to offices, and the high-ceilinged gymnasium, complete with a stage, became the sanctuary. Red velvet paper on the walls and red carpet on the floor set off the white, gilt-trimmed woodwork.

Gold tassels trimmed the maroon velvet drapes on the stage where a piano, an organ, and a set of drums stood. The Rev. Jenkins sent back to Ohio for an enormous crystal chandelier, a gift from his friend Mae West. He hung it in his new church in all its shimmering glory.

In a very short time, the staff moved to the new offices and took over the operation of the national ministry. The Rev. Jenkins' children—Theresa, Candy, Sharon, Dennis, and Danny—worked in the office, as did his sister, Polly Vickers. It was a tightly knit group under the supervision of Mrs. Buckingham. From the new offices, the Rev. Jenkins was able to assume leadership of the Association even though he was still a "guest" of the South Carolina prison system.

SPIRIT OF TRUTH CHURCH

The reverend was eager for the day when he would once again be back where God had put him, before God's people, preaching and teaching and praying for the sick and afflicted. As always, he intended to do it boldly and with his own special style.

At once, the church began to fill up. Some of the people had attended the Greenwood crusades, but others had never seen the prophet before. The fact that he was a convict did not overshadow his reputation as a great man of God.

Visitors included Alice Turner, the wife of Warden Olin Turner; and Addie Strickland, former wife of Deputy Commissioner Jesse Strickland. Mrs. Strickland was also employed in the office of the Evangelistic Association.

Dr. Gilbert Holloway, distinguished lecturer and pastor of the Christ Light Church in Deming, New Mexico, and his wife, June, had come to Columbia to help manage the Association office.

Eventually, the Rev. Jenkins made arrangements for men from Campbell to be allowed to attend the church, where they could meet their families and worship together. The prison van delivered them to church and took them back to prison after the service.

God did not disappoint his faithful. Hundreds received healing and deliverance at this wonderful church.

One day a lovely little lady, badly crippled and bent over a walker, walked haltingly into the church. After the reverend prayed for her, she ran to the back of the church and out the door. When she did not return, the ushers went looking for her. They found her a block away, still running.

A VENTURE INTO POLITICS

Tom Turnipseed, a state Senator and candidate for the Democratic nomination for lieutenant governor, visited the church on occasion.

Turnipseed had fought many a battle on behalf of consumers against the public utilities and insurance companies and was known for his tent revival-like speaking abilities.

One day, the tall, handsome politician strode into the Campbell Pre-release Center.

"I'm here to see Leroy," he announced. A member of Campbell's board of directors, he was immediately ushered into an office while guards fetched the reverend.

"Your lawyer in Ohio, Henry Eckhart, told me to look you up," he said, extending his hand to the preacher. "Henry is a topnotch lawyer and a friend of mine. He says you are tops in his book, and that makes you okay with me."

Offering the senator a chair, the Rev. Jenkins perched on the side of a table, one long leg swinging as he regarded this new acquaintance.

Turnipseed was fond of playing the role of the knight in shining armor to those the system had oppressed, and he found a kindred spirit in the young preacher, who had made a name for himself as a spokesman for the inmates at Campbell.

The senator became a regular visitor at the Prayer Breakfasts the reverend and Warden Olin Turner had inaugurated. The Rev. Jenkins was delighted when Turnipseed told him he was running for the office of lieutenant governor.

"I can help you, Tom," the Rev. Jenkins told Turnipseed. "I know how to present you and your ideals to the public. I will get my television production company to come down here from Ohio and make you a commercial that will emphasize the faith that you have in God. They will express your views perfectly, as they do mine.

"The public is tired of these crooks in politics," he said. "They want a Christian and a family man like you."

With this, the Rev. Jenkins was back in politics, behind the scenes this time.

The production company made three commercials for Turnipseed. They were very effective, showing his interest in the average family. A fourth was planned at the reverend's urging, which would highlight Tom Turnipseed's deep faith.

But nothing the Rev. Jenkins did escaped notice. The newspapers soon found out that he had a hand in the planning and presentation of the commercials, and headlines soon linked him with Turnipseed's campaign.

JENKINS AIDS TURNIPSEED CAMPAIGN

CANDIDATE DOWNPLAYS LINK

The State, May 21, 1982

Jerry Adams

The Rev. Leroy Jenkins has helped inject religion into the media campaign of lieutenant governor candidate Tom Turnipseed.

Jenkins, a faith-healing evangelist serving time on arson and assault conspiracy charges, recommended the firm that shot footage for the Turnipseed television advertisements, screened the results and then urged that another ad be produced because God hadn't been mentioned in the first three.

Turnipseed confirmed that he used an Ohio firm suggested by Jenkins to film the spots and that the 46-year-old evangelist had screened the ads.

He called Jenkins a client, a supporter, and "hopefully a friend" but said Jenkins hadn't contributed "financially" to the campaign and was just one of many to see the ads.

Turnipseed denied that Jenkins had an advisory role in the campaign but confirmed that a fourth ad - this one using a humanistic and religious approach - is being produced.

Jenkins was "not really" the basis for the fourth spot, Turnipseed said, adding that both he and Jenkins are "very much interested in religion and God."

Jenkins refused to be interviewed about his relationship with Turnipseed.

The fourth commercial "will be a reference to God that will help us create a better quality of life for everyone," Turnipseed said in an interview.

"TOGETHER, WITH GOD, WE CAN DO BETTER"

The 30-second ad shows the candidate leaving a church and delivering the following message:

"Understanding and communication are the keys to the survival of our families, our nation, and people everywhere. This golden rule of understanding others as we would like to be understood ourselves works. From it grows a spirit of co-operation. When we seek each other, we seek God. As we reconcile our differences and work for the common good we can raise the quality of life for everyone. Together, with God's help, we can do better."

Turnipseed acknowledged that the issue of religion is a touchy one, and said the ad is *"very, very honest."*

"You've got a large segment of the population out there that feels very comfortable talking about God," he said. *"Others don't."*

Jenkins' son, Dennis, who works as a volunteer driver and photographer for the Turnipseed campaign, was one of the photographers who spent a day and a half in the state shooting footage for the Turnipseed ad.

Turnipseed, who serves on the board of the work-release center, occasionally meets with Jenkins at the center's Prayer Breakfast Club. While the two men get together about every two weeks, they also talk by phone periodically in connection with Jenkins' legal affairs.

"He doesn't have any role, any type of advisory role at all. He's just a friend, someone I talk with," Turnipseed said of Jenkins.

"It would be easy to say, 'Aw, he's just friends and it doesn't look good to be involved with somebody who's in prison and I hardly know him.' But he's a friend," Turnipseed said. *"He's not a guy I consult with everyday or anything near that. But I know him.*

"If they could use that against me, we're in bad shape in this country, I'll tell you that."

A CLOSE RACE

Busy days followed, as Dennis Jenkins drove Turnipseed around in the Rev. Jenkins's limousine to political rallies throughout South Carolina. Traveling together late at night down country roads lined with pine forests and palmettos, the two became fast friends.

Turnipseed made several appearances at the Spirit of Truth Church, along with other churches, and gained substantial support, so much so that he may have become overconfident. On the last Sunday of the campaign, the Rev. Jenkins urged Turnipseed to come to church once again.

"Don't let up now," he said. "If you do come, I prophesy that you will win the primary election hands down."

Turnipseed did not heed the warning, and on election day, the heartbreaking results came in. He had lost by less than thirty votes.

TURNIPSEED REQUESTS PROBE OF VOTE-BUYING ALLEGATIONS

The State

Clark Surratt

Tom Turnipseed said Wednesday he has asked the U.S. Attorney's office to investigate possible vote-buying in Tuesday's Democratic primaries, but the once-more beaten politician said he has no direct evidence.

Turnipseed, who lost out in his bid for the Democratic nomination for lieutenant governor to state Rep. Michael Daniel, also said the Rev. Leroy Jenkins has authorized him to sue the Daniel campaign for libel.

Turnipseed said a Daniel campaign of "fear, deception and possible fraud" cost him the run-off.

The Columbia lawyer said he had no concrete examples of voting fraud, but he said he thought there are sufficient reasons for federal authorities to investigate.

"I have enough information that has been fed up to me to believe there ought to be an investigation," Turnipseed said.

But when asked how votes were bought, he said, "How they did it, I don't know."

Following a meeting with Turnipseed Wednesday, U.S. Attorney Henry Dargan McMaster said his office will conduct a routine preliminary investigation to determine if there have been any violation of federal election laws.

Turnipseed said there was too much of a turnaround in the voting patterns in some black precincts, especially in the Piedmont and PeeDee areas, for something not to be amiss.

Predominantly black wards in Richland County still went heavily for Turnipseed, but when asked about that he replied, "We can watch them (Daniel campaign workers) here."

Turnipseed said he had talked with Jenkins, an evangelist serving time in prison on a conspiracy charge, about the contents of a letter circulated against Turnipseed. He said Jenkins told him to bring suit because of one of the statements in the letter.

The letter, signed by eight black men, said in part, "Turnipseed has joined hands with the Rev. Leroy Jenkins, South Carolina's equivalent of Jim Jones of the Jonestown Massacre and constantly praised the work of Rev. Jerry Falwell and his moral majority crowd. The moral majority movement is more devastating to black people in 1982 than the Ku Klux Klan."

Turnipseed said he was infuriated by the letter.

Although beaten, Turnipseed seemed in no mood to end a political campaign Wednesday.

"We ran a good campaign," he said." The issue now is campaign tactics."

He said he wasn't sure whether to feel good or bad about Tuesday's outcome.

Turnipseed said the calls of support he's gotten "almost make me feel better than I have before."

Regardless of the charges of vote buying, the fact remained that had Tom Turnipseed made that one more appearance at the Spirit of Truth Church, as the Rev. Jenkins advised him to, he might have won the primary election.

Ultimately, the charges of vote buying were ignored, and Michael Daniels became lieutenant governor of South Carolina.

LEROY JENKINS SAYS HE'S STARTING 'NEW CHAPTER'

AFTER TIME IN PRISON

Columbia Record, December 4, 1982

Steve Smith

ANDERSON (AP) -To this day, the Rev. Leroy Jenkins maintains his innocence, says the 3 1/2 years he spent behind bars at the state penitentiary in Columbia changed his life and opened a "new chapter" in the story of the man who built his empire on "healing" the sick.

"It made me more aware of the needs of people," said the faith-healing evangelist whose nationwide ministry once added $3 million a year to his coffers in Greenwood - before its founder ran afoul of the law.

"I wasn't even aware of the insides of a prison. It's almost frightening to see how overcrowded it is - people stacked on top of each other."

He contended he won friends while in jail, preached to them and won a few over to the straight and narrow path.

"I slept beside them, ate with them, and I have a lot of respect for them," he said.

"I know in my heart that I did nothing wrong," said Jenkins in a telephone interview from his Spirit of Truth Church in Columbia.

This week, prison officials placed the preacher on an extended work release program which permits him to live outside the prison in custody of his daughter, Candace, provided he obeys some conditions.

Jenkins says he will work at building his church which he said already includes 1,200 members, including as many as 15 prisoners at a time with their families.

He wants to keep a low profile, while tailoring his preaching to reach more inmates. That's the "new chapter" he talked about.

"Publicity is one thing I'm trying to avoid," said a man who has seen his share of it over the past few years, much of it controversial. "I've done my time (in prison), did what I was supposed to do to earn this status."

He declined to discuss his plans for beginning his television ministry over, but promised that he would return to his former base in Delaware, Ohio if he wins parole in March 1984.

He had continued operating his church in Ohio and evangelical business while in jail, and turned the former Christian School in Columbia, into a church several months ago.

"I feel very good about it (work release)," Jenkins said.

"I'm proud that I went through almost four years in prison. It says in the Bible that the Lord will not put on you more than you can bear.

"I feel the only true rehabilitation is through church and Jesus Christ," Jenkins said." There's certainly not any in prison."

Copyright © Columbia Record

"HE'S OUT BUT NOT DOWN"

JENKINS GOING STRONG DESPITE PRISON YEARS

Columbus Dispatch, December 16, 1982

Julia Keller

He's out but not down.

Released from a South Carolina prison earlier this month, faith-healing evangelist Leroy Jenkins is full of plans, prayers and promises.

Those plans include returning to his church in Delaware, Ohio, as soon as he can, and continuing television pitches for new converts.

"I'm doing real, real good," Jenkins said during a telephone interview from his home near Columbia, S.C. "But I felt like God had it in his plans for me to be in prison."

His Spirit of Truth Church is just outside the Columbia corporation line. It is a large, white former school building with an adjoining wing for the offices of the Leroy Jenkins Evangelistic Association.

He preaches there on Saturday nights and Sunday mornings. He said it seats 800 and includes maroon velvet drapes, a large chandelier and red carpeting "with just a touch of maroon." His buildings in Delaware were known for their flamboyant furnishings.

Jenkins, 45, was released in the custody of his daughter, Candace, 23. He lives with her and his other children, in an apartment adjoining the church.

"I've had a hard time re-adjusting," he said. "Four years in prison - you could call it incredible. But I helped a lot of guys in prison, tried to make it better on them.

"Now some of them come to my church and bring their families, too."

His Holy Hill Cathedral in Delaware is still going strong, Jenkins said.

His first parole hearing is scheduled for April, 1984, the earliest possible time Jenkins could receive permission to leave South Carolina.

"Prison took the bitterness out of me. But I was bitter at first. I felt bitter against God, too. I couldn't understand why this was happening to me," said Jenkins who maintained his innocence throughout his imprisonment.

Jenkins has already made one television appearance, and plans to make many more, he said.

Copyright © Columbus Dispatch

JENKINS, REBUILDING MINISTRY, CAN'T EXPLAIN HOW HE HEALS

Columbus Citizen-Journal, December 27, 1982

John O. Meekins

COLUMBIA, S.C. - *Leroy Jenkins, the evangelist who once made Delaware, Ohio, his headquarters, stood beside his sleek, yellow Mercedes 450 SL parked behind his new church. (see photo on page 267)*

"From now on I'm going to keep a low profile," he pledged, looking at the $36,000 vehicle he said was a gift from an admirer.

It might be easier for a rich man to enter the Kingdom of Heaven than for Leroy Jenkins to keep a low profile.

He's been out of prison just a month, but already has an 800-seat church that he plans to expand to accommodate 1,200 people.

Jenkins already has aired the initial segments of what he says will be a weekly religious television show that will be beamed nationwide.

A computer whose memory contains 400,000 names and addresses is at work as boxes and boxes of envelopes containing $10, $20 and $50 contributions to his ministry attest.

That's a quick start - and not so low-profile - for a man who has just finished serving three years and eight months of a 12-year prison term.

Copyright © Columbus Citizen-Journal

JENKINS BUILDS DUCK PONDS LIKE JOHNNY APPLESEED PLANTED APPLE TREES

Jenkins actually started building his Spirit of Truth Church here about six months ago when he began a prison work-release program.

"I was passing by one day in a [prison] van with my hands cuffed and my legs shackled, and I looked up and saw this place was for sale," he recalled. "I said, 'I'm going to buy that place.'"

Today the former Seventh Day Adventist school already is beginning to resemble Jenkins's Holy Hill Cathedral in Delaware.

American flags and church banners flutter atop poles in front of the L-shaped white building.

Jenkins' faith-healing ministry is basic stuff, so if a passer-by believes Jenkins has erected a specific number of flag poles for an esoteric religious meaning, he is mistaken.

"I don't know," Jenkins said when asked how many flag poles guard his church. He counts to 14, then says, "I've got three more I might put on the hill over there. I think they make it look better."

Another Jenkins stamp is a large duck pond behind his church.

Jenkins builds duck ponds like Johnny Appleseed planted apple trees. He had several in Delaware, and South Carolina authorities commended the evangelist for beautifying prison grounds with flag poles and duck ponds everywhere he was imprisoned.

"I just like water, There's something spiritual about it."

Jenkins said he served time in several prisons, from maximum security to minimum security, "because they didn't know where to put me."

Despite all he's done since he traded his prison togs for the sharply cut suit of an evangelist, Jenkins still has a long way to go to rebuild his ministry.

At its zenith, Jenkins' Holy Hill Cathedral in Delaware attracted 5,000 people to Sunday worship services, and packed in thousands when he preached at the Ohio Theatre and Veteran's Memorial Auditorium in Columbus.

Now maybe 300 people attend worship services at Holy Hill, and on a recent Sunday in South Carolina, barely 200 people came to hear Jenkins preach at his Spirit of Truth Church.

Jenkins is not discouraged.

"Many churches with a pastor that's never been in jail don't have even 50 people, right? It shows me that, in spite of what people said or did to me, I still have a following, and I will have."

GIFTED EVANGELIST'S VOICE IS "PURE ELVIS PRESLEY"

Jenkins says his "gift of knowledge" from God is stronger today than ever. Jenkins says he regularly uses his "gift" - best described as a divine form of extrasensory perception - to heal everything from sore throats to cancer.

He readily allows that he doesn't understand what his power is, or how it works. In fact, he claims he is sometimes afraid of it.

"I see this woman and tell her she has two scars on her stomach. How can I know that? It's something inside me that knows it.

"There was this man with a perforated hip. I just ran over, broke his crutch in two and said, 'You're going to have to walk now.'

"He jumped up and started running around the church. I was worried he might slip and hurt himself because we didn't have the carpet down yet, and the floor was slick."

Jenkins said he discovered another facet of his gift in prison when he made weekly telephone calls to his congregation in Delaware.

"It hit me what I had been doing. I was able to tell people over the telephone where they were sitting and what they were wearing. It scared me when I realized what was happening, and the next Sunday I didn't call the church."

After that, he just accepted it.

Because of restrictions on his probation, Jenkins won't be allowed to set a foot out of South Carolina until 1984. But he still telephones the Holy Hill Cathedral on Sundays and shares his "gift of knowledge" with the congregation in Delaware.

The gift is one drawing card for his ministry, but another is Jenkins' showmanship.

Preaching at the Spirit of Truth Church recently, Jenkins, decked out in a three-piece suit, grabbed a microphone and sang a tune that reminded the listener of "My Way." His voice is best described as pure Elvis Presley. (see photo on page 267)

Music is an important part of his services. He sings both religious and secular tunes, and the soft tones of an organ and whispers from a snare drum accompany his preaching.

"I GIVE THEM SOMETHING I'VE BEEN LOOKING FOR ALL MY LIFE - PEACE OF MIND"

People who attend one of Jenkins' sermons may not always come away with a divine feeling, but at least they have been entertained.

They have paid for it though - passing the collection plate is also an important part of the services.

Before Jenkins went to prison, Internal Revenue Service records showed that his church's income was in the millions of dollars each year.

Jenkins claims he doesn't know how much he is making today. He said his church is solvent, and one of his workers in Delaware said the church repaid a $400,000 debt while Jenkins was in prison.

Records show that his taxes are current on his property in Delaware, although until recently they were a year in arrears.

Jenkins pays himself $250 a week, but the figure is meaningless.

"People give me clothes, houses, everything," Jenkins said. Cars, too, he said again, gesturing toward the bright Mercedes. "People give me things, but I don't steal anything."

Jenkins claims his beneficiaries are repaid for their generosity.

"I give them something I've been looking for all my life; peace of mind."

He said his years in prison mellowed him, helped him find some peace of mind, and made him decide to keep a low profile as he starts his ministry again.

ADJUSTMENT AIDS SURVIVAL OF PRISON LIFE'S DARKNESS

John O. Meekins

COLUMBIA, S.C. - Evangelist Leroy Jenkins seems to have depended upon himself as much as his God to carry him through three years and eight months in prison.

"None of the others (evangelists) have been through it, and I doubt they could have stood it - Billy Graham, any of them," Jenkins said." Because of my upbringing as a poor person, I could do it. I adjusted and came out of all that darkness."

But prison was tough, Jenkins readily admits.

"It was a very hard life to be perfectly honest with you," he said." First of all it was something very different.

"I'd seen all the movies and dramas of prisons and what they were like, and I actually thought they were overemphasized in many respects until I got there. Then I discovered they haven't even scratched the surface."

He groped for words, then said, "You have to be there to understand totally what I am saying. You see the world and everything in it is moving. It's just like watching television. You're a thousand times more aware of what's happening than the average person, but you can't participate."

Jenkins said he survived the experience, which included being attacked in the shower, because, "There wasn't a day that went by that I didn't expect them to come to me and say, 'We've made a mistake, you can go.' I never did give up. That's the reason I kept my sanity."

He said that seven men attacked him in the shower room.

"I thought it was all over, but I fought my way out of it. I had taught myself karate at my church, and at the time I didn't know why I was doing it because it was totally against my character."

He survived, but was stabbed in the back with a "shiv", a spoon handle that had been filed to a sharp point.

Jenkins said he also changed his attitude. Instead of fighting authority, as he had so much outside prison, he obeyed the rules.

"Everyone in jail knows that if you keep your nose clean, you can get out early for good time," he said.

It worked for Jenkins - he was released a day earlier than even he expected." I was supposed to get out on Dec. 1, but I got out the day before."

FURLOUGH ME

While the Rev. Jenkins served out his time in prison, his tiny-but-tough mother, Willie Mae Jenkins, held Holy Hill Cathedral together with her own fiery brand of preaching. But her age, her hard life working in the cotton mill and the stresses of her son's imprisonment took a heavy toll.

By the time her son moved to the Campbell Pre-release Center, Mrs. Jenkins lay in an intensive care room at Delaware's Grady Memorial hospital, hooked up to a breathing machine, nourished by tubes attached to her body.

Lying still, eyes closed, she appeared unconscious, past any hope of recovery.

"We might as well shut off these machines," one doctor said. "She is gone. Only the machines are keeping her body functioning. Let her just slip away."

But Mrs. Jenkins had the same can-do spirit the Rev. Jenkins had, and even in her unconscious state, her body fought the pneumonia that threatened to take her life.

"THEY'RE WELCOME TO HIM"

The Rev. Jenkins applied for a furlough to visit his ailing mother, but the prospects didn't look good. The state of South Carolina seldom granted furloughs except in the case of a death of a parent or family member. And Mrs. Jenkins was not dead—yet.

The reverend had already been refused a furlough to attend his sister's funeral in South Carolina.

The State newspaper in Columbia reported on February 14, 1984, that South Carolina was waiting for Ohio to give him permission to come there. The Rev. Jenkins' Ohio attorney, Henry Eckhart, was quoted as saying, "I think [the paperwork] is practically completed. Mr. Jenkins is a respectable citizen. He went down to South Carolina and got railroaded."

Sam McCuen, spokesman for the SC Department of Corrections, said in the article, "If the state of Ohio would like to have Leroy Jenkins, and if it can be worked out, let me put it this way, they're welcome to him."

"Because he is such a high image person, he's a lot of problem to take care of," McCuen said.

In truth, Ohio was perfectly willing for the Rev. Jenkins to make the trip. It was the State of South Carolina that refused to let him go.

LEROY JENKINS SHOWS FRUSTRATION, ANGER AS CAROLINA

AUTHORITIES REFUSE OHIO VISIT

Columbus Citizen-Journal, February 16, 1983

David Yost

The South Carolina Department of Corrections yesterday refused a furlough request by the Rev. Leroy Jenkins that would have permitted him to return to Ohio to visit his ailing mother.

In a telephone interview yesterday from his Spirit of Truth Church in Columbia, S.C., Jenkins expressed both frustration and resignation.

"I'm at their disposal....whatever they say, that's what I have to do," he said with a hint of sarcasm. "If they love me so much they don't want me to leave South Carolina, I guess I'll have to stay."

He said he has received more than 4,600 letters yesterday from people who heard he might be permitted to return to Ohio.

"They [his supporters] have been my only source of hope, really," he said.

Copyright © Columbus Citizen-Journal

HOME AGAIN

At last, thanks in part to public pressure, the reverend gained permission from South Carolina authorities to visit his mother. News that he had returned to Ohio made headlines. "Jenkins Gets Furlough to Visit Ailing Mother" beamed *UPI*. "Delaware Abuzz with Jenkins Back in Town" announced the *Delaware Gazette*.

JENKINS VISITING ILL MOTHER IN OHIO

The State, March 18, 1983

The Reverend Leroy Jenkins is on an emergency furlough from a work-release program to visit his ailing mother in Delaware, Ohio.

Sam McCuen, spokesman for the South Carolina Department of Corrections, said Jenkins' furlough to visit his mother, Willie Mae, began at 7 a.m. Wednesday and ends at 7 p.m. March 21.

Jenkins, who is about 45 years old, is the minister of the Spirit of Truth Church, off Broad River Road. His followers in Delaware, Ohio, have raised a banner in front of his Holy Hill Cathedral reading, "Welcome Home Leroy."

"She's (his mother) got pneumonia and her doctor wrote us to say that for a person of her age, this could be a life threatening situation," said McCuen. "State law does provide for that sort of visit with approval of the governor of this state and the governor of Ohio."

Copyright © The State

MOTHER JENKINS' MIRACLE

The moment the Rev. Jenkins arrived in Ohio, he rushed to his mother's side, bent over her, and placed his hand on her head.

"Mother, you're going to be all right," he said.

At that, Willie Mae Jenkins opened her eyes and looked around the room. Soon, she was doing so well that doctors removed the breathing machine, the oxygen tubes, and other life-support mechanisms. Within days, Mrs. Jenkins recovered completely.

"I saw an angel," she said of her recovery. "He touched my head, and I knew I was healed."

One of the young interns who had lingered by her side for several days was so impressed by the miraculous recovery he came to the church and gave his life to God.

Within a month, Mrs. Jenkins was off on a nine-month trip to Sweden. While there, she met a tall, handsome Swedish gentleman whom she later married. Although he spoke no English and she no Swedish, the two were blissfully happy. Mrs. Jenkins died after several more years but not before she enjoyed some of the happiest years of her life.

FIERY JENKINS STILL UNBOWED AFTER PENANCE IN PRISON

Columbus Dispatch, March 19, 1983

Nancy Nall

DELAWARE, Ohio - He was a little rusty at first, but before long things were rolling so smoothly he threatened to take up a collection.

Leroy Jenkins was back in the pulpit.

Just like old times, the millionaire evangelist was speaking from his cavernous Holy Hill Cathedral with the glitter-encrusted crosses, tufted-upholstery organ, and fire-engine red everything.

On Friday, though, the flock consisted of reporters anxious to talk with Jenkins, 45, back in Ohio for the first time since his release from a South Carolina prison in December.

"I'm just a wee bit nervous," Jenkins confessed. "After being in jail, you get that way."

He returned to Delaware on Wednesday on a special furlough from the work-release program that keeps him confined to Richland County, S.C. The furlough was granted to allow Jenkins to visit his ailing mother, Willie Mae, 77, who is suffering from double pneumonia. He will return to South Carolina on Monday.

"Everybody is just thrilled to death. The phone has rung off the hinges, so to speak, since they read just a little bit in the newspaper about me being here," Jenkins said of his congregation. He will preach Saturday night and Sunday at Holy Hill, and promised such evangelical pyrotechnics as faith-healing and the Ohio debut of Jenkins' latest song.

Jenkins lashed out at the South Carolina authorities he said "set up" his arrest and conviction, and said jail was "not a gravy train" but made him a better minister with a stronger following.

"All of my members that write to me now say my ministry's going to be greater than ever before and I believe that," he said.

"I guess they feel it's just like it was in the Bible days. They put all the Apostles in jail in the Bible days and we still read about them and the preacher preaches about them every Sunday. I'm no different than they are."

Jenkins said he is keeping busy in South Carolina with his church, a growing television ministry and preparations for a book and a movie about his life.

"I'm not in this to see how many dollars I can get. I'm in it because God put me in it 22 years ago against my will.

"I do not want to do what I'm doing. I enjoy it, but I don't want to do it," he said.

"I had a lot of friends in jail. It was a different group of people than I was used to associating with, but I didn't let them rub off on me. I let me rub off on them."

JENKINS BACK ON HOLY HILL

Columbus Dispatch, March 20, 1983

DELAWARE, Ohio - Evangelist Leroy Jenkins walked on stage before 1,500 of his flock Saturday night, fell on his knees, wept and blotted the tears with his handkerchief.

Jenkins was preaching once again in his Holy Hill Cathedral, the first time since his release from a South Carolina prison in December on a work-release program.

Jenkins was given permission to return to Delaware to visit his ailing mother, Willie Mae, 77.

The standing-room-only crowd greeted Jenkins with upraised arms, Halloween type noisemakers, and shouts of "Praise the Lord!"

Jenkins boasted that when he was in prison he had heavenly assistance in destroying a prison guard who told him a religious meeting he was holding was too noisy.

He said he told the guard, "I hope you fall dead in the tunnel, you S.O.B."

Later, someone told Jenkins the guard had died. "and then I said, 'Praise the Lord.'"[95]

"I'm just like Jesus, just like Him. You do Him wrong, and He'll send you to hell. If you do me wrong, you wish you were in hell," he said.

Jenkins told his followers of his trials and tribulations in prison. He said God had sent him there for a purpose - to preach to the prisoners. He said there a lot of prisoners filled with the Holy Ghost. "There are murderers now baptized."

Then Jenkins walked into the audience and approached a man who appeared crippled. Jenkins threw the man's cane down the aisle, and ran him around the cathedral.

During the "healings" Jenkins asked the audience to pledge $48,000 to defray the costs of his television ministry.

Copyright © Columbus Dispatch

---

[95] The guard had a reputation for making inmates' lives a misery. After he died, his wife filed suit with the South Carolina Industrial Commission, claiming damages for a work-related death because her husband was under the influence of the Rev. Jenkins' prayers. The suit was thrown out of court.

REVIVAL

As soon as the Spirit of Truth Church in Columbia opened its doors, God poured out blessings on the faithful who came seeking his help.

One of these was Carry Dixon, a small woman of great faith.

"Rev. Jenkins, please pray for my child," she said. "She's supposed to have her leg amputated in the morning, but I know that God can heal her."

As the evangelist approached the sixteen-year-old girl, Mrs. Dixon wiped her hands across her cheeks to brush away her tears.

"She's got leukemia, and her knee is fused so that she can't bend it. And it is so painful," Mrs. Dixon said.

The girl's name was Virginia. She sat in the front row of the church with her mother, her crutches on the floor beneath her feet, her leg propped up on a chair beside her.

"My son had the same thing, and he died when he was nineteen years old," Mrs. Dixon said. "I can't stand to lose Virginia too. In the morning, they are going to take off that leg to save her life."

Mrs. Dixon leaned over and removed the elastic bandage wrapped around her daughter's leg.

It was the first of May and very warm. The evangelist had removed his tie and opened the collar of his ruffled shirt. The service had been long, and many prayers were answered.

Unknown to anyone in the church, three young doctors from Richland Memorial Hospital watched the proceedings intently from the back row of the church. Responsible for Virginia's case, they wanted to see for themselves what would happen when the so-called faith healer prayed for her.

The Rev. Jenkins walked briskly over to the teenager, knelt before her, and placed his hand on her stiff knee. Suddenly, Virginia's knee bent, and her foot fell to the floor.

"Get up, honey, and walk. You are all right, now," the reverend said.

Hesitantly at first, Virginia rose to her feet. She took a tentative step and looked up, joy flooding her face.

"Go on, go on," urged the pastor. Virginia walked and then ran across the front of the church. The congregation erupted in cheers and shouts of praise to God. Mrs. Dixon jumped up and down.

"Thank God, thank God," she cried, "I knew God would heal her if you prayed for her. She's got sickle cell anemia too."

"You mean she *did* have sickle cell," said the Rev. Jenkins, beaming and shouting "alleluia," as he watched Virginia's joyful promenade.

Monday morning, Mrs. Dixon and Virginia kept their appointment at the hospital, and after tests and x-rays, doctors sent Virginia home. The leukemia and sickle cell anemia had disappeared. There would be no amputation.

The young doctors rejoiced with her and gave her the x-rays of the afflicted knee to support her testimony.

Today, Virginia Dixon has two adorable children of her own and is still well, with no sign of leukemia or sickle cell anemia.

KEEPING A LOW PROFILE

Not everyone was pleased with the spectacular miracles taking place in the new church. One prison official went so far as to warn the reverend to tone down his activities.

"Leroy, if you expect to have the parole board vote to have you put on parole this spring, you will have to keep a low profile," he said. "Stay out of the news, give up preaching in your church, and lay very low until next April," he said.

The official should have known better. Asking evangelist Leroy Jenkins to keep a low profile was like asking the earth to cease its orbit. He called a press conference to tell reporters he did not want to be in the news anymore.

As might be expected, this announcement had the opposite effect. Several other papers across the country picked up on the story, and the reverend was in the headlines again.

"I'm d____d if I do and d____d if I don't," the Rev. Jenkins said ruefully. Soon he returned to his pulpit and remained in the public eye.

BACK IN THE THICK OF IT

The Rev. Jenkins just couldn't seem to stay away from controversy. Due to prison overcrowding, the South Carolina Legislature was considering a proposal to shorten prison sentences. Instead of serving one-third of his sentence, a prisoner would have to serve only one-fourth of his time before he was considered for parole. To the Rev. Jenkins, that meant he could be out in five years instead of seven.

South Carolina senator Norma Russell came out as a vociferous opponent of the proposed change.

"Those prisoners need to be kept in there for their full time," she claimed. "They ought to lock them up and throw away the key."

One day the Rev. Jenkins stopped at a Waffle House for breakfast on his way from the prison to his job at his church. He spied Mrs. Russell sitting in a booth and, on behalf of the inmates, went up to her to speak in favor of the reduced required time.

Mrs. Russell knew who he was and was cordial but once again expressed her feelings that prisoners should serve their full time.

"Ms. Russell," said the Rev. Jenkins, "one day you are going to be very sorry that you feel that way. Your own son is going to be put in jail, and then you will feel differently about it."

"I doubt that," she said, smiling into her coffee cup.

Not long after, headlines carried the news that Norma Russell's son was arrested for a felony and was sentenced to serve time in the South Carolina prison system.

"Rev. Jenkins," said the shaking voice on the telephone, "this is Norma Russell. Remember you told me that one day my own son would have to serve time? Well, you see what happened. Of course, you know my son was not guilty."

"Now you know how I feel," said the reverend. "I wasn't guilty either, but I still had to do my time."

"Leroy," Mrs. Russell continued, "I have heard a lot about you, and I know that you are very influential over there at the prison. Can you help me get my son in a good institution, where he will not be harmed by the general population? A lot of people don't like me over there, and I fear for his life."

"I will do what I can," the reverend said. "But it would be a lot better for him if you withdrew your opposition to the reduced-sentencing bill."

Mrs. Russell did withdraw her objection to the bill, and it passed the legislature.

Because of his encounter with the senator at the Waffle House, the Rev. Jenkins would be released in a little over five years, instead of seven.

TENT REVIVAL

May is arguably the prettiest month of the year in South Carolina. The grounds around the Spirit of Truth Church were lush with spring-blooming flowers. The baptismal lake behind the church, with its fountain of softly splashing water, lured the congregation to sit on the grassy banks, while the children played on a small beach. (see photo on page 278)

As he had at Walden, the Rev. Jenkins plunged into the work of fixing up the grounds around the old school. He dug out a low-lying swale behind the church and found a spring that created the baptismal lake. He bought a used mobile home and installed it behind the pond where he could be where he wanted to be, right on top of things.

"Let's have a tent crusade," the Rev. Jenkins said one day. "It's time we did more for God. I have seen greater miracles under a tent than anywhere else," he said. "I believe God prefers a tent."

The Rev. Franklin Walden, who had been present many years before at A. A. Allen's crusade when the Rev. Jenkins was healed, had a successful ministry based in Georgia. He loaned the church a tent and sent his men over to help raise it.

The workmen set the center poles in the ground and then pulled the heavy ropes that lifted the canvas to the top of the tent. Heaving sledgehammers, they secured the tent by pounding yard-long steel stakes into the dry, hard soil.

Meanwhile, the evangelist's sons and daughters, Theresa and Candy, also jumped in, grabbing wheelbarrows and rakes to spread sawdust shavings over the gravel parking lot. (see photo on page 274)

"Boys, God told me to do my first things over," he told his sons, referring to his early tent crusades. "God is going to do great things under this tent."

He instructed his son, Dennis, to put up a refreshment stand that would sell hot dogs and soft drinks to the crowds. The refreshment stand did a good business since many who came to the afternoon services stayed over for the evening revivals as well.

Every night for a week, the faithful raised their hands in praise as God answered their prayers for healing and salvation. Hundreds were blessed and healed under that tent, but undoubtedly the most dramatic healing was that of Rose Marie Hoffman.

On the first day of June, the tent was filled to overflowing. A blonde lady in a wheelchair was rolled in, but the only vacant seats were at the back of the tent.

"Come on up here," said Willie Mae Jenkins, the reverend's mother. She instructed the ushers to crowd the wheelchair in beside her chair in the first row. "Sit right here where you can see everything."

The Rev. Jenkins delivered his sermon and prayed for members of the congregation. Then, toward the end of the service, he walked over to the wheelchair.

"What happened to you?" he said, bending over to speak to the woman.

"I fell down some stairs several years ago at work, and now I am completely disabled and on disability leave from Fort Jackson Army Base," she replied. "It's my back. I am in terrible pain. I was just getting ready to go home. I couldn't sit here another minute."

"Pull her up," the Rev. Jenkins ordered, motioning to the ushers. "Now, hold her, she can't stand up alone."

Holding her hand as she tottered back and forth, he said, "Now, take a step toward me."

Cautiously she lifted one shaky leg and planted her sturdy black shoe on the sawdust in front of her.

"That's right, come on, take another step," urged the evangelist.

As she moved out to take another step, a radiant smile spread across her face, and she looked up in delight. Another step and then another, and she was walking across the front of the tent, unaided.

Suddenly realizing the full extent of her healing, she ran over to the Rev. Jenkins, threw her arms around him, and lifted him up in the air.

"Oh, thank you, thank you," she cried, bouncing him up and down several times. Then, she turned and ran out of the tent, her mother rushing to catch up with her, the empty wheelchair sitting in mute testimony in the front row.

Later, she called the office and sent in her testimony:

My name is Rose Marie Hoffman. I was employed at Fort Jackson when I fell down the stairs. Since then I have been put on total disability.

I really had no life other than just existing. Totally disabled, unable to walk any distance, sit for any length of time, unable to stand for any period of time. When driving, (which I did very little of) the pain would be worse in my spine, back, right leg and foot and afterwards I would be sicker.

I was totally dependent upon medications to endure the severe pain which I had all of the time except when sleeping. I had reached the point where I could not sleep in the hospital bed, which I had in my bedroom at home, because of the muscle spasms cutting my breath off. I would sleep in a Lazy-boy chair.

When you prayed for me, it felt like an arm went across my waistline, in back, down to my right hip, pulled up my right hip, and it felt like the hip popped into the joint. It must have been the hand of God, because you did not touch me, you were holding my hand.

After taking about six steps with you, I felt God's power, fire and heat, hit the top of my head and soar through my body.

Now, several days have passed, and I still feel great! I haven't felt this wonderful since I was sixteen years old. My energy level is unlimited and the amount of sleep required even before I fell down the stairs has decreased considerably.

God has erased the memory from my body and mind the way the pain affected my body, resulting from the after effects of the two disc operations and the fall.

It is as though I had never been sick or crippled. Praise God! I am now a whole, well human being. No pain. No medications. No wheelchair. No TENS machine shocking the muscles in my back, legs and feet. No muscle spasms. I am able to do anything I so desire. Praise God!

After her healing, Rose Marie Hoffman gave herself a makeover. She lost the extra weight she had gained while sedentary, bought some stylish new clothes, and returned to work looking like a million dollars. No more sturdy oxfords for Rose Marie.

The report in her employee file said, "Healed of her disability by Leroy Jenkins."

Today, Rose Marie goes about to various churches and crusades, testifying to the miracle that God gave her years ago in the tent in Columbia, when a convict prayed for her to be healed.

MORE PRESS, MORE LIES

The Rev. Jenkins was set to go before the parole board in April 1984. So it was important that he stay out of the newspapers. This meant no press releases and no interviews.

Everyone in the Association office, as well as his immediate circle of friends, was warned not to make any comments to the media.

Despite these efforts, interest in the reverend's activities was so great that the *Atlanta Constitution* sent a reporter, Jim Galloway, to do a story on the pastor.

Galloway had been at the *Anderson Independent* during the Rev. Jenkins' time in Greenwood and had contributed to a number of negative articles about the evangelist.

The new stories were full of the same old gossip and careless reporting contained in those first stories.

Galloway repeated the lie that the reverend had taken out insurance just before his church in Delaware had been hit by a bomb blast. That lie had been refuted by the chief of the Delaware Fire Department, who affirmed that there had never been a bomb blast at Holy Hill. Like the *Independent*, the *Atlanta Constitution* failed to do some basic fact-checking before running with the story.

It would not be surprising to find out that the series of articles written about the Rev. Jenkins aided Galloway in procuring his job at the Constitution. The cleverly written, provocative articles certainly fattened his portfolio at the reverend's expense.

To add insult to injury, Galloway's apparent lack of belief or understanding of the healing aspect of the Rev. Jenkins' ministry came across as sarcasm. The following are excerpts of the two-page article.

A PRISONER IN THE PULPIT
CONVICT LEROY JENKINS IS REVIVING HIS EVANGELISM BUSINESS

Atlanta Constitution, September 26, 1983

Jim Galloway

COLUMBIA, S.C. -The preacher dressed in tight navy blue pants and ivory jacket, assured his Sunday congregation that the lyrics were original and eased into the throaty Elvis voice of a torch singer.

"Please release me, let me be, can't you see what prison's done to me...." The song finished, he discovered an ax handle behind his portable pulpit, and held it up for the crowd to see. There was black electrical tape on one end, and he put it back.

"We don't want no violence today," he joked. Deep in the audience the warden's wife laughed. Everybody laughed.

More than four years ago, television faith healer Leroy Jenkins was shackled and harshly introduced to South Carolina's prison system, where a judge had ordered him to spend the next 12 years. A jury had just found him guilty of conspiring to burn the houses of a highway patrolman and an alleged gambler, and of arranging an assault on a local newspaper reporter.[96]

---

[96] This statement begs clarification. The reporter should have noted that no homes were burned and no one was assaulted.

It was a blow that his $3 million-a-year evangelistic Association was not expected to survive.

But it has, and so has Jenkins - a charismatic man already elected to sainthood by his tight, passionately loyal group of followers. He is a man even his detractors grant a certain Rasputin-like ability to survive and mesmerize.

Today, though officially in state custody, Jenkins is in his 11th month of the state's work-release program. His full-time job is the supervision of his evangelism business from an old elementary school a mile from the prison, next to a National Pride car wash.

The Leroy Jenkins Spirit of Truth Church is a white-washed affair bordered in front by alternating American and Christian flags. Behind is a small pond with a fountain in the middle. Jenkins' churches have always been surrounded with flags and fountains.

Each Sunday he holds church in the converted gymnasium, conducting a red-carpet service that is a mixture of black Baptist, white Pentecostal and Las Vegas showtime.

The rest of his time is spent sending out videotapes and collecting the prayers and contributions that flow therefrom. (His tapes air in Atlanta every Sunday at 6:30 a.m. on WXIA-TV)

He has only 13 television markets now, down from 78 stations across the nation before his conviction. But the top-down Mercedes that inmate no. 96650 drives back and forth to work is evidence that his work is not failing.

"It's in better shape now that it's ever been. And that's no turkey. I don't owe as much money," said Jenkins, 48. "In fact I've paid off $448,000 of TV indebtedness that I had."

According to secular calculations, Jenkins will be eligible for parole in March 1984. But "the Rev," as he likes to be called, says God has revealed that he will be out on Jan. 1 ...

...Jenkins began his faith-healing in Atlanta during the early 60's. Damning movies and television as sins of the devil,

he was a hot-tempered and unschooled - but not unskilled - tent preacher, raising his living from collection plates.

At the height of his financial success he decided to move his headquarters back home. He bought the street where he had once lived, bought a church and turned it into a shopping mall, and imported vintage Chicago bodyguards - complete with three-piece suits and sunglasses - into a Southern mill town.

He promised to run for mayor.

But the glamour of coming home again came tumbling down with his arrest in April 1979.

His conviction a month later was sealed when the jury heard the tape of a whiskey-soaked conversation of the evangelist and his intimates planning revenge on a police officer who had arrested Jenkins' daughter for speeding. The conversation was interrupted occasionally by Jenkins' attempts to add a new song to his repertoire, "I Must Tell Jesus."

Other tapes documenting foul language, drinking[97] and debauchery[98] were capped by evidence that Jenkins had hired a federal agent to burn the home of the patrolman,[99] and as a favor to an employee, the house of an alleged gambler.[100]

The agent had infiltrated the organization to search for evidence that Jenkins had engineered the unsuccessful dyna-

---

[97] Foul language and drinking are not criminal offenses.

[98] This is a vague term. The reporter should never have mentioned the word if he was not prepared to give examples.

[99] This statement needs clarification: there was no fire.

[100] According to a sworn affidavit by one of the prosecution's chief witnesses against the Rev. Jenkins, the reverend had nothing to do with the planned arson or assault. See chapter, "A Witness Recants – Too Late."

miting of his church in Delaware, Ohio. In April, 1978, shortly after he took out a $1 million insurance policy on it.[101]

Jenkins was also convicted of hiring the agent to assault a local newspaper reporter[102] who had publicly noted the timing of the dynamiting, the insurance policy and the fact that Jenkins' home in Greenwood had burned three weeks later.[103]

"I was a poor nobody and came back and bought half the town, and they got jealous - the whole city did. And that's all it was, nothing but that," Jenkins said. "I wouldn't be feeding the poor over here on the right side and killing people on the left. I mean that just wouldn't be fair. And that's not in my character and never has been."

---

[101] As discussed in the previous chapter "Setting the Stage for Accusations of Arson", there never was a dynamite blast at Holy Hill Cathedral. Some burn marks in the church ceiling were considered by the Delaware City Fire Department to have possibly been caused by a welding tool used in repairs. The Association did take out a $1 million insurance policy on the church, but it had nothing to do with a bombing. The church had applied for a loan to pay a creditor and it was the lender who required the insurance coverage. No claim was ever made for the damage to the church ceiling because it was so minimal.

[102] There was no assault.

[103] The reporter who wrote this story, Jim Galloway, was also one of the reporters who wrote the story about the non-existent dynamite blast. He should have identified himself as such at the beginning of this story. If he really believed that the Rev. Jenkins was capable of having his fellow reporter assaulted, he might conclude he also would be assaulted. Galloway should have been taken off this story due to conflict of interest.

Jenkins hopes to prove someday that the tapes were spliced together to frame him.[104]

"They wanted me out of Greenwood and they did anything they could to get me out of Greenwood. But they opened up all kinds of new things when they did this to me," he said.

What they opened up was a chance to begin a prison ministry according to the evangelist. "It can be exactly what you make it. I took the barber shop. I painted it. I put drapes in it that I brought from my home in Greenwood," he said. "I painted some little guys sittin' in barber chairs on the wall, and made it real nice and clean.....And I counseled a whole slew of guys while cuttin' their hair." (see photo on page 278)

But Jenkins' emphasis was on keeping his evangelistic Association running. Jenkins was one of the few prisoners in the state who was allowed daily visitation. "I had a lot of mail coming in and they didn't want to handle it," Jenkins said.

Once he had earned his AA trusty status, Jenkins was allowed a 4 1/2 hour church leave every Sunday. Last November, he was released into his daughter's custody on the state's work-release program, and resumed full-time command.

"As you can see, the inmates and officials that are coming to church here obviously have been impressed by something or they wouldn't be here," Jenkins said.

He is subject to an 11 p.m. curfew, cannot touch alcoholic beverages and cannot enter the city of Columbia, even though the church is located a few miles outside the city limits. He can drive only to and from work, though he can be driven anywhere in the state, as long as he keeps in touch with correction officials.

A Jenkins-style church service can be summed up by the two most prominent images of his auditorium - a cross made of grey carpet on the floor, over which hangs a huge, bell-shaped, crystal chandelier ...His sermon is a defense of

---

[104]   See chapter, "A Witness Recants – Too Late."

himself, down to his characterization of Christ as a man brought down "because of jealousy and people in high places."

They warm to his tale of persecution. "I can say I haven't changed a bit. Whatever I was when I went in, I was the same when I came out," he tells them.

It is a sermon that does not draw any judgements that might make the audience uncomfortable. "It isn't what the judge says, it isn't what the police say, all that matters is what God says," he said.

There are a few more songs, and the healing begins. Curing an elderly woman from Freetown, Ind., of pain in her body nets a $100 check.[105] Her husband will later confess that his son is a "burned out drug addict in California." Jenkins will pray the boy out of that hedonistic territory.

Another man is promised a job by the end of next week. Toward the end, Jenkins confesses that he has shaken hands with a man who has just been cured of cancer, and never even knew he had it. The man's sister jumps up and begins praising the Lord.

Jenkins enjoys the next part—the collection plate. He cajoles checks and cash from his flock a la Don Rickles. "If you write me a letter and don't send me no money, wait till you have money and then send it. 'Cause I got a license to make money. You don't."[106]

There are more songs, bluesy and upbeat, and Jenkins begins to call up his closest supporters, to let them bask in his glory.

He assigns the benediction to an elderly woman, and disappears in the middle of her roaring prayer.

Copyright © Atlanta Constitution

---

[105] The Rev. Jenkins does not, and has never, charged a fee for prayer, despite the reporter's implication.

[106] As any evangelist, minister, priest or rabbi will attest, if you don't ask for money, you don't get it.

GOOD-BYE TO A GOOD FRIEND

The Rev. Jenkins had vowed he would not let prison officials forget about him. They couldn't have forgotten him even if they had wanted to.

Just across the street from the entrance to the department of corrections administrative offices, a large billboard displayed a photograph of the evangelist accompanied by the words "Leroy Jenkins Miracle Tent Crusade." Prison officials had to look at the billboard every time they passed through the prison gates.

In response to that billboard and others like it throughout Columbia, people flocked to the big tent that had been erected next to the Spirit of Truth Church.

It was hot under the canvas, and in the evening, workers rolled up the side flaps in hopes of catching a breeze. Cars lined up along the curb, windows rolled down as a number of people watched the service from a distance and listened to the gospel music.

A ramp ran across the front of a platform where the Rev. Jenkins stood. Those who elected to, walked up the ramp and stood before him as the preacher laid hands on them and prayed. Fragrant, golden sawdust lay several inches thick, cushioning the fall of those who were slain in the spirit after being touched by the "miracle arm."

"Now, folks, if you really mean business with God and want to free yourself of those chains that have you bound, come on up here, and I will ask God to move on your behalf," he said. Night after night, almost every soul under the tent heeded the call.

Olin Turner, superintendent of Campbell Pre-Release Center, had not attended the crusade, although his wife, Alice, and his daughter had not missed a single meeting. He finally found it in his heart to attend the last day of the crusade one Sunday afternoon.

When the alter call came, Turner stood and joined the line snaking up the ramp.

"Olin," said the Rev. Jenkins, "I pray that God will see your humble spirit and bless you in every way." Little did anyone realize that Turner had made his peace with God just in time.

Not long after that, the telephone rang in the Association office early one morning. It was Alice Turner.

"Get Leroy. Please, hurry," she said, crying. Turner had collapsed at a restaurant where they were eating breakfast on their way out of town for a vacation.

The Rev. Jenkins rushed to the hospital, but it was too late. Turner had quietly passed away. The reverend did what he could to comfort the family.

"He gave his heart to God," he told Turner's wife. "He is better off than we are."

But in his heart, he grieved for the warden who had become so dear to him.

FALSE WITNESS

As the day of his first parole hearing approached, the Rev. Jenkins asked officers and guards in the prisons where he spent time to write letters of recommendation for him. The letters were to be sent to Grady Wallace, commissioner of the South Carolina Board of Probation, Parole and Pardon Services. These men responded with glowing reports of the reverend's conduct and character.

The commissioner, assistant commissioner, several of the wardens, and many officers—sixteen in all—wrote to Wallace on his behalf. Two South Carolina sheriffs, several county officials, and prominent members of the community also pled for his release.

To the Rev. Jenkins' pleasant surprise, seventy-six inmates at Kirkland, the maximum-security prison where the reverend was sent right after his conviction, signed a petition on his behalf:

> We, the undersigned, do state that since Leroy Jenkins has been incarcerated in the South Carolina Department of Corrections he has personally assisted many persons in their efforts to change their lives. He has done this in several ways: He has provided means by which an inmate can work and receive commensurate benefits such as

employing other inmates, and banking funds for future needs.

He has freely distributed Bibles which have assisted inmates in their spiritual growth.

He has participated in programs such as work release which give credibility to the future status of the program.

He has ministered to employees and inmates alike in past Christian in Action Services as well as giving counsel and encouragement in the prison yard.

It is our opinion that Leroy Jenkins has contributed in a positive way to our lives and we feel that he is deserving of Parole and an opportunity to once again make a contribution to society.

We pray that the Lord's will be done as regards the future of Rev. Leroy Jenkins.

THE HEARING

The parole hearing was set for April 18, 1984. Hugh Beasley, Dennis Jenkins, and a staff member were ushered along with the Rev. Jenkins into a room where the parole board was seated around a table.

To the reverend's surprise and consternation, also present was a childhood friend, Durrell Smith, and his wife. The Smiths had threatened to appear in opposition to the parole if they were not given $11,000, which they claimed was owed them by the Rev. Jenkins.

Smith and the Rev. Jenkins had been friends when they were children. Many a day they played hooky from school, sneaked into the movies, and pulled the kinds of pranks young boys are prone to do.

Smith's mother, Pearl, was a proud and erect Pentecostal lady, hair neatly piled up in a bun, who had suffered many tribulations in her hard life. She told of raising her little ones back in the Carolina hill country, where she trudged through miles of fields lugging water home in a bucket.

When Leroy Jenkins returned to Columbia and opened the Spirit of Truth Church, Mother Pearl became a regular member. Prancing into church with a dramatic flair, always just a little bit late, Mother Pearl would perch her lanky bones on a chair on stage. She relied on the affection of the man she called "son" to let her be a part of the ministry. She often testified and sang her favorite hymn "Satisfied, I'm Satisfied."

She often spoke of her son, Durrell, in glowing terms. He had become a successful builder and had a lovely wife and child. One day, Smith visited the church with his wife, and both sat in the back, weeping, as they listened to the message and joined in the singing.

Smith was eager to renew his friendship with his old friend. He offered to drive the school bus that had been purchased to bring poor families from inner-city neighborhoods to the church. After a few weeks of this, his interest faded, and the church had to find another driver.

A TALE OF WOE

As Christmas 1982 approached, Smith came to the Rev. Jenkins with a pitiful tale. He was unable to work because of an injury to his back when he fell off a ladder. He was suing somebody for damages and would soon receive a large sum of money once the suit was settled.

Meanwhile, he was very ill, having seizures, and had suffered a heart attack. His little boy was in the hospital, seriously ill with pneumonia, and he was about to lose his home.

Smith wanted to borrow some money for thirty days—just to get through the Christmas holidays. Would the Rev. Jenkins lend him $5,800 for one month until the settlement money came in? As security, he would give the reverend some valuable jewelry, which Smith assured him he could keep if he did not pay back the money in a month.

The Rev. Jenkins arranged for an interest-free loan for his friend, believing that his childhood friend would not let him down. The reverend then took possession of the jewelry and had it immediately placed in a lock box.

One month passed, then six months. When staff members tried to telephone Smith to remind him of his promise to repay the loan in one month, they discovered his phone had been disconnected, and he had moved, leaving no forwarding address. He was not seen in church again.

Mother Pearl was questioned about the disappearance.

"Poor Durrell, he had to move because these people were hounding him for money," she said. "I can't tell you his phone number; he told me not to tell anybody. No, I can't tell anyone; Durrell wouldn't like it at all."

When asked if she knew his new address, she became agitated.

"Oh yes, I know where he lives," she said. "But I can't tell anybody. Durrell said not to, and honey, he has a terrible temper. I wouldn't dare tell," Mrs. Smith said.

Mother Pearl was asked to relay a message to Smith about the loan. Still, no one heard anything from Smith or his wife.

Finally, after more than a year had passed, the office wrote Smith at his last known residence, a rural route in a nearby town. The letter warned Smith if he wanted to repay the money he owed and reclaim his jewelry, he should do so within ten days, or the Rev. Jenkins would dispose of the jewelry and consider the matter closed.

The letter was not returned, and it was assumed to have reached its destination. Still, Smith did not contact the Association office. Finally, the Rev. Jenkins tried to recover some of the loan money by selling the jewelry to several of his friends.

EXTORTION

Suddenly, more than a year after receiving the loan, Durrell Smith showed up in the office and demanded his jewelry. This time his attitude was quite different from the humble, downtrodden person he was before he got the $5,800. He was roughly dressed and had a burly companion with him. In a threatening manner, he leaned over June's desk and demanded his jewelry. He did not offer to pay back the money he owed. He just wanted the jewelry.

Smith's timing was perfect. He knew the parole hearing was coming up, and he warned the Rev. Jenkins if he did not get his jewelry back or receive $11,000 for the "loss," he would appear against him at the hearing.

The reverend was incensed by this extortionist threat. But he was also puzzled. Why did Smith think the parole board would take his charges seriously? He had done nothing wrong. It was Smith who had failed to repay the interest-free loan.

ONE BAD APPLE

It came as a complete shock to see Smith at the hearing. He gave the parole board a fabricated account of what had happened, accusing the Rev. Jenkins of taking the jewelry and refusing to return it.

His wife also came before the board and wept as she told of the family heirlooms that had been unjustly taken by the evangelist. Mrs. Smith also claimed that he had made threatening phone calls to her. This was impossible, since no one had been able to find out whether Smith even had a telephone.

Additionally, Mrs. Smith claimed the reverend had driven a pickup truck into her yard and threatened her. This also was impossible since no one knew where they lived.

Mother Pearl could have rebutted all those charges. She knew everyone was trying to locate her son. She admitted she was in contact with him, and staff members asked her to deliver messages to him about repayment of the loan.

But Mother Pearl seemed to be terrified of her son's wrath, and she begged the reverend not to call on her.

Smith also told the parole board the Rev. Jenkins had asked him to plant cocaine on his son-in-law, Ricky Kernon.

Despite the fact that Kernon and his daughter were no longer married, the reverend and Kernon were on good terms. Hurt and shocked that this false charge should have been effective in keeping his father-in-law from getting parole, Kernon sent an affidavit to the parole board, saying that relations between them were friendly, and he did not believe the accusation.

"Dad," Kernon told his father-in-law, "I don't know why he would say that. You know I love you with all my heart, and I know you love me. You're the greatest dad in the world."

Sadly, the parole board allowed themselves to be swayed by the performance put on by the Smith family. They refused the reverend's parole without taking time to investigate the charges and without giving him a chance to rebut them. They told him he would not have another parole hearing for one year, until April 1985.

EVANGELIST WILL REMAIN IN CUSTODY

The State, April 19, 1984

COLUMBIA, S.C. (UPI) - A childhood chum of television evangelist Leroy Jenkins scuttled the preacher's hopes for parole when he told corrections officials Jenkins is capable of doing anything to "eliminate" his opponents.

The state parole board deliberated less than five minutes Wednesday before voting to keep the flamboyant evangelist in custody. Guards whisked the 44-year-old Jenkins away after the decision, and the minister made no comment.

A Greenwood County jury convicted Jenkins, who has churches in Columbia and Delaware, Ohio, of conspiracy to commit arson and assault in May 1979 and the preacher received a 12-year sentence.

"I've always lived a straight life, and I am grateful that I was about to keep a good record during five years in prison," Jenkins said during his 30-minute hearing.

But Durrell Smith, a Columbia construction worker who said he grew up with Jenkins in Greenwood, painted a different picture.

Smith said Jenkins recently offered to pay him $5,000 and cancel a $5,800 debt if he would plant cocaine on the minister's son-in-law in Tampa, Fla.

The witness said Jenkins wanted the man jailed because he had beaten the preacher's daughter and was trying to gain custody of Jenkins' grandchildren.

"I didn't want to get him in any more trouble," Smith said, explaining why he did not tell police. "At the time we were friends."

But he changed his mind and decided to testify against Jenkins when the preacher refused to let Smith's wife buy back the jewelry she had put up as collateral for the loan.

Parole officials then asked Smith if he considers Jenkins a dangerous man.

"I think he is capable to do anything to eliminate anybody that gets in his way," Smith replied.

But June Buckingham, the preacher's secretary, accused Smith of trying to blackmail her boss. She said Smith vowed to testify against Jenkins if he did not drop the $5,800 debt and return the jewelry.

"I can't imagine why they would do this," she said of the parole board's decision.

Jenkins is now participating in a work release program while in the custody of his daughter. Corrections officials said the denial of parole will not alter his work-release status.

Earlier Jenkins attorney, Hugh Beasley of Columbia, called the charges against the minister, "a pure set-up engineered by the government."

"It is a case of religious persecution," he said.

A NEW HEARING

It was only after the board received Ricky Kernon's affidavit and discovered that Smith had a two-page long criminal record that the Rev. Jenkins was granted another parole hearing in six months.

Later that year, Durrell Smith and his wife were successful in suing to recover $11,000, which they claimed was the value of the jewelry put up for collateral for the money they borrowed. It is inexplicable why the jury decided in their favor, especially since they were aware of Smith's police record, which included four separate counts of bank robbery, assault, and other crimes for which he served time in prison.

The case came to trial just before the second parole hearing in November 1984, and in order to get the matter settled without more scurrilous charges and publicity that might once again influence the parole board, the Rev. Jenkins paid Smith the money he demanded. Smith's tactics had worked before, and the reverend was now convinced his childhood buddy was capable of doing anything to achieve his end.

It is a wonder that God allows such things to happen. But the even greater wonder is how people can take the "slings and arrows of outrageous fortune" and go on to lead victorious lives, never allowing themselves to become bitter.

The stunning rejection by the parole board, which was based on the lies of a man he tried to help, could have crushed anyone's faith in mankind. But though he could not return to his church in Ohio, he determined to make the best of things and threw himself into planning the great summer tent revival of 1984.

FREE AT LAST

A SENATOR STEPS IN
TO RIGHT A WRONG

"Moving On" headlined *The State* newspaper on Wednesday November 21, 1984. Underneath, a photograph showed the Rev. Jenkins carting some boxes to a moving van:

> The Rev. Leroy Jenkins went to work when movers arrived at his Columbia church on Tuesday. The television evangelist, sentenced to 12 years in prison, won parole last week and is moving to the Tampa, Fla., area.

After telling the reverend he would have to spend another year in prison, parole board officials reversed their decision and granted him a new hearing. Evidence presented to the parole board discredited the testimony of Durrell Smith, the Rev. Jenkins' childhood friend who used the parole hearing to extort money from the evangelist.

Another factor in the parole board's decision to grant the reverend another hearing was the intervention of Sen. John Drummond.

Senator Drummond, a longtime friend of the ministry, suggested the strategy that finally won the reverend's freedom.

"Son," the senator said. "They would be glad to get you out of their hair in this state. You are a threat to them. Promise you will leave the state, and I guarantee you, they will let you go."

Just like Brer Rabbit in the briar patch, the wily preacher pretended to balk at the suggestion.

"What, leave the state where I could do so much good getting rid of these crooked politicians and the rotten police and law enforcement?" he said. He had no intention of remaining in South Carolina. But if prison officials thought he might stir up more trouble, they might be more anxious to get rid of him.

In the end, he took the senator's advice, and with the promise he would leave South Carolina and not come back, he won his release. He had served five years—twice the sentence served by someone convicted of an *actual assault*, and just eleven months less than the average convicted murderer.

LEROY JENKINS PREPARES FOR TRIP SOUTH

Greenville News, November 20, 1984

Marilyn Rauber

COLUMBIA–*The Rev. Leroy Jenkins spread thick, brown varnish over the trailer bed, as staff members hauled cartons onto the church porch and others hovered nearby to discuss moving strategy.*

A white bull dog named Toby watched the activity with confusion, prancing between moving legs and car wheels crunched over the churchyard gravel.

At the church entrance, a mop and pail stood behind the glass double doors. The pale blue "Spirit of Truth" sign above the roof, capped by the black, slanted scrawl of Jenkins' sig-

nature, competed for attention with the "For Sale 3.5 acres" marker above the fence.

Leroy Jenkins, the flamboyant faith healer and evangelist from Greenwood, is packing up and heading south.

After serving less than half of a 12-year sentence on 1979 charges of conspiracy to commit arson and assault, charges involving threats against a Greenwood law enforcement officer and an Anderson reporter, Jenkins last week agreed to be paroled on the condition that he get out of South Carolina.

With his houseboat—hence preparation of the trailer—four of his children, two truckloads of belongings, and most of his church staff in tow, he's heading for Tampa, Fla., where he already has leased a house and an office, Jenkins said Monday.

He's leaving behind 2,600 church members; a preacher, Alma Joe Brown, who will hold services in his absence; and promises to return to the flock when his parole expires in nine months.

Jenkins believes state officials are treating him more severely than they would a paroled murderer. He's asking a lawyer to check into the legality of his temporary banishment from the state.

"I sort of expected something like this to happen, "he said, "Because if they put you in prison for nothing, they'll do this to you for nothing."

Jenkins said his record in prison was "perfect", and his hundreds of followers who packed the Columbia church for his final appearance Sunday afternoon were angry and upset about the way he has been treated.

Jenkins hopes to rebuild his national following by holding crusades around the country. The first is scheduled for Dec. 23 in Atlanta, Georgia.

Copyright © Greenville News

"IT CAN'T BE TRUE"

No sooner had the Rev. Jenkins moved to Tampa than he was back in South Carolina. Parole and banishment from the state would soon seem minor aggravations in light of the tragedy that followed.

TRUCK CRASH KILLS LEROY JENKINS' SON

Dayton Journal Herald, November 23, 1984

COLUMBIA, S.C. (AP)—The 17-year-old adopted son of television evangelist Leroy Jenkins died Wednesday night when the pickup truck he was driving spun out of control on a curve and smashed into a tree.

Scott Dewayne Morgan suffered a broken neck in the accident, according to Trooper L.C. Hoover of the South Carolina Highway Patrol. A passenger in the car, Lilburn David Marsh, 30, suffered broken ribs and was treated and released at Lexington County Hospital, the trooper said.

"They had a wiener roast and a lot of his school friends were there," Jenkins said Thursday of the events preceding his son's death. He made the comment in Tampa, Fla., where he is under parole supervision.

Jenkins, 47, left the state Tuesday to move his family to Tampa, part of the conditions of a release from his sentence. He said Scotty wanted to finish school at Lexington High School and was living with his personal secretary.

Jenkins said he was uncertain whether the youth would be buried in South Carolina or Ohio, and added he was returning to Ohio for several days after stopping in South Carolina.

Jenkins "raised the boy since he was a baby," according to Jenkins' personal secretary, June Buckingham.

The accident occurred about 11:45 p.m. Wednesday in Ballentine, a community northwest of Columbia.

"We figured more than anything it was (caused) on the part of excessive speed," Hoover said.

The truck rounded a curve, ran off the side of the road, cut back across and struck a tree, pinning Scotty inside, he said.

"When he rounded the curve he lost it, the tree hit at the driver's door between the bed and the cab," Hoover said.

Buckingham said Jenkins planned to return for the funeral at 2:30 p.m. at his Spirit of Truth church in Columbia.

"I have permission to come back," a shaken Jenkins said. "My parole officer just left here."

But he said other members of his family "don't know about it yet. They're on their way down here."

Copyright © Dayton Journal Herald

NOT IN VAIN

The shock of Scotty's death, which happened as the Rev. Jenkins was on his way to Tampa, almost caused the preacher to collapse.

"No, June, it can't be true. It must be a mistake," he cried out when he heard the sad news. Prison had kept him apart from his youngest child for too long. Now he would never see him again. He could not accept the fact of Scotty's death until he had made several telephone calls to verify the incident.

The State newspaper ran the story on November 23, 1984, after calling the office for comment. It was difficult to gauge the loss everyone felt. Scott was a tall, good-looking young man with soft-brown eyes and an engaging smile. He was a sweet boy, very popular.

His father's travails had been hard on the teenager, but now that the reverend was free, he seemed to be optimistic about the future.

"Scotty was a very exceptional kid at school," the Rev. Jenkins told the reporter. "All the kids loved him. I know he had a lot of friends. Scott had talked about going into the ministry a couple of years ago, but I think he wanted to study to be a lawyer."

Though he normally avoided funerals, the Rev. Jenkins presided over that of his son.

"Young people," he told the hundreds of Scotty's classmates who attended the funeral. "I don't want Scotty to have died in vain. If you take this to heart and be careful and take care of yourselves, I will feel that his death accomplished something.

"Now all of you kids, if you want to give your lives to the Lord, quit drinking and smoking pot, come on down here, and we will pray together," he said. The entire church full of young people crowded around Scotty's casket at the front of the church. They sobbed together as they raised their arms to dedicate themselves to the Lord.

At first, the reverend could not decide where he wanted to bury his son. Oddly enough, one morning as Mrs. Buckingham was driving Scotty to school, he pointed out a beautiful cemetery along the route and said he wanted to be buried there.

"Why, Scotty, don't talk that way," Mrs. Buckingham said. "It will be a long time before you have to worry about that."

When the Rev. Jenkins heard of this conversation, he decided to bury Scotty in that Lexington County cemetery in a mausoleum where there was just one crypt remaining. He could not bear to put his son in the ground.

Years later, flowers still appear on Scotty's crypt, a gift from those who loved him and remembered what happened. (see photos on page 279)

MORE HEADLINES

Once again, the Rev. Jenkins found himself in the headlines. Newspapers were full of stories about his activities now that he was out of prison. As always, some of the reporters didn't even pretend to hide their cynicism.

The following are excerpts of several of these articles:

FRESH OUT OF PRISON

TV PREACHER BRINGS 'GREATEST GIFT' TO TAMPA

St. Petersburg Times, December 17, 1984

David Finkel

TAMPA–There's a new preacher in town. His name is Leroy Jenkins, and you'll please excuse him if he seems a tad out of breath and pinched in the voice, but he is a busy man these days, a man on a mission.

Don't know him? He's none other than the self-proclaimed healer of thousands, the Internal Revenue Service-proclaimed maker of millions and the sole possessor of what he calls "the greatest gift."

Still don't know him? That's why he's so busy.

He used to be known all over. Every Sunday morning he used to appear on television sets across the country, a likeable guy trying to heal the crippled and singing up a storm. A favorite was "I Did It Thy Way," which he delivered a la Elvis with his open shirt, flashy jewelry, and swept back, jet-black hair...

Copyright © St. Petersburg Times

REVEREND PLANS CAREER REVIVAL AS EVANGELIST

WHILE OUT ON PAROLE

Tampa Tribune, December 16, 1984

Daniel Alcorn

Rev. Jenkins was paroled last month in South Carolina after serving five years of a 12-year sentence. At one time he had the third largest evangelical Association in the country.

Rev. Jenkins, the faith healer with the "miracle arm," is back in Tampa, planning to continue his national ministry while serving out a prison parole.

The 46-year-old evangelist recently returned here from South Carolina where he was paroled in November after serving 5 years of a 12-year sentence. The parole requires him to remain in Tampa where he and his family previously lived...

PAROLED EVANGELIST SAYS HE'S REBUILDING MINISTRY

Charlotte News, March 11, 1985

Maggie Hirsch

Evangelist Leroy Jenkins, on parole from a S.C. prison, held his first healing service in Charlotte since his 1979 conviction on conspiracy to commit arson and assault charges.

In a 3 1/2 hour service at Ovens Auditorium, Jenkins spoke of his prison time and said he intends to rebuild his once-thriving television ministry, formerly reported to bring in about $3 million annually and, he said, played on 87 television stations and 43 radio stations.

"You don't know how long the nights get (in prison)," he told the audience. "They had to tell me what they locked me up for. I didn't know. They gave me 20 years for nothing."

Before Jenkins came on stage, his son Dennis asked the crowd if they knew about the preacher's prison stint. Most raised their hands.

"We didn't try to hide it, did we?" he asked. "God chose him to go to jail. He healed a lot of people in prison. He's got something you can't argue with. He's got a gift."

Leroy Jenkins said he was glad to be back in Charlotte. He expressed delight at the naming of the Billy Graham

Parkway, for "the greatest man in the world," Jenkins told the crowd.

During the afternoon he performed healing ceremonies, criticized some other preachers he said were building "billion-dollar skyscrapers on earth," and railed against the Russians, who he said, are "planning to take us over."

As the service drew to a close, Jenkins solicited donations from the audience. "It's going to take me a long time to get where I was," he said. "I'm gonna need a lot of people to stand with me for the next few months.... It takes a lot of money to come to an audience... I'm going to ask everyone in this place to give to God freely and quickly." Four young men carrying Bibles left, telling Jenkins, "You're serving money," and citing scripture.

Then he began walking off-stage singing the song, "My Way" made popular by Frank Sinatra. But Jenkins sang, "I Did it God's Way."

TRYING TO RECAPTURE THE LUSTER

Embarking on a whirlwind schedule of crusades, the Rev. Jenkins crisscrossed the country, praying, singing, renewing acquaintances, and gathering his flock of believers together once again.

His friend Jesse Strickland resigned his position as deputy commissioner of South Carolina's Department of Corrections and accepted a job working with the Rev. Jenkins to ease him back into life on the "outside."

"Rev," he said, "you won't make good decisions for a time. You have to give yourself some space to settle down. At least a year."

Despite this advice, the reverend rushed back into the mainstream of the evangelistic field, basing his office by turns in Florida, Ohio, and Arizona.

Every week Rev went to another auditorium in another city, glad to be free and able to bring the word of God, along with the demonstration of his power to heal and to deliver, to those who had been cheated of the ministry while he was incarcerated.

"How many kids could have been delivered from drugs? How many could have been saved and healed during these past five years?" he told Strickland. "I have a job to do, and I must do it, for I have to answer to God for each one I could have helped, and didn't," he said.

He appeared in Atlanta, Dallas, Detroit, Chicago, Louisville, Philadelphia, Baltimore, and Nashville, among other cities. He was a man on fire for God.

SETTING THINGS RIGHT

Even though the Rev. Jenkins was free, the rejection by his own people still stung. He had gone to South Carolina to rewrite the story of his youth. He purchased homes in his old neighborhood and turned a slum into a showplace. He opened a popular restaurant where diners could enjoy home-cooked meals in a jovial atmosphere. His evangelism attracted thousands to crusades in the Greenwood Civic Center, a fact that benefited Greenwood both spiritually and materially. He poured his heart and soul into the community and its people, seeking refuge for himself and his family in the warmth of its Southern hospitality.

As far as he was concerned now, he was through with South Carolina, and his home state was through with him. So it was with some surprise that the Rev. Jenkins received the news that the Hon. Marshall Williams, South Carolina's senior state senator, wanted to meet with him in the senator's Orangeburg law office.

"Rev. Jenkins," said the one-time chairman of the state senate's judiciary committee. "I have been following your case from the beginning. I believe you were unjustly imprisoned. Now, I want you to tell me all about it."

The Rev. Jenkins recounted the story of the harassment by Greenwood officials, the fire at his home, and the spying by the

ATF agent. He recounted the arrest and trial and the conviction for crimes he did not commit.

The venerable old senator listened and nodded. One of the most respected men in South Carolina, Sen. Williams served as president pro tempore of the senate and, at the time of his death, was the longest-serving state senator in the United States. He was a wise man, who recognized the truth when he heard it, and he had the power to make things happen.

"Rev. Jenkins," the senator said. "I am dying of cancer. And before I die, I want to make things right. I am going to ask the Board of Pardons to grant you full and unconditional absolution and to restore your civil liberties." (see photo on pages 261 and 262)

Normally, a convicted felon cannot vote or hold office, even if he has paid his debt to society. With his civil rights restored, the Rev. Jenkins could run for president if he wanted to. True to his word, Sen. Williams persuaded the parole board to grant the Rev. Jenkins a full pardon on September 28, 1993. The Hon. Marshall Burns Williams died on December 28, 1995. He had set things right.

A PROPHET AMONG US

Among the spiritual gifts outlined in 1 Corinthians 12:1 is the gift of prophesy. In the years following his incarceration, the Rev. Jenkins was able to predict events for nations as well as individuals. Members of his congregation are accustomed to hearing of upcoming events before they happen and take them in stride.

The year 1989 proved a great year for prophesies because of the tremendous upheavals that were taking place throughout the world.

"A great revival is going to break out in Russia, and Gorbachev is going to be the head of it," the Rev. Jenkins prophesied on April 26, 1989, during a tent crusade in Daytona Beach, Florida.

He repeated the same prophecy to his congregation at Healing Waters Cathedral on October 29, 1989.

"There are going to be such great world upheavals that the press will concentrate on those and let the preachers alone," the Rev. Jenkins said.

At the time, it seemed like an impossible prediction. Churches in Russia had been outlawed for seventy years. Christians were persecuted and were forced to meet secretly in members' homes to avoid being sent to the gulags. The communists held Russia, Poland, Latvia, Lithuania, and other satellite countries in an iron grip.

In Poland, clerics were beaten and murdered, and the church was driven underground. Lech Walesa, head of the opposition Solidarity movement and a staunch Catholic, suffered imprisonment and beatings.

However impossible the prophecy seemed, in December 1989, Soviet leader Mikhail Gorbachev traveled to the Vatican to confer with the pope. After that, the repressive rules against churches were revoked. For the first time in seventy years, Russians celebrated Christmas in St. Basil's Cathedral, just outside the Kremlin. Church bells pealed across Russia's vast expanse as neglected or damaged churches opened their doors to worshippers.

The Solidarity movement in Poland overwhelmed the communists, and it was revealed that the Catholic Church, with the cooperation of the United States, had sheltered Lech Walesa and his associates. *Time* magazine's January 1, 1990, issue carried a picture of the victorious Solidarity leaders, one of them carrying a large crucifix in the victory parade.

The revival that is now sweeping Russia, Poland, and other countries that were once a part of the Soviet Union was prophesied in the little town of Delaware, Ohio.

"The iron curtain is coming down in Germany," the reverend prophesied in the October 29, 1989, service. The world had been kept in darkness about the internal unrest in East Germany, but on November 9, just twelve days after the prophecy, Germans stormed the wall that separated East and West Berlin, tearing it down piece by piece. East Germans poured into West Germany by the thousands. The barb wire and the machine-gun toting soldiers vanished.

"A famous person is going to die," the reverend said in another prophecy involving Eastern Europe. "Their picture will be on the front page of the magazines. Everyone will be shocked," he told the church on October 29, 1989.

In January, a photograph of Nicholas Ceausescu, Rumania's ruthless dictator, appeared on the cover of *Newsweek* magazine. He was lying in a pool of his own blood. This unprecedented pictorial document shocked the world. He and his wife were tried, found guilty of numerous heinous crimes, and were executed by a firing squad from their own army.

Through the gift of prophecy, the Rev. Jenkins is able to predict events for nations as well as individuals.

In December 1989, the Rev. Jenkins predicted the attempt to overthrow Philippine President Corazon Aquino and her legally elected government.

The Panama Canal grabbed headlines during the last week of 1989, when the largest US military airlift since Vietnam carried American troops into Panama. Just as God had shown the reverend, the greatest upheavals in many years occurred in the last half of 1989.

The Rev. Jenkins told his church on January 6, 1991, that there was going to be a war, as he heard bombs and machine gun fire. He also said, "God is going to turn the White House upside down. There is going to be a change in people's attitudes." The Gulf war started on January 16, and President George Bush declared a day of prayer. Television screens showed him coming out of church in the company of the Rev. Billy Graham. The press announced that people all over the country were crowding into the churches to pray.

One Sunday shortly after the start of the war, the Rev. Jenkins said, "There is a wife here in Ohio who is grieving about her husband who is missing eight thousand miles away, and she is afraid he is dead. She should not worry, he will be all right." The next day television stations carried the news that an Ohio pilot had been shot down behind enemy lines in Iraq. He was not badly hurt and radioed out to his compatriots, who rescued him in a daring foray behind enemy lines.

FORECASTING WEATHER

In addition to political, religious, and societal events, the Rev. Jenkins also forecasts weather, often with greater accuracy than TV weathermen. In October 1989, God showed the preacher that a great storm was coming through Ohio and Michigan, and the winter would be very severe. On December 22, the record-breaking storm arrived, sending the temperature plummeting to a minus twenty-six degrees.

The evangelist said he saw a great earthquake coming, cities burning, and buildings falling. He saw the globe shifting and the sun falling closer to the earth.

"Watch what the news media says about the sun," he advised.

The December 1989 issue of *Reader's Digest* carried an article about the sun's unusual activity which they called "record-shattering, earth-shaking, solar storms raging 93 million miles away on the sun."

Further, the article said, "Within the next year or two... the gigantic invisible forces with boiling magnetic energy ... will approach record levels." Once again, the Rev. Jenkins foretold what science was predicting would happen.

"An earthquake is going to hit the Midwest in a few days, but you people will not be hurt," he said at a Dayton, Ohio, crusade on September, 19, 1990. Just seven days later, on September 26, an earthquake rocked parts of Illinois, Indiana, Kentucky, Missouri, Arkansas, and Tennessee. Ohio had been spared.

A NATION SEEKING GOD

In this age of preoccupation with science and computer chips, the reverend prophesied in November 1990 that the print medium would carry front page stories about God. In December, *Life* magazine's cover story was "Who is God?" The December 10, 1990, issue of *U.S. News* and *World Report* followed with a rendering of St. Matthew and the angel on the cover, and the words "Who Wrote the Bible?"

Newsweek's December 17, 1990, issue featured a picture of a young couple and their children standing in front of a stained glass window along with the words "And the Children Shall Lead Them–Young Americans Return to God."

People magazine got into the act as well when its December 21, 1990, issue carried the cover story "Miracle Baby." It was the story of little Weston Kilpatrick, born with a defective heart, who had a spontaneous recovery that the doctors termed "a little bit of a miracle." The news of a miraculous recovery from a fatal condition was not unique, at least to those who are accustomed to seeing such miracles all the time. But the fact that it was the cover story in a major magazine—especially one that normally featured gossipy stories about celebrities—was remarkable.

The July 1991 issue of *Life* magazine asked "Do You Believe in Miracles?" accompanied by a picture of a statue of the Virgin Mary.

Time magazine of December 9, 1991, carried the front-page story "One Nation Under God," with an illustration of a giant red-white-and-blue cross. On December 30, 1991, *Time* featured the Virgin Mary on the cover, with the heading "The Search for Mary."

On January 6, 1992, *Newsweek* magazine featured the cover story "Talking to God, an Intimate Look at the Way We Pray."

OTHER MINISTERS' TROUBLES

The Rev. Jenkins wasn't the only pastor to experience problems. In November 1986, he told his church that Jim Bakker would lose his television ministry and be driven from his church in disgrace. At that time, there was no hint of the scandal that led to Bakker's downfall. However, in early spring of 1987, Bakker's association with Jessica Hahn came to light, and he resigned his position at PTL on March 19, 1987.

After Jimmy Swaggart denounced Bakker and condemned him for his mistakes, the Rev. Jenkins told his congregation in April 1987 that Jimmy Swaggart would be caught in a scandal of his own. Just a few months later, in January 1988, he was photographed with a prostitute. Rather than face censure by the Assemblies of God, he resigned from that denomination.

"Jimmy Swaggart apologized, and God forgave him, and so should we," the Rev. Jenkins told his congregation. "He will be restored to his ministry for a time, but then he will fall again," he prophesied. On October 12, 1991, Swaggart's followers suffered another shock when he was found in the company of another prostitute. He resigned from his ministry.

"This is not the last of the scandals," the Rev. Jenkins prophesied. "Billy Graham is next. They will try to ruin his name too." Just a few months later, on October 2, 1990, the *National Enquirer* splashed his picture on the cover with the headline "Billy Graham Scandal–Ministry Cons 98-Year-Old Woman Out of $3 Million." These charges were never proven.

Once again the preacher's gift of prophecy proved true. Like the prophets of old, he has made prophesies that will undoubtedly come to pass in the future. His congregation depends upon his predictions, and many have profited financially as well as spiritually by his advice.

THE GREATEST GIFT

"He's got something you can't argue with," the Rev. Jenkins' son Dennis once remarked. That something is the gift of the Holy Spirit, manifested in the word of knowledge, healing, deliverance, and prophecy.

But perhaps the greatest gift God has given the Rev. Jenkins and members of his congregation is the knowledge that God loves each and every one of his own, that He knows their sorrows and can deliver them from anything this corrupt world dishes out. It is the peace that passes all understanding.

Though his enemies tried to silence him, the reverend's gifts were only enhanced by the suffering and mental anguish he endured. Today, he hears the voice of God more clearly than ever.

The trials and tribulation he endured have increased his compassion for those who are suffering.

He stands firm, true to the God he believes controls all things. He does not understand why people must suffer, why he had to go through such torment in this life. But he believes God has a plan and that he is part of that plan.

He believes God is the same yesterday, today, and forever. His faith is firm, and he is steadfast. There will come a time when God will make it all clear to him. Until that day, he will continue to serve his Creator.

A MAN OF GOD

Leroy Jenkins is God's man for the age. Having endured suffering and misunderstanding, he stands against the winds of time, still trumpeting the clarion call of the gospel, the salvation of the world.

Time spans the years since the Rev. Jenkins returned to the place of his birth. He left Greenwood a little better off than he found it, beautifying a decaying neighborhood, revitalizing an abandoned church and generally improving everything he touched.

But the truly lasting things are the things done in the name of Jesus Christ. During Leroy Jenkins' time in Greenwood many people received the gifts of faith, healing and salvation.

It would be difficult to think of a greater legacy than that.

Leroy Jenkins rode into town in a black limousine. He rode out in chains. He went to prison for the simple reason that he talked too much and made enemies of the wrong people. For this crime, he was separated from his children, his ministry and slandered, and he suffered horrendous abuse in South Carolina's worst prisons.

Evangelist Leroy Jenkins paid a high price for a few careless words. He lost his freedom.

> For now we see through a glass, darkly;
> but then face to face:
> now I know in part; but then shall I
> know even as also I am known.
> And now abideth faith, hope, charity, these three;
> but the greatest of these is charity.
> 1 Corinthians 13:12, 13 (KJV)

He lost precious years. But he did not lose his spirit. That, no one can take.

> If the Son therefore shall make you free,
> ye shall be free indeed.
> John 8:36 (KJV)

AFTERWORD

For fifty-three years, I have served God and my fellow man in the ministry. Much time has passed, and with it, reflection on my life's experiences. God works in mysterious ways, and I have experienced that in the end, truth shall prevail. I was wrongly accused and arrested on April 17, 1979. I was pardoned on September 28, 1993, by Senator Marshall Williams. It is my wish and purpose of allowing this book to finally be published to bring the truth to the thousands of my faithful followers.

On this, the twentieth anniversary of my pardon, I celebrate He who created all things, He who loves unconditionally, and He who forgives each and every sincere heart.

In serving the Lord, I have always known all mankind are created equal. We are all children of God under one denomination, and color is nonexistent. I have worked with and willingly served many of his children regardless of race or gender. It is with deep thought that I would like to mention a few of these relationships in my words now.

I want to express my greatest appreciation for a true lady, June Buckingham, who devoted forty years of her life in helping me. I will always be grateful for her dedication, loyalty, and love for me and the ministry.

My true friend Jesse Strickland, former Deputy Commissioner of South Carolina, helped me through some very difficult times. The extent of this help could have cost him his job. Our friendship went beyond being official as he allowed my nine-year-old son, Scotty, to live with him at one time. Also, after he divorced, he moved into my house to live, and later when retired, he came to work for me at the ministry.

Although it was unheard of to hold a trial where no one was allowed to testify on behalf of the defendant, my one-time enemy, Willie T. Jones, the solicitor, has been forgiven by me. I had the privilege of telling him so before he died. Willie T. Jones was deathly sick in the hospital with Lou Gehrig's disease. I asked him if he would like to make a statement of truth before he passed away. His response was, "I would be too embarrassed." He did, however, wish me and my family the best Christmas ever.

A few of the people who wronged me have asked for forgiveness; many have not. I must look beyond people like Judge Moore, the acting judge in my trial who was appointed by Willie T. Jones, who wrongly sentenced me.

I must look beyond the actions of Mayor Tom Wingard, who was serving as mayor during the time I was being set up. He attended many of my crusades to spy on me.

I must look beyond the behavior of Highway Patrolman Keesler who was violent with my daughter.

The stories could go on and on, but I do not wish to devote any more of my precious time on what I consider "bigger criminals" than what they tried to accuse me of being. I believe this book has proven beyond a shadow of a doubt who the real crooks were. I watched each one of these people take a big fall. Most of them are gone and dead, or in bad shape. After all is said and done, it states in Matthew 7:20, "Wherefore by their fruits ye shall know them" (KJV).

In closing, may I express gratitude to the National Christian Ministries Association for awarding me the Minister of the Year twice while I was in prison. I give thanks and appreciation to all my followers worldwide for their continued love and support. I thank God for His sustaining influence, which strengthened me during my toughest trials. The work must go forward as I continue to hold crusades, work in the ministry, and preach the word of God.

—Reverend Leroy Jenkins